Children, Schools, and Inequality

Social Inequality Series
Marta Tienda and David B. Grusky, Series Editors

Children, Schools, and Inequality, Doris R. Entwisle, Karl L. Alexander, and Linda Steffel Olson

Social Differentiation and Social Inequality: Essays in Honor of John Pock, edited by James Baron, David B. Grusky, and Donald Treiman

Can Education Be Equalized? The Swedish Case in Comparative Perspective, edited by Robert Erikson and Jan O. Jonsson

Generating Social Stratification: Toward a New Research Agenda, edited by Alan C. Kerckoff

The New Role of Women: Family Formation in Modern Studies, edited by Hans-Peter Blossfeld

Social Stratification: Class, Race, and Gender in Sociological Perspective, edited by David B. Grusky

Persistent Inequality: Changing Educational Attainment in Thirteen Countries, edited by Yossi Shavit and Hans-Peter Blossfeld

FORTHCOMING

Rational Choice Theory and Large Scale Data Analysis, edited by Hans-Peter Blossfeld and Gerald Prein

Children, Schools, and Inequality

Doris R. Entwisle, Karl L. Alexander, and Linda Steffel Olson

Westview Press
A Member of the Perseus Books Group

Social Inequality Series

Copyright © 1997 by Westview Press, A Member of the Perseus Books Group.

Published in 1997 in the United States of America by Westview Press, 5500 Central Avenue, Boulder,
Colorado 80301-2877, and in the United Kingdom by Westview Press, 12 Hid's Copse Road, Cum-
nor Hill, Oxford OX2 9JJ

A CIP catalog record for this book is available from the Library of Congress.
ISBN 0-8133-0831-3 (hc)   ISBN 0-8133-6651-8 (pbk)

The paper used in this publication meets the requirements of the American National Standard for Per-
manence of Paper for Printed Library Materials Z39.48-1984.

10   9   8   7   6   5   4   3   2

Contents

v

Tables, Figures, and Charts

Figures

Charts

Preface

The purpose of this book is to shed light on the process of schooling--how and why attending school affects children's cognitive and socioemotional development. Schooling is not the same as learning, although children do learn many things in school, including much that is not in the formal curriculum.

The sociopsychological basis of schooling has challenged researchers all through this century. For one of us (DRE) it has been the most important thread running through a career--beginning with a study of placebo effects in a field experiment in 1961 and continuing through to the present. Hopefully the work presented here, which is based entirely on observational data, will shed some new light on early schooling. It is truly astounding that so little sociological research directly concerns young children. Despite prodigious efforts by educators and by a wide group of social scientists, we know very little about schooling. To give an example, teachers for a long time have believed that children in small classes do better than children in big classes but only recently has robust evidence been marshaled to support this belief. (See Mosteller 1996.) Many other school practices like reading groups for first graders or curricular tracking in high school likewise are common but more because of opinions or custom than because of solid scientific evidence that tells us how these organizational devices actually work.

Politics and policy are part of the problem. When children *appear* not to be doing well in school, society blames the school and cries for change. Then, to placate constituents, school boards and departments of education order changes in schools, not because they know the changes will be effective but because making a change offers them a way to deal with political pressure. Likewise, policy makers in all sections of the government recommend changes, often well-intended, but again with no explicit scientific justification. In a country like the U.S., with grass-roots control of education and with almost everyone having a stake in the outcome, the cacophony is monumental. Fortunately, human beings would not have survived to the present if they could not learn under almost any conditions.

Our purpose in starting the Beginning School Study was *to look*--to watch children when they started school, catalogue their experiences, query their parents and teachers, and, with as few preconceptions as possible, to try to understand what helps or hinders their schooling. In short, the Beginning School Study was conceived as a multi-faceted longitudinal study to examine how a great many variables affected schooling under "natural" conditions. We did not try to alter how reading was taught, or how children were treated, or how schools were organized. We merely observed as closely as we could what was actually going on in a large urban school system.

Ideally, of course, we would have tried to "isolate" variables--that is, we would have randomly assigned children to segregated or integrated schools to evaluate effects of the ethnic composition of schools or randomly assigned children across schools to study variables like the socioeconomic mix of the student body. Or to study effects of retention we would have had randomly retained some children and promoted others. This being impossible, we tried to "isolate" variables statistically, that is, after the data were collected and refined, we examined effects of one variable (like the ethnic mix of the school) with other variables held constant statistically. The catch is, of course, that important variables can be left out, or variables can act so as to offset each other, or even the way a variable is sampled distorts the outcome. A persuasive example of the pitfalls in a strictly observational approach is that children's achievement varies by season, and seasonal differences in achievement vary by social class (summer learning). If test scores were examined only once a year, seasonal patterns would be missed. No amount of "control" on other variables or scrutiny of additional variables would solve this problem. It could only be solved when an astute investigator like Barbara Heyns pointed the way by conceiving of the school calendar as approximating a "natural experiment." Children attend school for only part of the year, so children's performance changes when school is not in session. In fact, schooling cannot directly affect children in summer when children do not attend. By comparing summer performance with winter performance, then, we can estimate school effects. Progress in winter when school keeps is greater than progress in summer, when school is closed. We can "isolate" school effects by comparing growth in winter with growth in summer. This strategy is not ideal but it has done a great deal to clarify the process of schooling, especially in helping us understand how family resources affect schooling.

This book brings together some key findings about children's elementary schooling derived from the Beginning School Study, but as we say in the first chapter, it is not meant to be a comprehensive report on that Study. Rather, it presents a set of findings that help clarify how *some* aspects of social structure affect schooling. Like many academic researchers, too often we can look only at the immediate picture and try to answer one or two major questions at a time. In this book we have tried to enlarge our horizons a little by taking a more comprehensive approach and weaving together findings of the BSS with findings from other studies.

We have made some suggestions about how schools could be altered in ways to help children do better. Still, our main purpose here is to explain how schooling proceeds in a large urban system over the elementary years. By demonstrating that even first-graders can be successfully interviewed and that school and family contexts for these children reveal consistent patterns, we hope to encourage other investigators to study social phenomena in middle childhood.

We owe a tremendous dept to the students in the Beginning School Study, most of whom have continued to help us up to the present. We are also grateful to their parents for allowing their children to be studied and for telling us about their own situations and hopes for their children. The cooperation we have enjoyed from the Baltimore City Public Schools has been absolutely splendid. Teachers, guidance counselors, and administrators at all levels have smoothed the way for us, often at considerable cost to themselves in time or in disruption of the workday.

We are grateful to several government agencies and private foundations, without whose support this work could not have been done: National Institute of Child Health and Human Development (HD29343, 23728, 21044, and 16302), National Science Foundation (SES8510535), Spencer Foundation (B1517), and the W.T. Grant Foundation (83079682 and 82079600).

It seems particularly appropriate here to recognize the key role that administrators of The Johns Hopkins University have played in helping us with this work. Grants with specific time boundaries are essential, and without them we could not have even started this work. On the other hand, a project like this, which already spans much more than a decade, and which has many ups and downs, requires the kind of commitment to individuals that only a university can make. We could not have devoted the effort to bring this project to a satisfactory conclusion without the University's consistent support, month in and month out. Over the years the University has unquestioningly provided the atmosphere we needed for research. There are relatively few places in the world where social scientists can work year after year on a project without an immediately visible "product." We would like to acknowledge here how important it has been for our work to have the kind of atmosphere that Hopkins has provided. We are truly grateful.

We mark it a privilege to have been associated with several colleagues who collaborated with us in many of the investigations summarized in this book. They include Aaron Pallas, Doris Cadigan, Maxine Thompson, M. Jane Sundius, and Patricia Gucer. We have also had the great good fortune to have a staff of assistants without whom this project, and this book, could not have been completed. First among them is Mary Ann Zeller, who has coaxed this book through many drafts and whose skill is entirely responsible for preparing the manuscript in camera-ready form. Her diligence and good humor are truly remarkable. Joanne Fennessey, Anna Stoll, and Sona Armenian have helped in every phase of the data collection and assembly of the data archive. Binnie Bailey, as department administrator, has guided us through the financial maze of university and granting guidelines and contributed her enthusiasm and support at every turn. Finally, we wish to thank virtually hundreds of patient and diligent field workers who have helped us gather data over these many years. Their enthusiasm and persistence were essential to the project.

Doris R. Entwisle
Karl L. Alexander
Linda Steffel Olson

1

Children and Inequality

Letitia is "8 years old, female, and the color of cinnamon... A few weeks ago she completed the second grade in a public school in one of Baltimore's most impoverished neighborhoods. For her good work she received a trophy inscribed with her name. But for a battery of tests, results were dismal...In four years Letitia won't need overt discrimination to stay glued to the margins of the American dream." --M. P. Fernandez-Kelly, Baltimore Evening Sun, July 12, 1991

This book is about social inequality and children's early schooling. Its purpose is to shed light on the many ways that social structure penetrates and shapes the *early* schooling of U.S. youngsters, especially in ways that are hidden or overlooked. The major question it seeks to answer is how early schooling may create advantages for some children and disadvantages for others, or put another way, why some children seem to derive more benefit from schooling than others do.

The intellectual legacies undergirding this book draw from three main traditions. The first, which could be described as "mainstream child development," picks up where projects like the Collaborative Perinatal Study leave off when they conclude that social factors far outweigh biological or medical factors in explaining children's success in school. The second is a subfield of status attainment in sociology that focuses on how social resources of families, schools, and communities support schooling and children's cognitive growth. The third tradition is research on human development that takes a life course perspective and emphasizes such things as how parents' sudden loss of income affects their children's psychological well-being, or how becoming a teenage mother affects a woman's work career. A few words will make clear how each of these legacies contributes to our understanding of social inequality and children's early schooling.

Somewhat belatedly, child developmentalists came to realize that, without doing long-term and large-scale research in natural settings, children's development cannot be fully understood. For example, in the mid-fifties, the National Collaborative Perinatal Study began to monitor children born into 50,000 families in fourteen sites scattered across the country. Its purpose was to see how specific medical events in the perinatal period affected developmental disorders in children over the long term. The implicit hypothesis was that there would be fairly clear connections between medical events and the disorders, one, for instance, being why some children of normal intelligence do poorly in school. It turned out, however, that by age four, the intellectual status of children in the study was far better explained by eight variables related to their family's characteristics such as lower socioeconomic status or less maternal education, than by any of the 161 biomedical variables that assessed the condition of mother and child through the first year after the birth (Broman, Nichols, and Kennedy 1975). At the age of seven, about one thousand of these children who had normal intelligence but poor school performance were compared with six thousand others in the same study whose school performance was "normal." Sameroff (1985, p. ix) summarized the findings as follows: The "primary causal factors [of poor performance] reside not in the child's biomedical history but in . . . the social context of development; . . . lower socioeconomic status, less maternal education, higher birth order and larger family size related to higher rates of academic failure." Similarly, Werner's (1980) research on Hawaiian children, which is also prospective and longitudinal, implicates social status and the family caretaking environment rather than severe perinatal stress as the most powerful predictor of childhood learning and behavior disorders.

At about the same time that studies like those just cited convinced mainstream child developmentalists of how strongly children's social environments could affect their development, sociologists began serious study of how one generation confers social status upon the next (Blau and Duncan 1967). Their research centered on how and why individuals sort themselves into occupations of varying prestige, and more particularly on how individuals obtain the educational credentials that govern this occupational sorting. With few exceptions, students in high school or college rather than students in pre- or elementary school monopolized sociologists' attention (see e.g., Sewell and Hauser 1976). Continuing efforts to model the process of secondary schooling with better and better data and with more elaborate models were not matched by efforts to understand schooling at the elementary level, however. In fact, until recently, sociologists left studies of young children and their schooling mainly to others, even though in the U.S. successive levels of schooling are tightly articulated. Curiously, the earliest grades, including the first-grade transition, have been the most neglected even though they set the stage for all that follows. In our opinion, this neglect of schooling in the earliest grades seriously undercuts understanding of how social inequality is created and maintained, for reasons that this book will make clear.

A third intellectual legacy, and in some ways the most fundamental, is the growing body of research on human development that takes a life course approach, beginning with Elder's (1974) *Children of the Great Depression*. These studies testify to the crucible nature of social context for children's early development. They also assume that development is to a considerable extent malleable, and in this regard they contrast sharply with earlier child development studies derived from a Freudian perspective which saw the quality of adult life as more or less fixed by early childhood events. The life course approach emphasizes the importance of social context for human development at every life stage and emphasizes change as well as continuity in development. For example, in early work that traced the connections between family income loss in the Great Depression and youngsters' life chances, Elder found that in families who suffered equally severe economic deprivation, daughters in working class families were given less chance for higher education than daughters of middle class families. More recent studies taking similar approaches examine why parents' marital disruption depresses children's school performance (Morrison 1992), or how a mother's being on welfare affects an adolescent's well-being (Furstenberg et al. 1987), or how gender differences in children's first-grade marks affect high school drop-out (Ensminger and Slusarcick 1992), or how quality of neighborhoods may affect children's cognitive development (Entwisle, Alexander, and Olson 1994). A life course approach thus focuses attention on the *social processes* that could explain why family economic status is associated with cognitive development, as found in the Perinatal Study, or on why gender matters for educational attainment, as in the status attainment research. All three traditions are dedicated to explaining human development, but the life course approach places more emphasis on explaining effects of social context on children's development than do the other two.

This book deals with children's schooling in their middle childhood years (ages 6 to 12). It examines how the inequity embedded in the various dimensions of social structure--school and family organization, family socioeconomic status, gender, and age--affect schooling. We picked these topics because we can add something new to the discussion of each drawing upon data from the Beginning School Study (BSS), a longitudinal prospective investigation of children's schooling, still in progress. Other important social inequities that affect children's schooling which are not on this list, like those created by women's labor force participation or children's physical impairments are omitted, not because we doubt their importance but because the Beginning School Study data can add little to what is presently known about them.

Social Stratification

Rigid social stratification begins when children start their formal schooling, or even before, yet much of the social sorting at this point in life is overlooked. For one reason, there are still few national data on children's schooling prior to kindergarten.   Sociologists have also been preoccupied with how socioeconomic stratification affects secondary schools rather than elementary schools.   Research with secondary students, however, can say little about schooling for younger students because of differences in the capabilities and developmental needs of children in middle childhood as compared with those in adolescence.   Also, although it tends to be overlooked, the organizational patterns of elementary schools are quite different from those of secondary schools (Chapter 4).   Having said that, we must add that the larger demographic trends that undercut children's performance in secondary school certainly have negative consequences for younger children's schooling as well. In what follows, a thumbnail sketch of recent population shifts and economic trends in Baltimore suggests why.

Baltimore and other cities like it have elementary schools that operate increasingly at the margins of society.   Instead of bringing various groups together--African Americans with whites and rich with poor--urban elementary schools are growing more and more isolated from each other and from the larger society.   They are not providing paths for children to take toward upward mobility and improved life chances; rather they are evolving more and more into institutions that embody the most intractable of America's social problems: racial segregation and economic polarization.   Increasing concentrations of poverty in inner city neighborhoods, as described by Wilson (1987) and others, lead to social isolation and neighborhood decay in U.S. cities. This isolation profoundly affects elementary schools because they are *neighborhood* schools, even in the largest cities.   When other institutions like churches, banks, libraries, stores, and recreational facilities are no longer in neighborhoods, the task of the elementary school is made that much harder.

A key way that the concentrated poverty in inner city neighborhoods touches not just those mired in poverty, but also children struggling to survive at its edges, is that the poorest of them attend elementary schools with others who,

like themselves, are severely deprived (see Neckerman and Wilson 1988). At
the elementary level, school demographics closely follow residential patterns.
For example, in 1970 Baltimore was still a majority white city (53%), but
between 1970 and 1990, the white population decreased to 39% while the
African American population increased to 59% (U.S. Bureau of the Census
1973; 1991a). This racial re-alignment was accompanied by a rise in poverty;
between 1970 and 1990 the percentage of the population in poverty rose from
14% to 22%. But the 1990 Census for Baltimore shows that for school
children, poverty was even worse: 31.5% of children were in poverty,
including about 49% of the female headed households with children under age
18 (U.S. Bureau of the Census 1991b). Not surprisingly, these demographic
changes profoundly affected the public schools, because the city's growing
concentration of poor led to a declining revenue base with which to finance
City services, including education. By 1983, the net taxable income of
Baltimore was 32% below the regional average and the 1984 local assessable
property base fell to 41% below the average for the region.

As the financial underpinnings of Baltimore City weakened, faith in the
public school system eroded. Between 1970 and 1987 the City lost 17% of its
population, but public school enrollment declined even more, by nearly 43%.
Part of this decline can be attributed to the nationwide baby-bust of the 1970s,
but the decline also reflects a determined effort on the part of some segments
of the population to avoid the public schools, either through migration from
the City or enrollment in private schools.

In 1980, whites made up 44% of Baltimore's population but their
representation in the public schools had fallen to around 22%. Only three-
fifths of white families with school-age children enrolled them in public
elementary schools. Ten years later, in 1989-90, white enrollment in the
Baltimore Public Schools stood at only 18% (Maryland State Department of
Education 1990). As the white public school population fell, racial
segregation intensified. By 1990, in 65% of the City's elementary schools,
over 90% of the students were African American, and a majority (58%) of the
white students attended the few elementary schools (14%) with white
enrollments of 75% or more (Baltimore City Public Schools 1992). Or, put
another way, by 1990, 12 of the 118 elementary schools in Baltimore (about
10%) had student bodies that were less than 10% African American; about
25% were integrated, that is from 11% to 89% African American, and over
65% were almost entirely African American (90% to 100%).

Besides becoming more segregated, Baltimore's public school population
has become progressively more disadvantaged. In 1990-91, 62% of public
elementary school students were receiving meal subsidy, a figure that

somewhat underrepresents the true need since not all of those who would qualify apply for the program. In elementary schools, the proportion of students on meal subsidy ranged from a low of 5% in some schools to a high of 100% in others, but in only 7 schools was the proportion below 25% (Baltimore City Public Schools 1991).

Increasing racial segregation has occupied center stage in school board directives and court decisions, but it is a serious mistake to downplay segregation by socioeconomic status (see Wilson 1987). Within elementary schools, segregation by socioeconomic status is much more pronounced than it is in secondary schools. For example, in the early '70s, almost half (47 percent) of the eight to eleven-year-olds in a random sample of Baltimore children attended schools where the variation in social class within the school was less than half of what it was for children fifteen years old or more in the same sample (Rosenberg 1979). Or, put more loosely, elementary schools were twice as segregated by socioeconomic status as high schools. The school-to-school variation in mothers' median education reveals this same cloistering by socioeconomic status. The average education of mothers *across* elementary schools ranged from 8.1 to 12.7 years, and exceeded the range for mothers (8.8 to 11.4 years) across secondary schools even though secondary schools are on average about 3 times as large as elementary schools (Maryland State Department of Education 1976). Similarly, the percentage of Baltimore students participating in the meal subsidy program also spanned a greater range (5% to 100%) across elementary schools than across high schools (8% to 65%) (Baltimore City Public Schools 1991).

These figures underline the extreme variation in socioeconomic status of children across elementary schools. The social climate in a small elementary school where the average student's mother has some college and where only a sprinkling of students are poor is quite different from the climate in a school where the average student's mother is a high school drop-out and where virtually all students are on meal subsidy. Johnson (1995), in interviews with about 100 white mothers of Baltimore public school students, found that mothers with less than a high school education typically worked at unskilled jobs such as custodian or grocery bagger, lived in sparsely furnished, rented houses, and even when they pooled income with a partner (who typically also held an unskilled job), their joint income barely exceeded the poverty line for a family of four (around $24,000 in 1992). By contrast, she found that mothers of public school students with some college typically worked as teachers or office managers, owned homes in middle class neighborhoods, and had a joint income more than twice that of the mothers with less than high school diploma (over $50,000). Because of the marked variability in family circumstances across elementary schools, almost all youngsters in some schools thus live at or below the poverty line with parents who are drop-outs, while in other schools, almost all youngsters live in settings that are financially comfortable with parents who have a high school education or better.

This book uses data for Baltimore children to show how differences in family circumstances translate into beliefs and activities that help or hinder children's development. (See Chapters 3, 5, and 6.) For example, if mothers have less than a high school education, children are less than half as likely to go to the public library in the summer after the second year of school as are children of mothers with 2 or more years of college (35% versus 78%). Or, to take another example, if mothers are drop-outs, they expect their children to get a C in reading on their first report card, while mothers with 2 or more years of college expect their children to get solid B's. Not surprisingly, activities like going (or not going) to the library, lead children to perform at the levels parents expect. *do not have high expectations for their children*

Schooling and Inequality

The literature on schooling and inequality builds on two recurrent themes. One involves identifying *family characteristics* like those just mentioned and others that could explain the link between socioeconomic status and children's success in school: parent's educational level, economic status, family type, and the like. The other theme involves identifying *features of schools* that help some students do better than others, such things as school size, school climate, grouping practices, and curriculum structure. This book will draw upon both streams of research, but with certain key modifications and changes in emphasis. A number of large scale studies show that family socioeconomic status is the key predictor of secondary school youths' educational attainment-- for example, the correlation between fathers' occupational status and the number of years of schooling their sons achieved is .42 (Duncan, Featherman, and Duncan 1972). But models to explain the schooling of poor elementary children are not necessarily the same as those that explain the schooling of relatively advantaged secondary students. For one thing, many young children these days lack continuous (or any) contact with their fathers, and therefore cannot draw upon the economic resources of fathers that play such a prominent role in the secondary school models. For another, family characteristics may relate differently to the schooling of younger as compared to older children. A mother's never having been married is associated very weakly with children's behavior problems at the preschool stage, but is more strongly linked to children's problems in adolescence, whereas a mother's being on welfare has negative effects at both stages (Furstenberg et al. 1987).

As far as features of schools are concerned, the extensive studies of high school tracking and school climate (Entwisle 1990) have little relevance because the organizational features of elementary schools are different from those of secondary schools. For example, students' social status vis-a-vis their peers in high school is determined in considerable part by their attractiveness to members of the opposite sex, whereas in elementary school children are mostly below the age of puberty. Nevertheless, because high schools are tracked, high school tracking prompted us to search out the hidden tracks in elementary school ("Special Education" and retention). Studies of high school climate call to mind other issues, such as teachers' differential grading of students of the two sexes (Chapter 6) and other contextual problems. In short, research from secondary schools could not be generalized directly to elementary schools, but pointed us in fruitful directions and suggested ways to proceed.

The Critical Period

Children's transition into full-time schooling, especially their progress over the first two grades, constitutes a "critical period" for their academic and social development (Entwisle and Alexander 1989). The "critical period" idea, which has its roots in ethology (see Brauth, Hall, and Dooling 1991; Newport 1991), is defined as a life stage of *limited duration* where an unusual response potential of an organism is coupled with very particular kinds of environmental stimulation. A well-known example of a critical period is imprinting in newborn ducklings. For a period lasting just 24 hours, ducklings instinctively follow and become attached to any large animal in their vicinity, including humans. They have the innate propensity to follow (an "unusual response potential"), and in most cases the female parent is there to be followed (a "particular kind of stimulation"), but this tendency is of brief duration.

The existence of true "hard-wired" critical periods in the development of children is debatable, but critical period imagery is nonetheless useful for thinking about early schooling. First, events during the earliest years of school provide a "particular" kind of stimulation; elementary schools are socially organized in ways children have not previously experienced and provide the kind of stimulation society believes is essential for children's optimum development; an unrelated adult (the teacher) is in control; children meet in classrooms with desks, books, blackboards, clocks, bells, maps, and often plants, animals, and mineral specimens designed for their instruction, and remain there for several hours each weekday; the presence of other children who share the same goals and who are at about the same level of competence provides strong incentives because human beings seek social approval (peers) and are at the same time profoundly rewarded by positive reinforcement from an authority figure (teacher). All these "particulars" provide an arena rich in learning opportunities that is unique to this life stage.

Second, the "particular" kinds of environmental stimulation coincide with important internal changes in children that produce an unusual "response potential." Children's cognitive development proceeds very rapidly over ages 5 to 8; they are beginning to test ideas of invariance and causality, and starting to form rudimentary conceptions of time, number, and logic, i.e., they are able to understand that the number of objects in a group is not changed when the objects are rearranged in space. A dramatic change occurs in their understanding of language because they reorganize their filing system for words. At age 5, when asked to give a word in response to "went," they say "home"--"went home." By age 8, when asked to give a word in response to "went," they say "go," ("went-go") showing they have learned the substitution privileges of these two verbs. "Go" almost never follows "went" in a sentence, so children cannot have heard these two words in contiguity, but they have nevertheless deduced how and when one word can substitute for the other. "Went" and "go" have the same privileges of occurrence in speech or text-- "they go home - they went home"--and the child not only has deduced this fact but has constructed a general theory of language. Children's memory span, their general learning capacity, and their speed of cognitive processing also increase over ages 5 to 8 (Varnhagen, Morrison, and Everall 1994).

The first two grades constitute a critical period because the child's external and internal worlds are undergoing profound change *in tandem*. Over this 2 - 3 year time span, when children are separated from their families and instructed in groups, their own capabilities are simultaneously changing in ways that are highly propitious for learning to read and reckon. As their memory span increases, for example, children find it easier to remember number series and are able to acquire the basic concepts of mathematics.

This ideal coupling of internal and external conditions for children's development is of limited duration, however, and begins to change as children progress through the upper primary grades. For one thing, there has been surprisingly little effort to understand children's attitudes towards school, but their enthusiasm for school does diminish as they go through the grades. Older children rate themselves as less smart, less good, and less hardworking than do younger children and are less likely to perceive themselves as able

(Blumenfeld et al. 1982; 1986). Children's self perceptions also become more negative between the second and sixth grades (Purkey 1970). Over the first couple of grades each child also compiles a school history and a set of expectations that begin to put constraints on the learning process. And over this time period, children who do not "catch on" are quickly left behind because if they are slow to learn to read they are hampered in the acquisition of many other skills. Children find it hard to do word problems in math, for example, if their reading skills are below par. Small wonder that the first few years of school make such a difference.

The critical period idea is useful because it directs attention to important issues that have been overlooked in contextual studies of education. Developmental research has focused much more intently on changes within the child than on the social environments surrounding the child (Bronfenbrenner and Crouter 1983), even though obviously learning does not depend wholly on the child. The primary grades are a special time because children's cognitive skills are increasing at an astounding rate, but these grades also provide learning conditions unlike those earlier or later. "Schooling" involves teachers and other persons with whom the child interacts, the ways curricular materials are presented, the general social climate, and the organizational features of the school. In the first couple of grades, most elementary schools, even those in depressed urban areas, go to great lengths to provide an emotionally supportive environment, but in later grades, this kind of sensitivity to individual children and their needs is much less in evidence.

Social Aspects of Critical Period

The transition into full-time schooling reconfigures the *child's social roles*. Social roles and expectations for children's behavior change a great deal over the primary school years, and social development accelerates partly because over ages 6 to 8 cognitive development accelerates. Six and seven year olds are becoming independent from their families: they learn how to find their way about the neighborhood, monitor their own activities in a limited way, and operate on their own and away from the family, at least during the school day. Teachers, who are the "significant adult other" during the school day, unlike parents, respond to children's social class and ethnicity. They constantly compare children against one another, if not always in terms of physical coordination or physical attractiveness, certainly in terms of mental quickness, cooperativeness, and savoir faire. Children who slip easily into the student role enhance their own development. A child who has the temperament and inclination to fit in well gets better marks and gains more on standardized tests in the early grades than does a child who has less of those qualities (Alexander and Entwisle 1988).

But "fitting-in" is a two-way street. Teachers' own social origins influence how they react to students. Other things equal, higher status teachers tend to rate poor and/or minority group children lower than they rate other children in terms of maturity and classroom behavior, and also hold lower expectations for these youngsters. Not surprisingly, children's gains on standardized tests and marks in first grade are depressed by such teacher disaffection (Alexander, Entwisle, and Thompson 1987). In short, social distance between teachers and their first grade students can lead students to achieve less: it generates inequality of outcomes. On average, a random sample of African American first graders in Baltimore in 1982 received marks about one-fifth of a grade lower than their white classmates did, with children statistically equated across a wide range of other characteristics including their standardized test scores when they began first grade and their socioeconomic backgrounds (Entwisle and Alexander 1988).

Still another part of "fitting in" is the "cum" for each child. Records of marks, school problems, and test data are accumulated in a folder that provides a paper trail from first grade upward. The second grade teacher sees all the information collected over first grade, the third grade teacher sees all the information collected in the first two grades, and so on. The setting is ripe for self-fulfilling prophecies and for labeling. Teachers' expectations in the early grades, which are shaped in part by these dossiers, can affect youngsters' school performance 4-9 years later, even taking youngsters' later ability level into account (Entwisle and Hayduk 1988).

"Fitting in" can be incredibly important for children beginning school. In fourth grade the effects of children's personal qualities on achievement in *that* year are small but carry-over effects from the impact of the same child's personal qualities on first grade achievement tests are substantial (Alexander, Entwisle, and Dauber 1993). A good rating in terms of classroom behavior by the first grade teacher not only leads children to do well in that first year but actually affects the gains they make in grade 4 more than does the rating of the grade 4 teacher. First grade performance is "critical" because the cumulative nature of the curriculum makes it hard for a child to achieve at a high level in fourth grade without having achieved at a high level in earlier grades.

The early administrative placements of children that reflect social structure in the larger society also have even longer-term consequences. Compared to other children and all else equal, males, minority group members, and/or children of low economic status, more often fail a grade or enter Special Education classes in elementary school (Bianchi 1984; Entwisle and

Alexander 1988; Alexander, Entwisle, and Dauber 1994). Later on these same children are thus more likely to discontinue high school (Consortium 1983). The early grades are thus "critical" in the ordinary sense of the word because whether or not children meet challenges at that point in time has serious and long-lasting consequences as far in the future as investigators have searched (e.g., Pedersen et al. 1978; Entwisle and Hayduk 1988; Ensminger and Slusarcick 1992; Kerckhoff 1993; Alexander, Entwisle, and Dauber 1994). While the cumulativeness of school performance has never been in doubt, the actual data to support this linkage is only now beginning to emerge.

It is becoming clearer and clearer that how well children do in the primary grades matters a great deal for their future success. By the end of third grade achievement test scores are fairly stable and the quality of children's performance by then is usually a good indicator of future school performance. In the standardization sample for the California Achievement Test battery (California Achievement Test 1979), for instance, grade 3 reading scores obtained in the fall correlate .87 with the score the following spring; the similar correlation for the mathematics scores is .84. These correlations are close to the reliability of the test, so they are at a practical ceiling. Husén's (1969) large cross-national study likewise shows that both intelligence scores and teachers' ratings in third grade are strong predictors of children's long-term educational careers, and Kraus (1973), who followed children in New York City for over 20 years, found that the most significant predictor of adult status was the score obtained on third grade reading achievement tests. Weller et al. (1992), likewise report a correlation of .57 between a reading readiness test given at the start of first grade and tenth grade reading and math tests (see also Butler et al. 1985).

As for marks, the child's first marks in first grade strongly forecast marks throughout elementary school and in some ways they are an even more reliable bellwether of future performance than test scores because they are sensitive to the child's gender, ethnicity, and economic background. For example, a random sample of African American youngsters in Baltimore got significantly lower reading and math marks than whites did, starting with their first mark in first grade, even though their beginning test scores and home resources *were not* significantly different (Entwisle and Alexander 1988). The cumulative nature of schooling and the persistence of early rankings make it essential to determine how social inequality affects children's early schooling. Long before secondary school, we believe the effects of social inequality on schooling have already taken hold. From this vantage point, it is ironic that studies of social inequality in education have focused mainly on high school, because by then the time for counteracting these inequities has mostly passed.

Transition Issues

Curiously, the transition when children begin their formal schooling has no generally accepted name.[1] Perhaps for this reason its significance as a life transition has attracted little attention. Children assume the role of student, with a new set of supervisors (teachers, principals, other school personnel), a new set of peers (fellow students), and a new set of role obligations. School forces children to expand and refine their concepts of themselves and to begin to monitor their relations with other people more carefully. The early days of school, in fact, provide an ideal "looking glass" for the development of the self, as outlined by Cooley, Mead, and others (Sullivan 1953).

Perhaps the most critical feature of the early school transition is that the basis of rewards changes. When children leave the protective circle of the family, they are rated according to how well they do compared to others, whereas they were evaluated before mainly in terms of how well they did with respect to their own past record and so always rated positively--as four-year-olds they were bigger and more capable than when they were three. Furthermore, success in school supposedly depends on academic performance, but children soon discover that they are rated on their ability to please the teacher, to impress peers, and to forecast others' reactions, as well as on their ability to read and do arithmetic. Feedback comes from many sources-- teachers, principals, and classmates--and much of it is evaluative. To be successful, they must learn to differentiate carefully among evaluators according to age and social status. Approval from some classmates does not carry the same weight as that from others.

The compulsory nature of schooling means that success is no longer guaranteed. Adults are free to move--from one house to another, one job to another, one spouse to another, or one hobby to another. A key consequence of this freedom is that adults can improve their odds of being successful. If promotion at the present job is refused, they can move to another job; if they are unhappy with their spouse, divorce or separation is an option. In fact, adults frequently respond to failure by trying another venue. Elementary school children do not have that luxury, however, because they are harnessed into a role at an institution that they must stick with, like it or not. Legally compelled to attend school, they usually have no choice about which school they attend, which teacher(s) they get, or what they will do while in school.

The shock of the first grade transition is hard for adults to appreciate. One way to imagine it is to recall their own reactions to being placed in a total institution, for example, how they felt upon becoming an in-patient in a hospital, or starting a new job, or going into the Army. Hospital admission

may be the best analogy. First graders, like patients, lose control over life's
small daily routines of eating or elimination. First graders have little control
over when they can get a drink of water or use the bathroom. First graders, like
patients, cannot leave the room without getting permission. They take a
prescribed curriculum (course of treatment), move through a pre-ordained
daily schedule, and are evaluated (poked or questioned) according to criteria
they do not understand.

Children quickly learn that they are being evaluated, but are often confused
about what matters (Dornbusch and Scott 1975). As Finn (1972) notes: "In
school [the child] first discovers that not all students receive the same
reactions from the teacher, the principal or from others. At this age, the
reactions to him are not colored by his achievement record so much perhaps,
as by his sex, color, physical appearance, or his exhibiting proper--that is,
docile--behavior" (p. 395). Children get marks in topics like "language"
without knowing exactly what "language" is supposed to be. They may be
placed in the lowest reading group merely by chance (see Chapter 4) and their
marks may even depend on what an older sibling has done (Seaver 1973).
Small wonder that on entering "big school," many children are seriously
threatened and fear failure for the first time. Only one child in a class can be
"best" in reading: with thirty children in a class, twenty-nine are bound to
suffer some loss of reward. Furthermore, the possibility of an unfavorable
comparison is outside of children's control, because it depends on how talented
their classmates happen to be. Elementary schools enroll students who tend
to be much alike, so small differences among children are magnified. The
absolute differences among the top fifteen students in an arithmetic class may
be small, but these differences loom large in the eyes of children, teachers, and
parents.

The most credible evidence supporting the seriousness of the first grade
transition is that relatively small differences at this time among children's
performance levels and adjustment to school not only persist but enlarge.
Children's gains on standardized tests over elementary school vary directly
with their families' economic resources and those whose families have more
resources show more growth, so differences among children of various
socioeconomic status levels get larger.

As children age, however, the number of test points they gain each year gets
smaller and smaller (Entwisle and Alexander 1996a; Schneider 1980). The
deceleration in children's cognitive growth over the grade-school years is not
a new phenomenon (see Stephens 1956, pp. 162-163), but its implications for
schooling are generally overlooked.[2] If *increments* in test scores are much
greater in the lower than in the higher grades, the effects of social inequality

on development are bound to be greatest in the early grades. As one corollary, the short-term pay-offs for interventions designed to help children in the early years are likely to be greater than they would be later on. As another corollary, as yearly gains diminish, the variance across test scores inevitably gets larger. A larger variance in the later grades of elementary school leads the predictability from first grade scores to grade 5 or 6 scores to be even better than the predictability from grade one to grades 2 or 3. One implication is that the effects of early interventions may be underestimated if students are not followed long enough (see Butler et al. 1985).

Because the inequities in social structure emphasized in this book are firmly in place over the beginning school transition, they have a serious prognosis for long-term life chances. This transition has important implications for children's future well-being mainly because achievement trajectories tend to fall within certain limits--children who do not perform well early in school have limited life chances and those who do not perform well because of social structural inequities could no doubt perform better. The organization of elementary schools closely parallels the social fault lines in the larger society, yet how elementary schools are organized is virtually ignored. The major finding of the book is that schools themselves go far toward mitigating inequality but are not perceived as being capable of doing so.

Plan of the Book

For all the reasons so far outlined and others, the overall purpose of this book is to turn a powerful lens on how certain aspects of social structure affect children's early schooling. This chapter and the next set the stage by discussing the nature of early schooling and how social inequality impinges on it. Chapters that follow take up various facets of inequality in turn. Socioeconomic status is probably the largest source of inequity in elementary schooling, so it is taken up in Chapter 3. Chapter 4 focuses on school organization, and following it are chapters on family organization (Chapter 5), and gender (Chapter 6). Chapter 7 reviews and integrates the discussion in earlier chapters. Appendixes provide information about the design and procedures of the Beginning School Study carried out in Baltimore, and about how Beginning School Study variables discussed in this book were measured.

A word of caution. This book is not meant to be a balanced or encyclopedic treatment of schooling. Rather it is a highly selective discussion of some aspects of elementary schooling that are linked to social inequality and that, to our way of thinking (1) have effects on young children which are either currently underestimated or misunderstood, and (2) about which we have something fairly new and sometimes counter-zeitgeist to say. The book is also not meant to be a report on the Beginning School Study (BSS), but we draw heavily on data from that study to fill gaps in the literature or to provide specific examples.

We began the Beginning School Study in 1982 in order to gain a better and more specific understanding of how social structure helps or hinders young children's schooling. This study is longitudinal: it followed 790 randomly selected Baltimore youngsters from the time they started first grade in 1982 (age 6) and at this writing is still on-going. This book draws mainly upon information collected in the first six years of the BSS. To return to where we started, this book concerns some of the social forces, identified by mainstream studies in child development and by sociological status attainment studies, that produce inequities in children's schooling over the elementary years. A life course approach joins these two traditions and makes clear how profoundly some of the events and situations in middle childhood affect children's development in both the near and the longer term.

Notes

1. Notwithstanding lack of a name, in considering moral education Durkheim (1973) emphasized this developmental stage: "One can distinguish two stages in childhood: The first taking place almost entirely within the family ... the second, in elementary school, when the child... is initiated into a larger environment"(pp. 17-18).

2. See 1916 data on speed of silent reading or 1944 Stanford Achievement Test scores.

2

The Nature of Schooling

not very helpful

The nation remains skeptical that schools can reduce social inequality among children. Historically, this skepticism springs from two main sources, one, the early evaluations of Headstart that reported little benefit for children attending preschools, and the other, a consensus inherited from the Coleman Report (1966), that said differences in school quality had little bearing on students' achievement. These two lines of research strongly deflected public policy analysts and laypersons away from seeing schools as institutions that could reduce social inequality. In order to set aside old shibboleths and move ahead toward a fresh and more realistic view of children's early schooling, each of these lines of research will be briefly summarized and reinterpreted in turn.

Headstart

According to early evaluations, Headstart programs raised disadvantaged children's IQ's by only a few points and for only a relatively short period of time (Cicarelli 1969; McDill et al. 1969; Bronfenbrenner 1974). These conclusions, which were widely disseminated, were mistakenly pessimistic, and taking them at face value even led some commentators to conclude that children's IQ's responded mainly to genetic rather than to environmental factors (Jensen 1969). These conclusions were modified a decade or so later when the early Headstart reports were re-evaluated by pooling data from all the major Headstart experiments, concentrating on those in which students were *randomly* assigned to experimental (preschool) and control (no preschool) groups (Lazar and Darlington 1982). The re-evaluations verified that preschooled children's IQ gains amounted to about 8 points in first grade and gradually faded after 2 or 3 years. But these re-evaluations found benefits that had not been uncovered earlier: compared to the control children, the Headstart children had better math achievement up through grade 5 and had more pride in their accomplishments throughout elementary school. Parents

17

of Headstart children were also affected. Compared to mothers of control children, the mothers of the preschooled children were more satisfied with their children's school performance, even allowing for the level of that performance; also mothers of preschooled children had higher occupational aspirations for their children than other mothers did, and higher aspirations for their children than their children had for themselves. Most impressive, when the Headstart students reached seventh grade, only 14.6% of them were in Special Education compared to 34.9% of the control children, and only 19.9% had been retained compared to 34.9% of the control group. By twelfth grade, 18.9% more of the preschooled than the control group had avoided Special Education.

These findings in favor of Headstart are impressive because they come from hard experimental data analyzed by careful investigators who had no part either in designing or running the original Headstart programs. In addition, the re-evaluation included *every* experiment before 1969 in the United States that involved more than 100 children. It is hard to overrate the importance of helping youngsters avoid being held back or placed in Special Education because avoiding these placements makes a tremendous difference in their long-term life chances--more of them will continue in school, and not drop out before high school graduation, for example.

Still, what about the IQ effects? The short term boosts in IQ scores did fade. But such short term boosts could produce the long term benefits mentioned above. Woodhead (1988: p. 448) suggests how. The temporarily elevated IQ's of Headstart children could have helped them do better in school if during the early grades teachers saw these children as smarter and better adjusted to the demands of school. These teacher perceptions, furthermore, could have triggered a more positive cycle of achievement and expectations that helped the child do better in the later grades, long after the initial IQ benefits had faded. In other words, because preschooled children did better in first grade while their IQ's were temporarily elevated, they were enabled to do better in later grades. Preschooled children may have been easier for the first grade teacher to teach, or their parents may have become more favorably impressed with their abilities, or they themselves may have sensed their increased capabilities. Whatever the case, the temporary Headstart advantage could have been converted into a longer-term advantage by several plausible routes.

It is key to realize that only modestly better achievement in the first couple of grades might be enough for children to avoid retention or Special Education. More children are held back in first grade than any other grade (Shepard and Smith 1989), and nationally the ultimate retention rate approaches 50% for children like those in the Headstart experiments who were African American, male and disadvantaged (Bianchi 1984). Therefore, even modest improvements in first grade achievement could lower retention rates.

Some additional long-term effects also have emerged subsequent to the time of the 1982 evaluation. Headstart youngsters were more likely to graduate from high school, and after they left high school, 66% of the graduates who had no retentions were employed compared to 41% of those who had been retained (Consortium 1983: p. 443ff). The Headstart youngsters also adapted better to "mainstream society": they were more likely to be in some type of educational program, including high school or the military; they were more likely to be either employed or temporarily laid off; they were more likely to be living with a working spouse/companion. By contrast, the non-Headstart group was more likely not to be employed or looking for work, and more likely to be in prison or a non-student on public assistance. Many of these positive findings come from the Perry Preschool Project (Berrueta-Clement et al. 1984), one of the experiments with the longest time frame and a particularly intensive intervention.

What were the Headstart programs like? Actually, they were extremely varied. Beller's (1983) program in Philadelphia, for example, enrolled low income 3 and 4-year-olds, mainly African Americans, who then attended a sequence of nursery, kindergarten, and first grade programs that were well staffed and "child-centered," with a social worker and "home-school coordinators" to help establish close relationships between families and schools. Another one-year program in ten Louisville schools (Miller and Bizzell 1983) involved kindergartners in four different kinds of curricula: two (Bereiter-Engelmann and Darcee) used small groups and emphasized direct instruction; two others (Montessori and Traditional) were oriented toward "long-term development" and did not involve group instruction. A third program (Gray, Ramsey and Klaus 1983) consisted of two or three summer sessions of 10 weeks each, followed by weekly or bi-weekly sessions with a trained home visitor during the school year, with students staying in the program for 2 or 3 academic years. Still another program (Schweinhart and Weikart 1983), probably the best known, consisted of group preschool that met five weekday mornings for about 30 weeks in two successive years and also included weekly visits with mothers at home.

These Headstart programs varied so widely in content, enrolled students in so many different sections of the country, and enrolled students so varied in age that to identify which elements of the Headstart programs are responsible for positive effects is impossible. Indeed, because each program was relatively small--a maximum of around 100 students--only when data were pooled did the positive effects of Headstart on retention rates and Special Education placement become apparent. Nevertheless, the conclusion is now secure that high quality preschools can have significant long-term positive effects on children's life chances. The early Headstart children were almost all disadvantaged and African American, yet they were more likely than their counterparts who did not attend Headstart to graduate from high school and to graduate on time. It took many years to be sure about benefits from preschools, but it is now clear that they do help children who are socially and economically disadvantaged to profit more from their subsequent schooling. Headstart did reduce social inequality in schooling by enabling poor and minority group children to perform when they began school at a level more nearly like that of better-off majority children.

Secondary Schools

Another large-scale and famous study, the Coleman Report (1966), can also be interpreted to support the idea that schools reduce social inequality, although originally it was taken to prove the opposite. Coleman et al. concluded that *differences* among youngsters' families and not differences among their high schools affected students' achievement. Narrowly interpreted, this conclusion is correct: secondary school quality does account for less of the *difference* among high school students' achievement than do personal and family background factors (see also Hauser 1971; Jencks et al. 1972; Mosteller and Moynihan 1972; Alexander and Eckland 1975b). Still, to say that secondary schools have little differential influence on students' learning is not to say that attending high school has no influence: if children who attended one high school gained 100 points on some standardized test while those who attended another high school gained 98 points, the 2-point difference is rightly judged negligible, but the 98-point gain that they all make is not negligible. If schools act to negate social inequities, they *would* produce this lack of variability in achievement across secondary schools because they would boost the performance of the less advantaged children to equal that of the more advantaged.

Unfortunately, the negative interpretation of the Coleman data discouraged similar research at the elementary level, so that, without directly examining new data, Jencks wrote (1972, p. 89): "Differences between elementary schools may be somewhat more important [than those between high schools] . . . but the average effect of attending the best rather than the worst fifth of all elementary schools is almost certainly no more than 10 [IQ] points and probably no more than 5."[1] At the same time though, Jencks (p. 89) was careful to note the early work of Hayes and Grether (1969), which shows that children's differential growth in summer is the major source of the differences in achievement between children of different socioeconomic levels. (See also Mosteller and Moynihan 1972 p. 48.) In this sense, Jencks anticipated Heyns' (1978) Atlanta study that demonstrated substantial effects of schooling independent of home background for sixth and seventh graders. She brought to light seasonal differences in learning that make the school's contribution much clearer.

Seasonal Learning

Heyns' research provided a major breakthrough. By comparing children's cognitive growth when schools are open (in winter) to children's growth when schools are closed (in summer), she separated effects of home background from effects of school. In winter both school and home can affect children's growth but in summer only home influence can affect their growth.

Heyns determined that attending school reduces the achievement gap separating economically advantaged from disadvantaged children, a gap which increases as they progress up through the grades, i.e., she demonstrated that the distance between the achievement of well-off and poor students narrows during the school year. She showed (see Table 2.1) that the *school-year* gain for white children from the most favored backgrounds is 1.00 grade-equivalent unit, and is very close to the 0.96 unit gain seen for those in the next lower income category (a difference of only .04 units). Over the summer, however, the better-off white children in her study gained .11 units more than students in the next lower economic category (.29 versus .18). For African Americans, the seasonal contrasts were even more striking; gains in the school year for children in the highest income categories differed by only .03 units (.62 and .59), but differed by .34 units in summer (-.12 plus .22). Thus, achievement differences between children from advantaged and disadvantaged home backgrounds emerged mainly in the summer months when schools were closed. When schools were open, poor children gained just about as much as better-off children did. Rather than making no difference, it seems Atlanta schools actually made up for shortfalls in resources in low socioeconomic status children's homes.

Heyns was not the first to identify seasonal differences in learning (see Hayes and Grether 1969; Murnane 1975), but she developed a conceptual framework, including multivariate models with "summer parameters," and carried out a large scale study on summer learning that produced two solid findings: (1) the gains children made in the school year exceeded those they made in the summer, and (2) children's summer gains were inversely related

Table 2.1   Mean Grade Equivalent Scores and Gains by Race and
                 Family Income for Metropolitan Achievement Test, Word
                 Knowledge, for Sixth-Grade Atlanta Students[a]

Race and Income	Fall 1971	Spring 1972	Fall 1972	School Yr Gain	Summer Gain
National Average[b]	5.10	5.80	6.10	0.70	0.30
Total Atlanta Sample	4.25	4.87	4.86	0.62	-0.01
White	4.96	5.80	6.04	0.84	0.24
Less than $9,000	4.21	4.86	4.93	0.65	0.07
$9,000-$14,000	4.77	5.73	5.91	0.96	0.18
$15,000 +	5.86	6.86	7.15	1.00	0.29
African American	3.93	4.44	4.32	0.51	-0.12
Less than $4,000	3.62	4.04	3.76	0.42	-0.28
$4,000-$8,000	3.84	4.35	4.23	0.51	-0.12
$9,000-$14,000	4.08	4.67	4.55	0.59	-0.12
$15,000 +	4.57	5.19	5.41	0.62	0.22

[a] The sample consists of all students with test scores available at all three points in time. Totals include those for whom family income was not available.

[b] These means are predicted from the norming population for the particular test date.

Source: Adapted with permission from Heyns (1978, p. 45).

to their socioeconomic status; that is, poorer children gained about the same amount as other children in winter but gained less in summer. In summers, almost all the African American children in Atlanta *lost* ground, in fact.

A subsequent study of summer learning (Klibanoff and Haggart 1981), based on three years' data for more than 100,000 students in over 300 elementary schools, bore out Heyns' conclusions. Economically disadvantaged students grew at a slower rate over the summer than did their more advantaged counterparts, and as in the Atlanta sample, the least advantaged children consistently lost ground over the summer in reading and math (see Heyns 1986).

Why have these findings about "summer learning" not energized educators and policy makers? Mainly because in most educational research, children's school progress is assessed only once a year. Any variation in rates of learning during the year is thereby obscured. If students are tested every June, then the annual increment in their achievement is computed as this June's score minus last June's score. The relationship between social background and learning is then necessarily assumed to be constant throughout the year, and all the causes of that learning are necessarily taken to operate in the same way over that period. Only when score gains are computed by season, separately for winter and summer, is the strong inverse relation between socioeconomic status and children's lack of summer achievement apparent.

To understand how schooling counteracts social inequality, it is essential to separate "home" from "school" learning. The effect of schooling *by itself* is hard to isolate, because children learn around the clock, and on week-ends as well as on week days. Indeed, they spend more time outside school than inside, and much of that time is spent at home. Accordingly, much of what children learn could be learned at home, not at school. Better-off families travel, go to museums and libraries, and spend time with youngsters in ways that could enhance their cognitive growth, while families who are not so well-off have fewer resources to help children develop. It would not be surprising then, if children from relatively advantaged backgrounds improved their academic skills substantially over the summer, when school is closed, while children from poorer backgrounds did not. (See Entwisle and Alexander 1992, 1994; and Alexander and Entwisle 1996b.)

Seasonal patterns in learning square well with the long-time impression that schooling helps disadvantaged more than it helps advantaged children (St. John 1975; Coleman 1966). In fact, in periods when school is open, disadvantaged children in Baltimore learn as much as their more advantaged counterparts do (Alexander and Entwisle 1996b). Only when school is closed does Baltimore children's achievement vary by socioeconomic status level. - The seasonal variation in learning seen in Heyns' and other data (Entwisle and Alexander 1992, 1994; Murnane 1975) highlights the idea that schools *mitigate* social inequality because differences in children's learning across socioeconomic status groups are virtually absent in winter. Table 2.1, which is adapted from Heyns (1978), shows that African American children with less than $4,000 income have a "school gain" (.42) plus a "summer gain" (-.28) that produces a net gain of .14 points. Parallel gains for African Americans in the highest income group came to .84 points. The highest and lowest income groups are thus separated by .70 points, but the "winter" part of that differential is .20 while the "summer" part is .50. Therefore, most of the difference in gains between the two groups (71% of it) comes from the considerable progress that better-off children made in summer when school was closed. All but the very poorest African American children in Atlanta gained roughly the same amounts of word knowledge when school was in session (.51, .59, .62). In summer, however, all of the poorer groups lost ground; only the most affluent group gained. The major differences in children's overall achievement are thus traceable to family background, as the Coleman Report concluded, but when schools are in session they are highly successful at reducing effects of social inequality. Seasonal learning data thus provide a strong counterpoint to the Coleman Report and other large national studies that have been interpreted so as to negate the role of schools in reducing inequality.

The Beginning School Study that we carried out in Baltimore builds directly on Heyns' research. It sees children's cognitive development as temporal in two key respects. The first is consistent with Heyns--schooling occurs in some seasons of the year, not in others, and the pace of children's cognitive growth reflects the school calendar. The second emphasizes that cognitive growth is temporal in quite another sense: it is much more rapid early in life than later. Jencks (1985) estimates the rate of cognitive growth in first grade is ten times the rate in high school. Consistent with this, Beginning School Study data show that children's cognitive growth is much more rapid over the first two elementary years than the later years. The reading comprehension gain that children made in year one (64 points) is well over twice the gain in year five (26 points), for example (see Entwisle and Alexander 1996a). Because students' capacity to profit from schooling is greatest in the early primary grades, their rapid rate of growth in the early years means that effects of social inequality are probably greatest in the early years of schooling.

Dimensions of Inequality

This book, as we said, covers just a few dimensions of social inequality: children's socioeconomic status, age, and gender, plus school and family organization. The first three of these are characteristics of *individual* children and are closely related to the "risk factors" often discussed in connection with schooling (Pallas, Natriello, and McDill 1989). As we will later point out, organizational factors in school and family also impose "risks" that can help or hinder children's schooling. Before considering these, a few words are needed about the individual risks, however, especially socioeconomic status.

Children from families of low socioeconomic status suffer from multiple risks including two major ones that overlap: family economic status or income, and the level of their parents' education. Low family income and reduced education go together, because, other things equal, persons who finish high school or better can anticipate a much higher standard of living throughout their lives than those who do not. In 1992, for example, for U.S. families in the lowest income quintile, 22% of household heads had less than a 9th grade education and only 5% had earned a bachelor's degree. By contrast, among

Really a shame get the impression that
Because they do not receive
high expectation their consequently
result in them not wanting
the try as hard.

families in the highest income quintile, 54% of heads had at least a bachelor's
degree and only 1% had not reached the 9th grade. Similarly, high school
completion rates for household heads in the highest income quintile stood at
96%, while among those in the lowest income quintile, only 57% had earned
a high school diploma (U.S. Bureau of the Census 1993).

Children who come from economically disadvantaged families are at greater
risk of failing a grade, getting low test scores and marks, or having behavior
problems in school. (See Zill 1996.) The odds are 8% greater that a child
from a higher income family will be in the upper half of the class than a child
from a lower income family will be, for example. Children in low-income
families are also more likely to fail a grade, and those whose families were in
the lowest income quintile in 1992 had a dropout rate of close to 25% versus
a rate of only 2% for children from families in the highest income quintile
(Smith et al. 1994). (See also U.S. Department of Education 1994.) Bianchi
(1984) used national school enrollment data to show that among sons of high
school dropout parents living in poverty, retention rates reached 50%,
compared with rates of 18% to 19% for sons in an "average household" (a
husband-wife family with income above the poverty level, in which the wife
had a high school education and either did not work outside the family or
worked part-time). Similarly the NELS-88 survey shows that, in the lowest
quartile of family socioeconomic status, over 31% of children had repeated a
grade versus 8% in the highest quartile (National Center for Education
Statistics 1990).

Parental education level is an alternative measure of family socioeconomic
status that also predicts children's school performance. The proficiency tests
administered in 1990 by the National Assessment of Educational Progress
reveal a consistent relationship between achievement and parental education.
Among 9 year olds, scores in reading ranged from 193 for students whose
parents did not have a high school diploma, to 218 for those whose parents
had more than a high school education. Math scores ranged from 210 for 9
year olds whose parents lacked a high school education, to 238 for those
whose parents were college graduates (U.S. Bureau of the Census 1994). The
relationship between students' achievement and how far their parents have
gone in school is thus strong and consistent. (See also U.S. Department of
Education 1994; U.S. Department of Education 1991.) As a consequence,
research studies often merge family income and parent education level, as
happens when father's occupation is used to measure family socioeconomic
standing.

Baltimore data clearly illustrate the specific risks posed by low family
economic status for young children's school achievement in reading and math.

Grade equivalent scores[2] in reading and math in all 122 elementary schools in Baltimore in the spring of 1987, classified by quartiles according to the percentage of children in the school eligible for subsidized meals, show that in schools where less than 50% of the children were on subsidy, scores are above grade level in every year (see Chapter 4, Table 4.2). At the end of grade 2, for example, these children were already reading above the third grade level (3.19), and by the second semester of grade 5, they were reading above the seventh grade level (7.15). At the other extreme, however, in schools where almost everyone (89% or more) was on subsidy, children at the end of grade 2 were reading almost half a grade (2.53) below the third grade level. By the end of elementary school, the difference in reading proficiency was well over one full grade equivalent between children in schools where students were at the two extremes of meal subsidy rates.

The risk factor approach is unattractive for many reasons, however, one being that this approach focuses on characteristics of *individual* children. Many influences on children's schooling are organizational or institutional, a prime example being the school's socioeconomic mix. The "risk" associated with childrens' low economic status could be mitigated or reinforced depending upon the fit between the socioeconomic characteristics of the school and those of the child who attends. On the one hand, placing poor children in schools where the majority of other children are well-off can promote higher achievement in those who are poor (Coleman et al. 1966). On the other hand, placing first grade African American youngsters in integrated schools (where they are often poorer than their white classmates) may make it harder for them to learn to read than it is for their counterparts in segregated schools (Entwisle and Alexander 1994).

The risk factor approach is limited for another reason, too. A risk factor is essentially the kernel of a probability statement where "risk" means an elevated probability of some event. It is easy to slide into causal imagery--that is, to say "low economic status causes children to drop out." To invoke causality requires more than an elevated likelihood, however; it requires pinpointing why and how low family income hinders children's schooling. Does family economic deprivation shunt children away from attending "good" schools, does the lack of infrastructure in poor children's neighborhoods undercut their learning outside of school, do poor families lack books and other learning materials in the home, or what? Rating individuals according to risks is a useful starting point in terms of suggesting hypotheses to test, but this approach cannot shed much light on social processes or social contexts. Also, so far the risk factor approach focuses mainly on *negative* relationships. The "risk" of doing better in school than would be predicted is hardly ever considered even though many children from economically disadvantaged and/or single-parent families do well in school (Pallas et al. 1987). The "risk" label has a negative ring to it, which is not necessary but which, nevertheless, leads to a neglect of "upside" risk.

Life Course Perspective

Issues related to social inequality and schooling can best be joined by taking a life course perspective. Risk factors, as just noted, somehow direct attention to shortfalls or failure, while a life course perspective directs attention to *all* outcomes, the positive *and* the negative. Many economically disadvantaged youngsters manage to finish high school, complete college, and go on to successful careers. A key question is how these children manage to do well despite economic disadvantage. Also a life course approach requires thinking in terms of how early schooling affects students over their entire life span. The schooling process in adolescence and early adulthood can be understood only in light of students' earlier school histories. In middle school, for example, children who take a foreign language and algebra and so are in line for the college preparatory program in high school, are those same students who have done well in elementary school (Dauber et al. 1996; Dauber 1993). Thus, to understand high school tracking requires an assessment of where students stood before they started high school. As yet, however, a dearth of longitudinal research with elementary school children examines effects of economic disadvantage, minority status, family type, and other social inequities in relation to school outcomes over the long term. In fact, to our knowledge, no national study of test scores in elementary schools continues into secondary schools even though various local studies suggest the correlation between early test scores and educational attainment is greater than .50, perhaps almost .60 in some instances (see Jencks, p. 323, also Chapter 3, this volume).

A life course approach also highlights the importance of school transitions. School transitions are times when children's social roles and obligations change, so they provide a window through which we can get a clearer view of how social forces affect schooling. They are strategically advantageous because they are points of maximum continuity/discontinuity in people's lives. In a bicycle race, it is hard to make distinctions among people when all are pedaling ahead on the straightaway and so bunched close together. Encountering a hill, however, spreads cyclists out, and it is easier to see who is ahead or behind as they pump uphill. Likewise, it is hard to tell who is ahead or behind when children stay in the same school, but school transitions are like "hills" when people are challenged and the differences among them tend to widen. Expanding the range along which people can be measured (spreading them out) is a technical advantage, because when people are more spread out we can estimate their positions relative to one another more accurately and so have a better chance to identify what propelled them ahead or behind. For example, if children are only one or two points apart on an achievement test, say 300 versus 302 on the California Achievement Test in reading when they began first grade, we cannot tell who is doing better or worse because the random error in the test is bigger than one or two points. If John gets 302 and Harry gets 300, we are hard pressed to say John's true score is actually greater than Harry's because if the test were repeated, Harry could easily outscore John. If scores are separated by many points, however, we have more confidence in our decision as to which person is first, which is second, and so on.

Children's long term success can be made more certain or placed in jeopardy by how they negotiate school transitions. By studying the details of their performance over such problematic periods, researchers usually can learn more than they learn from studying a life period that is static. The beginning school transition is a very difficult transition for children. Because of the way schools are organized, it is also the time when social inequality may exact its heaviest toll on their long-term life chances. As noted earlier, the rate of retention is higher in first grade than in any subsequent grade (Shepard and Smith 1989; Reynolds 1992; Alexander, Entwisle, and Dauber 1994). With other things equal, poor children are more likely than better-off children to be held back, so socioeconomic inequality at this stage can exact a price that may never be repaid (Pallas 1984).

The "excess" retention rate in first grade for children from poor families illustrates how social inequity present at the time children begin school can provoke serious consequences for later schooling. Or, to take another example, single parents have lower expectations than married parents do for children's school performance at the beginning of first grade (Chapter 5), and lower parent expectations act to depress their children's reading marks. Given the importance of early reading skills for all other kinds of academic performance, a small difference in parents' expectations for their children's reading performance at the start of first grade, when added on to the debit linked to the low income of single parents, can make the difference between children who pass or fail first grade (Sundius 1996).

It is puzzling why so little research examines children's success in negotiating the transition into full-time schooling because children's starting points are strong determinants of their trajectory patterns. Those who have an early lead have a marked tendency to stay ahead (Ensminger and Slusarcick 1992; Harnqvist 1977; Husén and Tuijnman 1991; Kraus 1973; Alexander, Entwisle, and Dauber 1994; Kerckhoff 1993; Luster and McAdoo 1996). As discussed earlier, the advantage of Headstart youngsters in the early grades that put them just slightly ahead of their non-preschooled counterparts persisted far into adulthood. The Consortium (1983) and other related analyses (Luster and McAdoo 1996) provide a compelling example of how even a slight edge early in the game can mediate remarkable long-term advantages.

Children's personal characteristics are easier to study than the social contexts of schools, and so are more often investigated, but the two are intertwined. If two children of the same ability attend different schools, for example, such that one school has a student body of higher socioeconomic status than the other, the student attending the "low" school could well receive less instruction than the student in the "high" school. Yet because his/her reference group could contain many more students of lower ability than him/herself, the student's academic self-image in the "low" school could exceed that of the student in the high school. The social milieu as well as the student's individual characteristics need to be considered in understanding schooling.

Teachers' personal characteristics are part of the school milieu that students experience. All else equal, higher status teachers in the Beginning School Study rated disadvantaged or minority children lower than they rated advantaged or majority children (Alexander et al. 1987). Compared to children with the same test scores but of higher socioeconomic status, high status teachers held lower expectations for the future performance of students from low social backgrounds and saw them as less active participants in class.

Teachers' feelings about their work environment can form still another part of the school's social milieu. Beginning School Study first graders who did exceptionally well in first grade had teachers who rated the social climate of their school higher than did other teachers (Pallas et al. 1987). Specifically, if teachers found teaching in their school "pleasant" (versus "unpleasant") and found trying to do their job right as "very rewarding" (versus "frustrating"), their students did better than did students of less satisfied teachers. Perhaps the enthusiasm of teachers who think well of their school spreads to their students, or perhaps these schools provide settings that make teacher-student interactions more productive. Whatever the case, these examples show how subtleties of the school context can help or hinder young students.

Social Inequality and Early Schooling in Perspective

This chapter started by looking back at two large research studies, one on Headstart and the other the Coleman Report, which both initially seemed to provide strong evidence that schools do *not* mitigate social inequality. The consensus about these earlier studies has now changed: attending high quality preschool programs certainly reduces effects of social inequality on students' later school success, and secondary schools serve to equalize the achievement of students of varying economic backgrounds in winter when they are open (Heyns 1978). In fact, as this book will make clear, schooling at any level probably offsets effects of social inequity because home resources are critical for students' development mainly when schools are closed.

The chapters to follow will show that organizational features of schools and families, such as the grade structure in schools or the parent configuration in families, do make a difference for children's schooling, but some things still matter more than others, in particular students' socioeconomic background. Family economic resources, however, do not affect how much student's learn when schools are in session, as the next chapter will show.

Notes

1. His emphasis on the "smallness" of 10 IQ points can be questioned. The standard deviation of most IQ tests is 15 points--two thirds of a standard deviation on each side of the mean includes 49% of the population. Or, from another point of view, the 10 point difference between an average score (100) and the score (110) is often cited as appropriate for a cutoff for college admissions.

2. Grade equivalents classify test scores by grade level. For example, a child who can complete tests in reading at the beginning third grade level is rated at 3.0 Grade Equivalent Units (G.E.'s). One who can complete tests equivalent to those of children in the middle of grade 3 would be rated at 3.5 G.E.

3

Low Socioeconomic Status

As the 20th Century ends, the U.S. economy is more and more taking on the shape of an hourglass, with families at the high end of the income distribution doing better and better and those at the low end doing worse and worse. This economic polarization has deepened and intensified children's poverty. Between 1970 and 1992 the median income of families with children rose from $10,227 to $33,659 in current dollars, but allowing for inflation, this represents no increase at all. To make matters worse, persistently poor children have become less dependent on income from the labor market and more dependent on income from public assistance (Duncan and Rogers 1991). With poverty now greatest among the young, the very youngest children are the worst off. Among all children under 18, median family income in 1992 was $33,659, with 21% in poverty. For children under 6, however, median income was only $30,697 and the poverty rate was higher (24.4%). In fact, the U.S. children's poverty rate is over twice that in the U.K. or Canada (Corbett 1993) and the relative gap between poor and affluent children is greater in the U.S. than in any other western country (Rainwater and Smeeding 1995).

A dramatic change between how poor children were raised in prior decades and how they are being raised today is the higher likelihood that they will live only with their mothers. In 1969, two-thirds of poor children under six lived in two-parent homes, while in 1991, 65% of them lived only with mothers (Brandon 1993-1994). Sex differences in wages thus produce some of the economic disadvantage that children suffer because women's earning power is still only two-thirds that of men's (Sorenson 1991). But patterns of fertility, divorce, and remarriage also generate a concentration of one-parent families at low levels of income. Eggebean and Lichter (1991) estimate that child poverty rates would have been about one-third less in 1988 if family structure had not changed since 1960.

Official poverty rates, though sobering, do not tell the whole story, however, because they are not well calibrated to *present-day* housing or food costs. Poor families today pay a much higher proportion of their income for housing than they did in 1963 when federal poverty guidelines were set, with the consequence that in terms of current costs for housing and food, Ruggles (1992) estimates the true proportion of children in poverty is about one-third.

Poverty and Schooling

There is no doubt that family economic status is strongly correlated with children's schooling. Children from impoverished backgrounds do not stay in school as long as their better-off classmates. Study after study links income and other measures of family economic status to the amount of schooling children obtain (e.g. Garfinkel and McLanahan 1986; Haveman and Wolfe 1994; Elder 1974; McLoyd 1989; 1990), with those living in poverty for at least one year 6% less likely than those not raised in poverty to graduate from high school (Haveman and Wolfe 1994). Children from impoverished backgrounds also do not do as well as their better-off classmates on achievement tests. Although research on young children's school achievement is not extensive, family background probably matters more for their test scores than it does for older children's (Alwin and Thornton 1984; Marjoribanks 1979). The strong relationship between family economic background and children's school outcomes begins early (e.g. Murnane 1975; Marjoribanks 1979; Alexander and Entwisle 1996b), because children from advantaged homes arrive at first grade with their verbal and math skills at a higher level than do children from disadvantaged homes (Smith 1972; Huston 1994).

Many hypotheses could explain the correlation between parents' economic status and children's cognitive growth, the most common one being that better-off families have more resources to buy games, computers, and other things, and having these possessions helps children learn more in school. We believe that the learning that goes on in school is not directly affected by economic conditions in the home, however, at least for children in the early grades. In other words, socioeconomic resources in the home do not potentiate learning in the elementary classroom. We think instead that the process of cognitive growth is not the same for children in poverty as for those who are better off. The main difference, which is not yet widely recognized, is that poor children's cognitive growth is more episodic than that of better-off children--it virtually ceases when schools are not in session. Better-off children's growth is continuous over the year because their families and neighborhoods can supply the resources needed to support their growth when schools are not in session, while the families and neighborhoods of poor children cannot supply the needed resources. (See Heyns 1978; Entwisle and Alexander 1992; 1994.) That is, over the summer when school is closed, or before first grade when children do not attend school, poor children do not have the resources they need to promote their full development. Poverty limits cognitive growth mainly by denying young children the resources they need to grow *outside* school, especially in summer. So young poor children and their better-off counterparts differ in how much they learn when school is closed, and the single factor associated most strongly with how much children learn over the summer is family socioeconomic status.

The idea that home resources affect learning over the summer is not new (see Heyns 1987), because for some time it has been clear that well-off children improve their verbal and math skills over the summer almost as much as they do in winter when they are attending school, while poor children gain little or nothing over the summer (see Entwisle and Alexander 1992; 1994; Murnane 1975; Heyns 1978). What is new is the idea that these resources matter *mainly* in summer.

Seasonal Learning

The main outcomes considered in this section are the seasonal gains in Beginning School Study children's California Achievement Test (CAT) scores in reading comprehension and math concepts/applications. These tests were administered to Beginning School Study students in fall (October) and spring (May) of each school year. By subtracting fall scores from spring scores, we obtain a measure of gains over "winters" (school in session). By subtracting spring scores from those of the following fall, we obtain a measure of gains over "summers" (school vacation).

Individual Gains

Clear patterns of seasonal learning can be seen in comparisons of the school-year gains of Beginning School Study children in math and reading when school was open (winters) versus the gains they made when school was closed (summers) (Table 3.1). Children from both high and low socioeconomic status homes moved ahead substantially in the first winter: low socioeconomic

Table 3.1   School Year and Summer Gains on California Achievement Tests in Reading and Math over Elementary School by Family Socioeconomic Status (SES) Level[a] (N's in parentheses[b])

	Reading			**Math**		
	SES Level			SES Level		
	Low (327)	Medium (165)	High (161)	Low (340)	Medium (166)	High (158)
School Year Gains						
Year 1	56.7	68.6	60.8	49.0	52.9	45.0
Year 2	48.0	45.4	40.1	42.9	43.5	42.2
Year 3	31.2	35.6	33.7	36.0	35.9	35.6
Year 4	33.1	41.0	31.7	33.2	33.6	35.7
Year 5	24.3	29.1	24.6	24.7	30.7	27.8
Total Gain	193.3	219.7	190.9	185.8	196.6	186.3
Summer Gains						
Year 1	-3.7	-2.1	15.0	-4.8	-6.8	8.8
Year 2	-3.5	1.8	8.5	-5.2	-0.6	3.3
Year 3	1.6	2.5	14.9	-1.9	5.1	1.3
Year 4	4.5	1.6	10.4	4.8	4.8	5.6
Year 5	1.9	-4.1	-2.2	-0.9	1.6	5.9
Total Gain	0.8	-0.3	46.6	-8.0	4.1	24.9

[a] Composite family SES measure for students in "low" category mean mother's education is 10.0 years; for "medium" category, 12.0 years; for "high" category, 14.6 years. See Appendix B for full definition of composite socioeconomic measures.

[b] Sample sizes vary year to year. N's in parentheses represent the maximum in each SES category.

status children gained 57 points in reading comprehension and 49 points in math concepts between the fall and spring of first grade (winter) and their high socioeconomic status counterparts gained about the same number of points (61 points in reading and 45 points in math) (top half of Table 3.1). However, the low socioeconomic status children lost ground in the summer between the first and second grades (4 points in reading and 5 points in math), while students from high income families gained ground (15 points in reading and 9 points in math).

Children's growth decelerated markedly as they progressed up through elementary school, so the gains or losses grew smaller year by year but the seasonal patterns continued through the five-year period. Pooling test gains over all 5 *summers* shows that the low socioeconomic status students gained a total of less than one point in reading comprehension and they lost 8 points in math in the periods when schools were closed. By contrast, over the same 5 summers high socioeconomic status children gained a total of 47 points in reading and 25 points in math when schools were closed (lower panel, Table 3.1).

Pooling test gains over all 5 *winters*, shows that both the low and high socioeconomic status groups gained almost the same number of points (193 points for low socioeconomic status versus 191 points for high socioeconomic status children in reading and 186 points for both groups in math). Entwisle and Alexander (1992; 1994) provide multivariate analyses of variance showing that these seasonal differences interact significantly with family socioeconomic status over the first two years of school. In winters when school was in session both socioeconomic status groups gained the same amounts, but in summers they gained different amounts. The generally higher level of test scores of the high socioeconomic status children thus accrues entirely from gains made in the summers.

School-Level Gains

The seasonal patterns in young children's test scores are also related to the *average* socioeconomic status level of the school they attended. When the 20 Beginning School Study schools are divided into two groups--the 10 schools with the highest percentage of students on meal subsidy versus the 10 schools with the lowest percentage of students on meal subsidy--the average test score gains for children in the "high" and "low" schools in winters are virtually the same. (Table 3.2.) A significant difference between "high" and "low" schools appears only in year 2, and in that year students in *low* socioeconomic status schools did better. Over the entire 5-year period, students in the "high" schools gained an average of 37.9 points in reading per winter while those in the "low" schools gained 41.3 points. Students' gains in achievement *during the school year* were thus equivalent whether they attended low or high socioeconomic status schools.

When the performance of the same students is examined over the summer, however, students in the 10 "high" schools gained about 7 points per summer in reading and about 3 points in math. Students in the 10 "low" schools *lost* 1.7 points in reading and 1.5 points in math per summer. Students from

Table 3.2   Seasonal Test Score Gains in Reading and Math for Years 1 through 5 by Average Meal Subsidy of School[a]

	Winter Gains			Summer Gains		
	"Low" SES Schools	t-test	"High" SES Schools	"Low" SES Schools	t-test	"High" SES Schools
Reading						
Year 1	59.9		61.7	-7.3	*	12.0
Year 2	50.6	*	38.8	-5.5	*	8.7
Year 3	33.8		31.3	-0.5	*	11.4
Year 4	36.5		32.2	4.4		5.4
Year 5	25.5		25.7	0.4		-1.5
Average	41.3		37.9	-1.7		7.2
Math						
Year 1	50.4		47.1	-7.7	*	5.3
Year 2	43.6		41.6	-6.1	*	3.1
Year 3	35.2		36.9	1.0		-.5
Year 4	32.0		36.3	5.6		4.0
Year 5	25.0		29.4	-0.4		3.0
Average	37.2		38.3	-1.5		3.0

* $p \leq .05$

[a] Percent of children on meal subsidy used to define SES level of school.

"high" socioeconomic status schools thus made greater gains in summer than did students in "low" socioeconomic status schools despite the equivalent gains of the two status groups in winters.

The correlations between the average meal subsidy rate in each school and the amounts students gained by season are shown in Table 3.3. To remove the influence of individual family socioeconomic status, partial correlations controlled on the composite measure of family socioeconomic status. Again, with effects of family socioeconomic status controlled, the same pattern of seasonal gains by school meal subsidy rate appear as in Table 3.2. In winter there are no significant relationships between children's reading or math gains and the meal subsidy level of the school, except in the second winter in reading (children in schools with *higher* rates of meal subsidy gained more). However,

Table 3.3 Partial Correlations of Seasonal Reading and Math California Achievement Test Score Gains with School Meal Subsidy Rate, Controlling for Students' Family Socioeconomic Status[a]

	Winter Gains		Summer Gains	
	Reading	Math	Reading	Math
Year 1	-.02	.03	-.12*	-.14*
Year 2	.09*	.01	-.10*	-.06
Year 3	-.02	-.05	-.04	.04
Year 4	.06	-.07	-.01	.03
Year 5	.01	-.04	-.01	-.03

* $p \leq .05$
[a] Family SES status measured by composite family SES measure.
Note: Positive correlations favor lower SES schools

in summer the trend favors schools with fewer children on meal subsidy. In reading, all the correlations favor high socioeconomic level schools and the correlations attain significance in the first two years. In math trends are similar but less pronounced (see Table 3.3).

The Faucet Theory

We propose the "faucet theory" to make sense of the patterns in children's cognitive development summarized so far. It says that when school is in session, the faucet is turned on for all children, the resources children need for learning are available to everyone, so all children gain. When school is not in session, children whose families are poor stop gaining because for them the faucet is turned off. The resources available to them in summer (mainly family resources) are not sufficient to promote their continued growth. To make this pattern clear, Figure 3.1 plots Beginning School Study children's winter gains (between fall and spring) over the first 5 years of school separately from their summer gains (between spring and fall), with the lighter lines representing the growth of low socioeconomic status youngsters and the heavier lines representing the growth of high socioeconomic status youngsters. The lines representing children's winter gains are close together: low and high socioeconomic status students make similar gains. However, the lines representing summer gains are much further apart, especially in the early grades, because in summer the high socioeconomic status students gained consistently more than the low socioeconomic status students did. As we said, in reading both low and high socioeconomic status children gained almost the same number of test points when gains over all five winters are combined (193 and 191). Adding their summer and winter gains together, however, shows a total gain in reading over the five year period of 194 points for low socioeconomic status children compared to 238 points for high socioeconomic status children. Summer gains account for the entire difference.

The sawtooth pattern of seasonal test gains for low socioeconomic status children--moving smartly ahead in winter but stopping or retrogressing in summers--is thus far different from the pattern seen when data are pooled over winter and summer seasons. The pooled gains--summer and winter added together--are effectively what we see when students are tested only once a year, however. Once-a-year tests do not distinguish between children's progress in winter and summer, so yearly test scores give the distinct impression that high socioeconomic status children are gaining at a more rapid rate than low socioeconomic status children i.e., there is a positive correlation between children's social backgrounds and their annual progress on achievement tests. When seasonal differences in growth rates are ignored, the differences in children's achievement in summers favoring those who are better off are hidden, as is the equality of their achievement in winters.

The seasonal data derived from the Beginning School Study archive in Baltimore agree with similar data for children in Atlanta (Heyns 1978), New Haven (Murnane 1975), and many other localities (see Hayes and Grether 1969; David 1974; Hayes and King 1974; Pelavin and David 1977; David and Pelavin 1978; Hammond and Frechtling 1979). They strongly suggest that the process of schooling has been misconceptualized, at least for young children. Home resources do not "add on" to school resources in winter, because poor children do as well as those who are well off. Only in summer do home resources come into play. When children's cognitive gains are measured yearly by using test scores procured once every 12 months, however, researchers "see" relatively slower progress of the poorer children all year, and then conclude that poorer youngsters derive less from school than do their better-off classmates. Actually, of course, poorer children derive as much or more from attending school than do their better-off classmates over these years. As a consequence, most models of school learning mistakenly imply that there is a constant relationship (i.e. a constant slope) between the level of home resources and children's school achievement. This implication leads to the erroneous conclusion that a family's higher socioeconomic status boosts school performance by helping these children do better in school (Alexander and Eckland 1975a).

Figure 3.1 Seasonal Test Score Gains for High and Low SES Children, Years 1 through 5

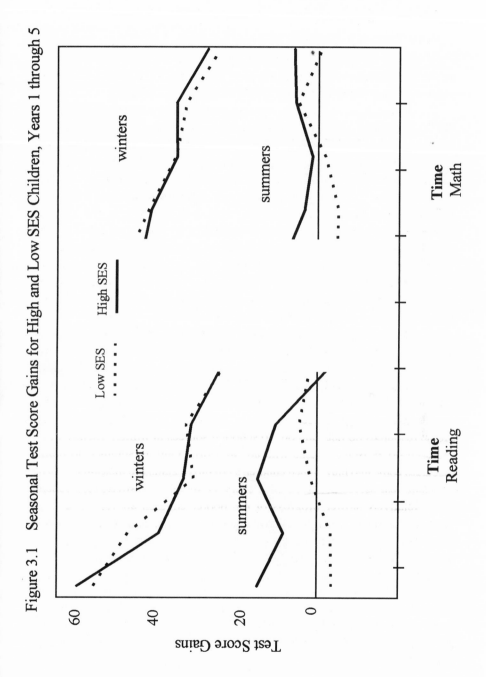

Family Socioeconomic Status and Children's Schooling

Exactly what happens in better-off families in summer that enables children in these families to continue to learn while those in poor families do not? What are the necessary "resources" in families? A number of explanations come to mind.

Expenditures

A common hypothesis to explain the link between a family's socioeconomic status and children's learning in summer is that the resources parents need to promote children's learning require expenditures, and higher socioeconomic status families have more income. Books, games, and computers top the list, but family trips to museums, zoos, science centers, historical sites, and sporting events, summer camp attendance and tutoring as well as the purchase of bicycles, musical instruments, and hobby equipment are often mentioned as resources that better-off families are better able to provide (Heyns 1978; Saxe et al. 1987; Schneider and Coleman 1993; Entwisle and Alexander 1995).

Beginning School Study data are consistent with this coupling of economic resources and learning materials in high socioeconomic status homes. Beginning School Study children *not* on meal subsidy in 1990 were more likely to have a daily newspaper, magazines, encyclopedias, or an atlas in the home, also more than twice as likely to have a computer as those on subsidy (38% versus 17%). In summers during the first few grades, Beginning School Study children not on subsidy were also more likely than those on subsidy to go to state or city parks, the zoo or science center, fairs or carnivals, or to take trips or vacations, and also more likely to play sports, go to the library and take books home, or to take music or dance lessons. The number of books Beginning School Study children read and their use of the public library both correlated strongly with socioeconomic status, and predicted summer gains (see also Heyns 1978, pp. 119). For Beginning School Study children, library use in the summer and children's meal subsidy status correlate 0.25. Taking a trip also contributed to summer gains, and Beginning School Study children's summer day trips and overnight vacation trips were both less numerous for children on meal subsidy (r=.41 and .37, respectively). (See also Heyns 1978.)

Expectations

Higher family socioeconomic status implies more than having extra learning materials available in the home or taking more trips, however. As McLanahan and Sandefur (1994) say, more income also can mean a better neighborhood

Table 3.4   Parent's Psychological Resources, Years 1-4, by Student's Meal
Subsidy Status

	On Meal Subsidy Mean	t-test[c]	Not on Meal Subsidy Mean
Parent's Educational Aspirations for Child[a]			
Year 1	2.8	**	3.5
Year 2	3.1	**	3.7
Year 3	2.9	**	3.7
Year 4	2.7	**	3.5
Parent's Job Aspirations for Child[b]			
Year 1	57.0	**	66.0
Year 2	55.0	**	64.0
Year 3	58.3	**	67.7
Parent's Estimate of Child's Ability			
Year 1	3.6		3.7
Year 2	3.6	**	3.8
Year 4	3.6	*	3.8
Parent's Expectation for Math Mark			
Year 1	2.6	**	2.9
Year 2	2.9	**	3.1
Year 3	2.9	**	3.1
Year 4	2.7	**	3.1
Parent's Expectation for Reading Mark			
Year 1	2.6	**	2.9
Year 2	2.9	**	3.2
Year 3	2.9	**	3.2
Year 4	2.7	**	3.1
Parent's Classroom Behavior Ratings			
Year 2 Interest-Participation	24.3		24.7
Year 2 Cooperation-Compliance	19.0	**	20.0
Year 2 Aggression-Restlessness	19.1	**	20.2

* $p \le .05$

**$p \le .01$

[a] Parent's educational aspirations are coded 1-5, with 2=high school graduate and 3=1 or 2 years of college.

[b] Featherman-Stevens Occupational status scores (Featherman and Stevens 1982) based on earnings and educational characteristics of both men and women workers. Typical job scores are: clergy=66.0, dentist=89.6, librarian=65.6, social worker=66.1, elementary teacher 70.9, nurse=46.4, police=38.0, waiter=18.9.

[c] t-tests compare means of students on meal subsidy with those not on meal subsidy.

and the financial security that enables children to expect to go to college. Knowing that college lies in the future raises both youngsters' and parents' goals. In line with those ideas, Beginning School Study parents of varying socioeconomic status levels differed in their psychological resources, including their expectations for their children's school performance. Before their children started first grade, poorer Beginning School Study parents expected their children to get lower marks in both reading and math and aspired to lower status jobs for their children as adults than did the better-off parents (Table 3.4). Even though children who were on *or* not on meal subsidy had gained equal amounts on standardized tests (see Tables 3.2 and 3.3), the poorer parents rated their children as lower in classroom cooperation and higher in aggression at the beginning of the next school year. Over the first four years of school, the mark expectations of the better-off parents and their estimates of their children's abilities rose a little more than did the parallel estimates of the poorer parents, even though the expectations of the higher socioeconomic status parents were considerably higher to start with.

Parents' expectations for their children's school performance relate to the quality of the parent-child relationship (data not shown). Beginning School Study parents with higher expectations tended to have warmer feelings about their children than did parents with lower expectations. In the second year, Beginning School Study parents rated their children's favorable and unfavorable qualities on three scales that focused on children's socioemotional status, for instance, whether children were "enthusiastic and liked to do things," "high-strung or fidgety," or "happy and well-liked." Parents who held high expectations for their children in reading also rated them at almost the maximum on these scales, while parents with low expectations rated their children a full standard deviation lower (data not shown). In essence, parents who expected their children to get high marks saw them as appealing *personalities*, while parents who expected low marks saw their children as considerably less appealing. Whether children with appealing qualities do better in school or whether those who do well react by being easier to get along with, there is little doubt that a warmer or more positive relationship between parent and child would support children's achievement growth.

Beginning School Study parents' expectations in year one also matched the actions they took (Table 3.5). For example, 81% of the parents who expected children to get an "excellent" rating reported they read to their child more than 10 minutes a day compared to 54% of the parents who expected an "unsatisfactory" rating; 59% of the parents who expected an "excellent" rating had seen their children's school records during the past year versus 27% of the parents who expected an "unsatisfactory" rating; 63% of parents who expected

Table 3.5   Parental Involvement and Student's Summer Activities by Level of Parent's Reading Mark Expectations in Year 1 (N's in parentheses)[a]

	Parent Reading Mark Expectations, Year 1			
	Unsatisfactory	Satisfactory	Good	Excellent
Year 1				
% Read story (more than 10 min/day)	54%* (26)	67% (230)	70% (306)	81%* (83)
% Parents seen school records	27%* (33)	41% (277)	46% (340)	59%* (99)
Year 2				
% Read story (more than 10 min/day)	43%+ (23)	58% (205)	61% (283)	66%+ (87)
% Parents seen school records	61% (23)	66% (205)	63% (284)	64% (88)
Child's Activities, Summer After Second Year				
% Children borrowed library books	31%* (13)	39% (97)	41% (160)	63%* (49)
No. of child's summer activities (swimming or music lessons, organized sports, go to library, etc.)	1.9+ (13)	1.9 (97)	2.0 (160)	2.9+ (49)
No. of child's summer trips (day or overnight)	3.2* (13)	3.7 (97)	4.1 (160)	5.6* (48)
No. of hours watching TV on weekdays	3.8 (13)	3.7 (95)	3.7 (156)	3.0 (47)

*$p \le .05$

+$p \le .10$

[a] Significant differences reflect t-tests comparing mean values for parents with highest ("excellent") and lowest ("unsatisfactory") reading mark expectations.

their children to get an "excellent" rating reported that their children had borrowed books from the library in the summer compared to 31% of the children whose parents expected an "unsatisfactory" rating; parents who expected an "excellent" rating reported that their children averaged nearly 6 summer trips while those who expected an "unsatisfactory" rating reported only 3 summer trips.

Do these parent opinions and activities matter? First, for every school outcome, whether marks, test scores, retention in grade, or drop-out, prior Beginning School Study research shows parents' expectations to be among the strongest predictors, and stronger by far than children's own expectations. (See Alexander and Entwisle 1988; Entwisle and Alexander 1990; Alexander et al.1994; Pallas et al. 1994; Entwisle and Alexander 1996b.)   Second, as Table 3.6 shows, parents' initial expectations when children started school-- before any report cards were issued--predict a number of students' characteristics important for schooling such as their academic self-images and feelings of competence. These parent expectations also have large *negative* correlations with the academic or other problems that children develop in first grade, and with whether or not children are held back or placed in Special Education.

Structural models to explain Beginning School Study children's cumulative gains on standardized tests over the first two years of school point to parents' expectations and family economic status as the two *major* explanatory variables (Entwisle and Alexander 1996b). These two kinds of resources are roughly of the same importance and largely independent of each other in explaining Beginning School Study children's school achievement. Better-off parents have more reading materials in the home and visit more places, but they also tend to have more of the psychological resources that foster children's development, such as higher expectations.

The family's willingness to make large investments in children *relative to the resources available* nevertheless probably deserves more attention than particular family activities (Heyns 1978). For example, a high-income family may purchase all kinds of educational books and toys but have little day-to-day contact with children, while a low-income family may not be able to buy books but can take children to the library and read to them. Parents of all economic levels, including those of the most limited circumstances, can supply the psychological supports to help young children do well in elementary school and these supports have strong positive effects that are virtually independent of effects of financial supports (Lee, Bryk, and Smith 1993; Entwisle and Alexander 1996b).

In sum, Beginning School Study parents' expectations vary by economic

Table 3.6   Correlations of Parent's Expectations for the Child's First Reading Mark in Fall of First Grade with Student Characteristics and Performance and Teacher's Ratings of Students, Years 1-5

	Years in School					
	1	2	3	4	5	1-5
Student Characteristics and Performance						
Absences	-14*	-.10*	-.09*	-.09*	-.09+	
Referrals for Academic or Other Problems	-.28*	-.18*	-.26*	-.23*	-.23*	
Academic Self-Esteem (Dickstein)	.18*	.10*		.13*		
Academic Self-Image (Harter)		.11*		.18*		
Student's Own Reading Expectations	.12*	.01		.11*		
Number of Retentions						-.35*
Special Education Placement						-.25*
Teacher's Ratings of Students						
Reading Marks	.42*	.40*	.30*	.29*	.31*	
Conduct Marks	.14*	.17*	.09*	.11*	.11*	
Work Habits	.32*	.24*	.23*	.24*	.23*	
Reading Level (Instructional Level of Reading)	.33*	.40*	.40*	.46*	.38*	
Personal Maturity Scales						
Interest/Participation	.38*	.24*		.30*		
Cooperation-Compliance	.18*	.15*		.16*		
Attention Span-Restlessness	.32*	.21*		.20*		

* $p \leq .05$
+ $p \leq .10$

status and represent a psychological resource that is positively and strongly related to children's school performance. Expectations reflect both parents' attitudes *and* behaviors: they index the parents' aspirations for the child and the emotional quality of the parent-child relationship as well as the specific actions parents take to help children learn. Parents who expect children to do well encourage them to have high expectations for themselves (Entwisle and Hayduk 1982), and when children have high expectations they are more likely to raise their hands and otherwise participate in class (Entwisle and Webster 1972). Also parents' early expectations have profound and long-lasting effects: Beginning School Study parents' expectations for children's first-grade marks correlated with how far they expected their first-grade children would go in school ($r=.30$) and with how far they expected their children to go in school when asked that same question eight years later ($r=.51$). First-grade children whose parents expected them to go to college were twice as likely to take algebra in eighth grade as a lower-level math class, with family economic status and the child's ability and performance in first grade controlled. These findings suggest that policies leading to parent involvement in school may be successful mainly because they channel parents' expectations and suggest specific ways for parents to implement their expectations.

Putting these various ideas together, we believe that family socioeconomic status affects children's achievement growth in summer mainly because it produces or reflects parents' psychological and economic resources. Despite children's equal progress in winter, low socioeconomic status parents continued to hold lower expectations for their children's school performance than high socioeconomic status parents did, no doubt in part because, like everyone else, they "saw" lower levels of achievement, not the actual test gains matched to the times when their children were or were not involved in school. That is, teachers' marks, children's reading levels, and children's promotion levels are in parallel with parents' expectations (Table 3.7), even though the growth rate of low socioeconomic status children *during the school year* equaled that of high socioeconomic status children.

Because poor children do as well or better than their wealthier classmates when school is open, the conclusion that home resources facilitate school learning is not warranted. The socioeconomic status of the family does not matter when school is open, and the conclusion instead is that the *process of achievement changes from winter to summer.* Resources possessed by higher socioeconomic status families do not enhance regular schooling, at least at the elementary level, but instead keep the resources faucet open when school resources are cut off in summer. Family resources matter relatively little in winter because then the school faucet is open, but in summer, when the faucet

Table 3.7   Ratings of Children's First Grade Performance by Socioeconomic Status (SES) Level of School

	SES Level of School, Fall 1982 (% Meal Subsidy)[a]			
	Low SES[c]		High SES[c]	
	Mean	S.D.	Mean	S.D.
Reading Mark, Qtr 1	1.64	.58	2.15	.74
Reading Mark, Qtr 4	1.94	.73	2.65	.95
Math Mark, Qtr 1	1.99	.75	2.52	.85
Math Mark, Qtr 4	2.26	.86	2.88	.90
Proportion Retained, Year 1	.22	.42	.11	.31
Reading Instruction Level, Qtr 1[b]	1.93	.51	2.21	.80
Reading Instruction Level, Qtr 4[b]	3.69	1.12	4.29	.96

[a] Percent of children on meal subsidy in each school used to define SES level of school. The 20 schools are divided into "low SES" (10 schools with highest meal subsidy rate) and "high SES" (10 schools with lowest meal subsidy rate).

[b] 1=readiness; 2=preprimer; 3=primer; 4=level 1; 5=level 2; 6=level 3.

[c] For low SES schools, sample sizes range from 355-405; for high SES schools, sample sizes range from 332-349.

is turned off, family resources are critical. To repeat: *home resources do not cause students to learn more during the school year. Rather, home resources provide students the opportunity to continue their learning outside school over summer periods when schools are closed.*

The flavor of day-to-day interactions and psychic investments that better-off parents make in their children may be the critical issue rather than the specific items they can purchase. Resources that promote cognitive growth in children involve activities with parents and other persons whose interactive style is conducive to learning. Better-off parents have more reading materials in the home, visit more places, and do more things, but they also tend to have the kinds of interpersonal skills that foster children's development, such as avoiding negative feedback (Hess and Shipman 1965). Parents with more income are also likely to have more rewarding and intellectually complex jobs, and the quality of the home environment when parents have more rewarding jobs (higher paid) is better than that of homes where parents have lesser jobs (lower paid) (Menaghan and Parcel 1991). This line of reasoning argues that children in better-off families learn more in summer because their parents have the needed psychological resources to prompt the kinds of interactions and activities that promote children's learning. They know how to "turn on the faucet" while parents who are less well off do not.

Neighborhood Resources

Lack of resources in neighborhoods is still another dimension of poverty related to family socioeconomic status (see Wilson 1987; Sampson 1992) that could affect children more in summer when schools are closed than in winter when schools are open. Because poor neighborhoods lack appropriate role models, safe streets for children to play in, a network of local institutions like libraries, stores and banks, or adults outside the immediate family who are invested in children's well-being, they accentuate and perpetuate the disadvantages of family poverty (Jargowsky and Bane 1990). In "ghetto neighborhoods," defined as areas where 40% or more of the families are below the poverty line, churches, book clubs, scout troops, community associations and other voluntary groups are absent or weak. These neighborhoods, which typically have high rates of crime and delinquency, provide little supervision for children, either formal as in organized sports, or informal as by the concerned neighbor over the back fence. For these reasons, concerned parents in poverty neighborhoods even try to shield their children from direct contacts with the neighborhood or its other residents.

Ghetto neighborhoods are qualitatively different from middle class neighborhoods (Wilson 1987). Seemingly, the absence of better-off families rather than the predominance of poor families explains much of the negative effect of these neighborhoods on children (Brooks-Gunn et al. 1993). Put another way, the pooled psychological resources of parents in ghetto neighborhoods are weak.

The faucet theory would predict that neighborhood resources matter more in summer than in winter, because when children are not in school, resources in high socioeconomic status neighborhoods could supplant the resources furnished by the school, but resources in ghetto neighborhoods could not. Beginning School Study schools were located in neighborhoods which ranged from very low socioeconomic status (close to 40% of families in poverty, the average parent a drop-out, and only 5% of workers in professional/managerial jobs) to relatively high socioeconomic status (2% of families in poverty, the average parent close to a college graduate, and 64% of workers in professional/managerial jobs). Surrounded by poverty, Beginning School Study children in the poorest neighborhoods presumably had few resources to support their academic growth in summer when school was closed.

To test the hypothesis that children's growth on achievement tests would depend on neighborhood resources mainly in summer, we computed partial correlations between Beginning School Study children's test score gains in summer and several measures of neighborhood quality. Over the first three years of school, after removing effects of both student level meal subsidy status and parents' education (Table 3.8), children's achievement gains in summer are inversely related to both the percentage of families below the poverty line in neighborhoods where Beginning School Study schools are located and to meal subsidy rates by school. Likewise, in five of six instances, median family income of the neighborhood is positively correlated with children's summer gains. Thus, *after family resources are taken into account*, the summer gains Beginning School Study children made on standardized tests were significantly higher in neighborhoods where the poverty rate was lower.

The linchpin of this demonstration is that in winters when schools were in session, neighborhood resources had either negligible or inverse effects on childrens' school progress. The partial correlations between gains in children's test scores and measures of neighborhood quality in winter (left side, Table 3.8) are either close to zero (not significant) or in many instances inverse--that is, children who lived in poorer neighborhoods gained *more* than did their counterparts in better neighborhoods. Beginning School Study schools were thus making up to some extent for the lack of neighborhood resources in winter, just the opposite of the pattern seen in summer. When the faucet was open in winter--and widely open for the poorest children--neighborhood resources are less important.

Definitions of Neighborhood. Baltimore is a patchwork of clearly recognizable neighborhoods, and the City's official planning agencies have developed a network of health, recreational and social services around these neighborhoods. The effects of neighborhoods on Beginning School Study children's achievement gains as just summarized are all the more persuasive because the neighborhoods mapped by the Regional Planning Council of Baltimore or by the Baltimore City Department of Planning and used in our analyses have to do with socially distinct neighborhoods, not zipcodes or other indices unrelated to social structure. Baltimore neighborhoods vary socially and culturally, and the ghetto neighborhoods in Baltimore clearly differ from the better-off neighborhoods. For example, when Study children started first

Table 3.8   Correlations of Seasonal Gains on California Achievement Test Subtests in Reading and Math with Measures of Neighborhood Quality[a]

Gains	Winter Gains			Summer Gains		
	Meal Subsidy Rate[b]	Neighborhood Income[c]	Family Poverty[d]	Meal Subsidy Rate[b]	Neighborhood Income[c]	Family Poverty[d]
Reading, Year 1	-.01	-.02	-.02	-.14*	.15*	-.12*
Reading, Year 2	.10*	-.04	.08+	-.10*	.01	-.04
Reading, Year 3	.02	-.02	.05	-.09*	.09*	-.12*
Math, Year 1	.07+	-.18*	.11*	-.13*	.17*	-.14*
Math, Year 2	.00	.07+	-.04	-.07+	-.04	-.01
Math, Year 3	-.02	-.05	.02	.03	.09+	-.09*

* $p \le .05$ + $p \le .10$

[a] These correlations partial out both family economic status and parent education level.

[b] Percent of children in school who receive meal subsidy, 1982 (Baltimore City Public Schools 1988).

[c] Median household income for neighborhood in which school is located (Regional Planning Council 1983).

[d] Percent of families below federal poverty level for neighborhood where school is located (Baltimore City Department of Planning 1983).

Note: For meal subsidy rate and family poverty, positive correlations favor lower socioeconomic level neighborhoods; for neighborhood income, positive correlations favor higher socioeconomic level neighborhoods grade, close to 50% of all Baltimore residents over 25 had completed high school (U.S. Bureau of the Census 1983) compared to only 20 to 30% of the residents in ghetto neighborhoods, and in these same neighborhoods, less than one-third of families with children included a married couple as contrasted with 55% of families for Baltimore as a whole. In the three poorest neighborhoods where Beginning School Study schools were located, male labor force participation was about 50% compared to 67% in Baltimore as a whole; also of persons age 16 and 19 in these neighborhoods, one-quarter to one-half were neither in school nor employed, compared to 20% for Baltimore as a whole. Probably most important, the percentage of households in ghetto neighborhoods relying on public assistance (41%) was more than double the percentage in the City as a whole (18%) and ranged up to 58% in some cases (Baltimore City Department of Planning 1983).

A number of recent studies point to negative effects of poor neighborhoods on the children who reside in them (e.g. Duncan and Laren 1990; Spencer 1992), but the other side of the coin is that strong neighborhoods should confer benefits. A few studies also show this. In Chicago, for example, political power of African Americans in neighborhoods was inversely correlated with infant mortality rates even though poverty and segregation rates were the same across neighborhoods (LaVeist 1992). Also, because boys spend more time out in neighborhoods than girls do (Heyns 1978; Medrich et al. 1982; Furstenberg and Hughes 1995), when neighborhood resources are plentiful, boys apparently profit more from these resources than girls do. (See Spencer 1992; Entwisle, Alexander, and Olson 1994; Connell, Clifford, and Crichlow 1992)

Explanations for Neighborhood Effects. The pooled psychological resources of adults in neighborhoods are probably the "faucet" that supports some of the summer growth of Beginning School Study children in better-off neighborhoods. Several of Jencks and Mayer's (1990) explanations for how bad neighborhoods could hamper children's development can be turned around to suggest why good neighborhoods would help children: (1) institutional influences--the presence of small businesses, good schools and the like, implies that some gainfully employed persons are nearby to support children's development: (2) epidemic effects--children whose peers are involved in travel or who read books may "catch" these good habits: (3) competition effects--children who must compete with older persons for resources are at less of a disadvantage when resources are plentiful: (4) relative deprivation--youngsters can be helped by their perception that they are relatively well-off compared to other students or families: (5) collective socialization--in good neighborhoods children profit from the monitoring and role modeling of neighbors.

In studies to date, collective socialization explanations have the edge over epidemic theories in explaining neighborhood effects. For example, neighborhood quality affects the number of years of schooling completed by Panel Study of Income Dynamics youngsters at *all* economic levels, not just the disadvantaged (Brooks-Gunn, Duncan, and Klebanov 1993). Also greater concentrations of low as compared to middle income families are not detrimental even for economically disadvantaged youngsters, we would say because the basic resources to support summer learning are provided by the presence of a core of affluent neighbors, which helps almost all groups. Negative effects traceable to competition with more affluent classmates are apparently more than offset by the benefits of living with more affluent neighbors (role models, mentoring). The faucet theory likewise favors collective socialization because an "epidemic" is not analogous to turning resources on or off, but collective socialization can be seen as a community resource that turns on when school closes. The main addition we would make to Jencks and Mayer's (1990) thinking is timing: neighborhood resources matter more when school is closed, at least for cognitive growth.

Other Hypotheses and the Faucet Theory

Parents' School Involvement

An alternative hypothesis to explain how a family's economic resources could support children's schooling focuses on parents' interaction with school personnel (Lareau 1987; Stevenson and Baker 1987). Lareau found that 100% of the middle class parents in her sample appeared for parent-teacher conferences and attended "open houses" at school, while only 65% of the working class parents appeared for conferences and 35% attended open houses. While her observations have led to the conclusion that parents' school visits improved children's learning during the school year, the face-to-face interaction between parents and school personnel she describes during the school year could also help children learn more in summer because parents' role enactment, rather than any direct effects of parents visiting school and the like, could explain why parent involvement in school helps. Specifically, working class parents in Lareau's study defined education as a process taking place on school premises and on school time, under the direction of a teacher. They did not believe that children's learning depended on activities at home and, in fact, encouraged their children to ride bikes after school and otherwise entertain themselves rather than spend time studying. Middle class parents, on the other hand, looked upon themselves as being partners with teachers in promoting children's academic growth. By visiting school, middle-class parents could learn what the curriculum is about, how teachers approach various topics, what kinds of projects are suitable for children of various ages, and perhaps the academic strengths and weaknesses of their own children. In summer when school is closed, they could put what they know to good use. In short, because they view themselves as partners with teachers in the educational enterprise, they could successfully promote learning activities in summer. Working-class parents who do not visit school would not be prepared to help in summers, nor would they see it as a time when they might take over the teacher's job. When school is not in session (in summers), middle class parent involvement could be helpful because then parents take over the role of teacher and their close contact with school in winter informs them of the level and kind of learning experiences their children are ready for. In short, they are in a position to turn on the faucet.

Stress in the Home

Still another hypothesis to explain why family socioeconomic status level correlates with children's school performance is that low family income produces high levels of stress in the home that interferes with children's schooling. DuBois et al. (1992; 1994), for instance, found that school-based supports buffered or compensated for hazards in the home and other places outside school, *and* that disadvantaged youths had a greater potential than their better-off classmates to benefit from adults' social support in school achievement. Although direct evidence is thin, maternal stress does interfere with mothering, in terms of both the quality of care and maternal sensitivity to the child's needs (Pianta, Sroufe, and Egeland 1989). Poor children could thus experience double jeopardy, first because they are exposed more frequently at home to family stress and other negative life conditions; second, because they experience more serious consequences from these risks than do children of higher socioeconomic status, particularly if poverty is long term (Parker et al. 1988). For these reasons, stress created by financial problems at home could have negative effects on children's school performance.

This hypothesis can also be seen as consistent with the faucet theory, however. The number of negative life events for Beginning School Study families of low socioeconomic status exceeded the number of such events for high socioeconomic status families,[1] but when school was in session, as we have seen, children in low and high socioeconomic status families gained on standardized tests at about the same rate. This parity in outcomes during the school year for children from different "life event" backgrounds suggests that in addition to serving as a forum for learning, the school may also serve as a social environment that neutralizes or buffers stress in the home. The summer differences in learning between high and low socioeconomic status children could then come about because poor youngsters are stressed in summer by negative life events that schools cannot buffer. When children are around home all day, as low income children tend to be in the summer, stressful conditions there could interfere with their development, whereas in winter they spend time in school, away from these stresses.

Asian Data

In Asian countries the school "faucets" rarely close, so the faucet theory is also consistent with the observation that Asian children achieve at consistently higher levels than American children do (Stevenson and Stigler 1992). U.S. schools close for long summer vacations--about three months--while Asian schools close mainly for the month of August, and even during vacations, Chinese and Japanese students have assignments to complete. Also when schools are in session, Asian children are in class 8 hours a day on week-days and 4 hours on Saturdays and spend "vastly more time on homework" than American children do (Stevenson and Stigler 1992, p. 54). Spending more time in school is not the only difference, and probably not even the main difference between the schooling of Asian and American students, but the faucet theory suggests that year-round schooling could act to improve the achievement of the *less* well-off Asian children and thereby raise overall levels of children's achievement.

Overview

Annual test scores give the distinct impression of a positive correlation between children's social backgrounds and their progress in school, but seasonal test scores show that annual gains have two components. In one component (winter), the correlation between children's social background and gains on achievement tests is essentially nil.[2] In the other component (summer), the correlations are strong, especially during the first three years of school. When seasonal differences in growth rates are suppressed, however, the differences in children's achievement in summers favoring those who are better off are hidden, as is the equality of children's achievement across socioeconomic status groups in winters.

Typically, school achievement has been studied in single snapshots, as in cross-sectional studies (Coleman et al. 1966), or in longitudinal studies tied to an annual or biennial testing schedule, as in High School and Beyond. Either approach misses the substantial seasonal variation in children's learning rates. Equally important, in prior studies of "summer learning" the invariance in winter learning rates has been glossed over. We believe that schools account for little of the variance in young children's achievement because when they are open they furnish sufficient resources so poorer children can learn as much as other children. Schools are *not* unimportant, however. Rather, they are so effective that when they are open the differences among them are inconsequential for children's learning.

Achievement Models

One major implication of seasonal learning patterns is that the process of schooling has been misconceptualized, at least for young children. Home resources do not "add on" to school resources to support achievement in winter, as implied by the constant coefficients associated with socioeconomic status in most models of school achievement, because when school is in session, poor children gain as much as those who are well off. Only in summer do home resources come into play. However, as we said, when children's cognitive gains are measured yearly, as happens when test scores are procured once every 12 months, researchers "see" relatively slower progress of the poorer children on a 12-month basis and then conclude that poor youngsters derive less from school than do their better-off classmates. This false conclusion leads to the mistaken notion that a family's higher socioeconomic status level boosts school performance by helping high socioeconomic status children do better during the school year as well as during the summer (Alexander and Eckland 1975c). If family socioeconomic status does not influence learning when school is open, as seems to be true for young Beginning School Study children, and also for middle school children (Heyns 1978), the conclusion instead should be that the *process of achievement changes from winter to summer*, i.e., the slope of the relationship between family socioeconomic status level and children's school achievement changes by season. In her study of seasonal differences in gains on word knowledge tests for sixth- and seventh- graders in Atlanta, Heyns shows clearly that effects of home resources are not constant throughout the year. She says (p. 82) "Schooling consistently dampens the impact of parental status [for both blacks and whites although] the magnitude of this effect achieves significance only for the complete sample..." And later (p. 92) "Unless one assumes quite implausible correlations among the residual determinants of income, it is not possible to replicate the observed correlations between income and achievement by assuming that the true effect [of income] is constant and of equal magnitude in the fall [after summer] and spring [after school year]...family income is more highly related to fall achievement than to spring scores."

There is no question that family economic status correlates strongly with all school outcomes for Beginning School Study children: their achievement, whether measured by test scores, marks, retention, or drop out; their teachers' opinions of them, whether indicated by conduct marks, group placement, class interest/participation, or attention span/restlessness ratings. Still, the question remains as to how family economic resources or parent education are transduced into various levels of school performance. Two major hypotheses that could explain this linkage have been emphasized, one involving material possessions or family activities that require expenditures and the other involving psychological attributes of parents. The seasonal patterns in achievement growth, however, argue that family resources of both kinds are redundant with those provided by the school when schools are in session. Only when school resources are cut off do family resources come into play. Then many factors correlated with both parents' economic resources *and* their psychological resources underwrite children's cognitive growth.

How family economic resources, parenting style, and children's school performance interrelate needs to be worked out in detail, but we agree with Walberg (1984) who concluded that the "alterable curriculum of the home" is more important than family socioeconomic status in promoting children's achievement. Informed parent-child conversations about school and everyday events, encouragement and discussion of leisure readings, monitoring and joint critical analysis of TV viewing, deferral of immediate gratification in favor of long-term goals in education, and expressions of affection and interest in the child's academic and other progress as a person, are just as accessible to low as to high socioeconomic status parents. Parents' socioeconomic status is correlated with the home atmosphere they provide but "... some low-socioeconomic status parents (defined in terms of income, education, and/or occupational level) are very good at creating a home atmosphere that fosters learning (e.g., they read to their children, help them with their homework, encourage them to go to college, and take them to the library and to cultural events), whereas other low-socioeconomic status parents are not" (White 1982). The affective quality of the mother-child relationship seems especially critical for young children's cognitive growth because it predicts children's ratings of their own competence (Cassidy 1988), as well as their school readiness at age 5-6 and school achievement at age 12 (Estrada et al. 1987).

The Role of Schools

A major implication of the faucet theory of children's schooling is that schools are doing a far better job than they have been credited with. Equally important is the implication that parents' attitudes toward, activities with, hopes for, and psychic investments in their children are a major reason for the variation in children's cognitive growth when school is not open. At present, because of misperceptions about the process of schooling, poorer parents' psychological resources are needlessly depressed. Their children do as well as other children do when school is open, but at the beginning of first grade, poorer children's marks and other ratings are a little lower than those of better-off children and their scores continue to reflect where they started rather than what they have gained. This mismatch between children's actual school performance and society's views of that performance is a gross form of inequity because, while in the early grades, low and high status children's *gains* on standardized tests are actually equivalent, their reading and math marks are not. Probably even more important, in the Beginning School Study twice as many low socioeconomic status as high socioeconomic status youngsters are retained in first grade.

When children start school their pre-reading and pre-math skills reflect their uneven family situations, but despite their uneven family situations, Beginning School Study children of all socioeconomic status levels progressed at the same rate over first grade. At the end of first grade, though, the unevenness in test scores that was present at the start is still there, despite all children's having moved ahead by the same amount once they began school. Children of both socioeconomic status levels have done equally well, on average, over the first year but since they started from different points, at the end of the school year they end up at different points. Observers then mistakenly conclude that poor children have derived less benefit from attending school than better-off children have, and look to the school for remedies.

The perception that children's gains during the school year are proportional to their starting scores (Coleman's notion of "fan-spread) is incorrect. (If anything, gains are inversely proportional.) Gains calculated on the basis of *only* the school year show that all children make equal progress. Nevertheless, and despite this equal growth, in schools that poor children attend, children's marks are lower and parents' and teachers' expectations are lower than they are in schools that better-off children attend. Children whose progress in school is equivalent are being treated differently on the basis of their family resources.

Summer School as a Remedy

The general profile of children's achievement growth in grade school and immediately before suggest that if economically disadvantaged children were provided with suitable resources, their achievement levels could be brought in line with the levels of more advantaged children over the first few years of school. Careful evaluations of Headstart programs in the 1960s (experiments with random assignment of youngsters to preschool or non-preschool groups) encourage this approach because the long-term follow ups of Headstart youngsters show that they do better than their non-preschooled counterparts in terms of retention in grade and Special Education placement (Consortium 1983). The short-term follow-ups (as is more widely known) show an IQ test advantage of a few points in first grade that tails off over the next couple of years. For purposes of this discussion, however, the demonstration that disadvantaged children's test scores *can* be elevated prior to the time they start formal schooling is key: the preschool period is a time when the faucet *can* be turned on.

An obvious further application of the same notion is that disadvantaged children need to be provided with resources to support their cognitive growth in summer. However, the outcomes of a number of studies in various areas of the country (see Heyns' 1987 review) that have experimented with this approach are exceedingly perplexing: so far summer school attendance or special summer programs have not boosted the achievement scores of disadvantaged children. Most of these programs have been short (6 weeks or less), not well-designed academically, and aimed mainly at "problem" students. Still, in the largest effort to date, the national Sustaining Effects Study (Klibanoff and Haggart 1981; Carter 1983; 1984), which was thoughtfully designed and carefully executed, summer school attendance did not accomplish the desired goal of helping poorer students catch up. Heyns' (1987, p.1155) reanalysis of some of these data shows that in the Sustaining Effects Study the racial gap actually increased during the summer.

Why has summer school proved ineffective in boosting scores of disadvantaged children? We do not have the answer, but one possibility not yet investigated is that the timing of these programs is largely out of phase with children's growth trajectories. The temporal aspect of children's schooling so far considered in this chapter relates to seasons, i.e. whether or not schools are in session. Young children's learning is "temporal" in another respect, however, which is not widely appreciated: achievement test data for Beginning School Study children and for national samples of children show that their scores increase most in first grade, next most in second grade, and continue to decelerate each year thereafter. These decreasing rates are visible in the upper (winter) or lower (summer) portions of Table 3.1, but are visible as well in standardized test data more generally. While psychometric issues of how these tests are scaled are complex and worrisome, the general observation that there is a spurt in children's cognitive growth at the time formal schooling begins is not in doubt. One reason that summer programs have been ineffective, then, may be that they are inappropriately timed. If reading achievement moves up twice as fast in grade one as grade three, as is true for Beginning School Study children, then the optimum time to intervene would be in the summer after (or before) grade one. Very few summer programs have targeted children this young. Table 3.1 shows that the differences between low and high socioeconomic status children's average growth rates in summer are 11.0 points in math over years one and two combined but only 3.5 points over years 3, 4, and 5 combined. (Reading growth rates are 15.8 points versus 5.0 points for the same two time spans.) Furthermore, the first two school years are periods when we see losses in low socioeconomic status children's scores over the summer. With only small differences in children's summer growth present in the later three years, it would be unlikely to see much change as a consequence of a six-week program.

Another issue is the nature of the program provided. Summer school programs tend to drill on material covered in the previous school year, but the summer activities that better-off families arrange for their children are varied. Better-off children do things in summer that are *different* from things they do during the school year. Heyns' (1978) data, like Beginning School Study data, reveal that better-off families provide visits to relatives, summer camp, music lessons, trips to the zoo, organized sports, and the like in summer periods. All these activities would offer children a different sample of experiences to learn from than the structured experience provided by summer school classes.

It would also be a mistake to overlook parents' psychological resources. The studies of Hess and his colleagues (1984) show that, compared to lower socioeconomic status mothers, higher socioeconomic status mothers interact with their children more often in ways that prompt children's cognitive growth--give them positive rather than negative reinforcement, encourage them to be self- rather than teacher-directed when they start school, teach them productive problems solving strategies, and emphasize less the superficial than the deeper structure of language when opportunity offers. In short, summer school instructors may need to adopt some of the qualities of higher socioeconomic status parents. As the Beginning School Study data attest, higher socioeconomic status parents have higher expectations and tend to be better informed about their children's school progress than are lower socioeconomic status parents. The parental interest to which this knowledge testifies may be more potent in stimulating children's development than the actual knowledge parents acquire. Beginning School Study data indicate as well that the neighborhoods better-off children live in also foster more growth than do the neighborhoods of poorer children, through organized sports and other programs specifically provided for children and/or through casual contact with positive role models in the community (see Entwisle, Alexander, and Olson 1994).

One possibility worth trying is to design summer programs for first and second grade children that contain some of the ingredients of life in better-off families and neighborhoods--a variety of activities, away from classrooms, where children can often choose what they wish to do, and with adults who are not cast in the role of "teacher" but rather in the role of adult companions who have a sincere interest in and liking for the child.

Another important consideration is the basis upon which teachers award marks. At present the emphasis is on absolute levels of achievement, but for young children especially, marking systems should incorporate rewards for growth and improvement. This is not an easy solution but one that merits careful study. Also important would be a general "news" bulletin to parents and teachers. Parents could easily be informed about the range of marks awarded in any school. Parents could also be informed about the importance of conduct and the standards for judging conduct in the school their children attend. We suspect that if parents' expectations for children's first marks in the low socioeconomic status schools were more accurate, their expectations would be even more potent.

Teachers could also be informed about the distribution of marks being awarded in their school and in other schools in the same system. We conjecture that, if they were told that marks over the entire school average 40% D's, teachers would mark less stringently. Without knowing what other teachers are doing, one teacher can believe that his/her class is not performing at the same level as the other classes in the school, and therefore it is possible for him/her to be less disturbed by a negative skew in the mark distribution than he/she would otherwise be. It is doubtful that teachers in low socioeconomic status schools are clearly and unequivocally aware of how low the marks given by all teachers to first-grade children actually are and of how confusing their marking criteria are. There must be ways to put low socioeconomic status children and their parents in better tune with their elementary schools.

Summary

The faucet theory can explain a large body of evidence--some of it counter-intuitive--concerning the schooling of U.S. children. It calls into question widespread assumptions about the nature of the relationship between family socioeconomic status and children's schooling. It suggests that schools have been doing a better job than they have been credited with and also why the timing and the nature of summer school programs as implemented so far could have undercut their effectiveness.

Research is needed to identify the specific influences that affect children's cognitive growth in summer, not only with respect to the attitudes and atmosphere within the family, but with respect to the neighborhood, especially influences that are "organized." Children tend to spend more time out in neighborhoods in summer than in winter so organized neighborhood activities could prompt summer growth in ways that summer school may not.

Notes

1. Negative life events include death or injury of a close family member, trouble on the job or with the law, and so on (Holmes and Rahe 1967).

2. Heyns (1978, p.82-83) discusses a linear model that captures this same effect over a single year by including an interaction dummy with values of 0, 1 depending on whether or not school is open.

4

Elementary School Organization

It is no accident that the rise of universal schooling in the 19th century parallels the social recognition of childhood as a clearly demarcated period in the life span. In the 20th century, the distinctiveness of many other life periods has faded, but not that of middle childhood, mainly because elementary schools match the physical and cognitive capacities of youngsters in this age range. In fact, over this century as the age of menarche declined from an average of 14 years to about 12.6 years (Tanner 1973), the organization of schools has responded. Since 1960 the number of grades in elementary schools has decreased from 6 to 5 or 4, as middle schools have replaced junior highs. Still, how the structure of schools maps onto children's development has traditionally been more of an administrative than a scientific concern.

This chapter examines issues related to how elementary school organization affects children's development. Because elementary schools seem to have a simple flat plan of organization--a string of self-contained classrooms with individual teachers--their structure has prompted relatively little sociological research, the main exception being studies of ability grouping. Nevertheless, these schools do have complicated organizational patterns. In the first place, because elementary schools reflect the characteristics of the neighborhoods in which they are located, students are tracked *between* schools by socioeconomic status (Dauber et al. 1993; Entwisle and Alexander 1993). Then, *within* schools tracks emerge starting in first grade: children are held back and placed in Special Education and both of these administrative decisions often segregate students by classrooms and by age. *Within* classrooms, children are usually also grouped for instruction in reading and sometimes in math. The upshot is that socioeconomic status tracks children by school, administrative decisions track students into separate classes within schools and instructional grouping tracks children within classes. The purpose here is to examine how such facets of school organization affect students' development in both the near and the longer terms.

Socioeconomic Status and Tracks Between Schools

Elementary schools appear to have the same general structure because the topics covered in their curriculum look much the same across grades and across schools. With the exception of grouping within classes, society perceives them as "untracked"--one program fits all. The major thesis of this chapter is that this perception is wrong: elementary schools are *not* the same, they are rigidly tracked by family socioeconomic status level and by administrative fiat. Their tracks are not labeled as such, however, perhaps because society prefers to repress them from view.

Variability Between Schools

The small size of elementary schools, plus their 3R's curriculum helps support the myth that all have the same structure, and that not until middle school does "tracking" begin. Quite the opposite is true, however.

The variation in socioeconomic level *between* elementary schools actually outstrips that between secondary schools. In 1990-91, for example, the proportion of Baltimore children participating in the subsidized meal program varied across elementary schools on average from 5% to 100%, but varied only from 8% to 65% across high schools (Baltimore City Public Schools 1991).[1] This greater socioeconomic variation across elementary schools is mainly a consequence of their small catchment areas which differ sharply by family income level. Neighborhoods, in other words, differ in terms of the socioeconomic status of the families that inhabit them and therefore so do their elementary schools. The correspondence between socioeconomic level of neighborhoods and schools is illustrated by Table 4.1 which ranks the 20 Beginning School Study schools by the average number of students on meal subsidy, an indicator of the average socioeconomic status level of students' families. This ranking corresponds well to 3 measures of neighborhood socioeconomic status: median household income, percentage of families below the poverty level, and the percentage of workers with professional or managerial jobs. The rank order correlations between meal subsidy level and the neighborhood indicators are: .86 (median household income), .66 (percentage of workers with high status jobs), and .83 (family poverty level).

Table 4.1   Mean California Achievement Test (CAT) Reading and Math Scores when Beginning School Study Students Began First Grade and at the End of Year 5 and Neighborhood Characteristics[a]

% Students in School on Meal Subsidy	CAT Reading Score		CAT Math Score		Neighborhood Characteristics		
	Begin Yr 1	End Yr 5	Begin Yr 1	End Yr 5	% Workers Professional/ Managerial	Median Househld Income (in thousands $)	% Families Below Poverty
11%	302	531	316	504	63.5	22.7	2.0
13%	317	567	340	516	57.2	24.2	2.9
14%	285	544	303	519	20.0	17.7	1.8
17%	297	510	294	507	15.9	14.4	11.1
30%	283	489	299	488	31.0	16.3	8.6
30%	292	505	286	505	16.9	14.5	10.2
33%	268	479	290	493	11.0	16.7	7.0
39%	283	482	298	484	7.5	12.1	11.7
43%	289	489	304	478	28.6	16.5	3.7
50%	259	478	283	481	8.3	12.1	16.4
52%	290	495	298	495	17.8	15.6	6.2
53%	284	474	302	471	5.0	14.4	9.9
68%	278	465	289	476	11.7	11.6	20.4
76%	289	480	300	460	9.4	11.6	14.6
77%	245	450	283	470	6.4	10.5	22.5
79%	286	461	297	462	10.8	7.4	38.2
82%	266	462	275	446	7.5	12.1	11.7
83%	266	448	279	448	9.2	11.6	33.7
88%	272	459	273	454	11.9	10.1	39.4
90%	265	465	273	456	9.9	7.4	39.0
Mean	281	482	293	476	18.3	13.7	16.8

[a] Neighborhood SES measures are for the neighborhood in which the school is located. See Appendix B for full definition of neighborhood measures.

Differences in Student Characteristics by Neighborhood²

Beginning School Study students who lived in the better-off Baltimore neighborhoods began school with higher test scores than students who lived in the poorer neighborhoods (Table 4.1). For instance, of the 20 Study schools, which were randomly selected to participate in the study, the school with only 11% of students on subsidized meals enrolled children whose average California Achievement Test score in reading comprehension at the beginning of first grade was 302 and average math concepts score was 316. However, in the school with 90% of students on subsidized meals, reading scores averaged 265 (37 points lower, about .9 S.D.'s) and math scores averaged 273 (43 points lower, about 1.3 S.D.'s). The rank-order correlations between the percentage of first-grade students on meal subsidy in a school and students' average reading and math California Achievement Test scores when they began first grade are .65 in reading and .72 in math.

The achievement test differences across Beginning School Study schools when children began formal schooling enlarged as children progressed up through the grades. By the end of year 5, the average difference in standardized test scores between Beginning School Study children in the highest and lowest socioeconomic status schools was 66 points in reading and 48 points in math.

As would be anticipated, the figures for *all* Baltimore City elementary schools show the same patterns as those in the 20 Beginning School Study schools. The gradient in children's reading achievement across schools follows the gradient in meal subsidy. In schools with 50% or fewer of students on meal subsidy, children were reading at grade level 3.19 by the end of grade 2 and over one year above grade level (7.15) by the end of grade 5 (first column, Table 4.2). In schools where 89% or more of students were on subsidy (last column, Table 4.2), children were reading at half a year below grade level at the end of grade 2, and slightly below grade level at the end of grade 5. The gap in reading achievement between the highest and lowest socioeconomic status schools in Baltimore increased between the end of grade 2 and grade 5 from about 2/3 of a grade level to 1 1/3 grade levels three years later.

Other studies also reveal strong patterns of socioeconomic stratification across elementary schools (see e.g., Rosenberg 1979). Although it tends to be overlooked, the Coleman Report (1966) also shows this stratification clearly. Based on a nationwide sample of over 400,000 children, it found greater school-to-school variability in standardized test scores for children in their elementary years (grades 1, 3, 6) than for children in their secondary years

Table 4.2   Mean Grade Equivalent Scores for Reading and Math California Achievement Test (CAT) Scores , Baltimore City Elementary Schools (N=122) 1987, by Percent of Students on Meal Subsidy

	Percent of Students on Meal Subsidy in School			
	11-50% (N=31)	51%-73% (N=30)	74%-88% (N=31)	89%-100% (N=30)
Mean	33.4	61.0	81.0	92.4
CAT Reading Comprehension Score				
End of Grade 2	3.19	2.86	2.81	2.53
End of Grade 3	4.29	3.71	3.67	3.41
End of Grade 5	7.15	6.30	5.92	5.85
CAT Total Math Score				
End of Grade 2	3.33	3.13	3.08	2.93
End of Grade 3	4.48	4.09	4.01	3.83
End of Grade 5	7.30	6.82	6.58	6.46

Source: Baltimore City Public Schools 1988.

Table 4.3   Percent Between-School Variation in Achievement by Grade Level, Coleman Report (1966)

Grade:	12	9	6	3	1
Nonverbal ability	13.99	13.97	22.29	17.33	18.16
Verbal ability	16.61	15.61	21.36	22.41	17.78
Reading comprehension	13.24	11.98	18.54	20.86	-
Mathematics achievement	10.55	11.97	18.41	21.48	-

Source: Adapted from Coleman, J. S. et al. 1966, p.293.

(grades 9, 12). In fact, variation in reading scores is almost 60% greater at grade 3 than at grade 12, and in math the variation is over 100% greater. (See Table 4.3.) Similar stratification by socioeconomic status characterizes schools in Britain, where primary schools are also much smaller than secondary schools. Teachers' salaries, the proportion of oversize classes, and expenditures for fuel and the like, all vary *more* among primary schools than do the equivalent indices among secondary schools (Central Advisory Council for Education 1967, pp. 618-619).

The point of these examples is that elementary schools are typically organized tightly along lines of family and neighborhood SES, so that socioeconomic status of elementary children differs markedly between schools.

Socioeconomic Status and Children's Learning

In spite of the pronounced variation in their standardized test scores by socioeconomic status when Beginning School Study children started first grade, those of different socioeconomic status levels progressed at the *same* rate during first grade, as we saw in Chapter 3. In winters (when school was in session) the yearly gains of the children in the high and low socioeconomic status groups were equivalent. We saw the same seasonal patterns in school-level data. When the 20 Beginning School Study schools were divided into two groups--the top 10 schools in terms of percentage of students on meal subsidy and the bottom 10 schools--students in the "low" schools gained even more in reading over second grade than did students in the "high" schools (51 versus 39 points). These data lend strong support to the conclusion that students' gains in achievement *when school is open* are equivalent irrespective of family economic status.

Socioeconomic Stratification and School Contexts

For a long time it has been known that secondary students' track placement is not simply a consequence of youngsters' prior achievement or ability (Kilgore 1991), and often follows social class lines (Heyns 1978; Jencks et al. 1972; Alexander, Cook, and McDill 1978). The *perceived* single curriculum of the elementary school, however, has tended to conceal the extreme tracking *between* elementary schools that actually exists. This variation by socioeconomic status leads to differences in how elementary schools function. Parents, aware of these school differences, use many strategies, including illegal ones, to get their children into high socioeconomic status schools.

Mainly they try to locate their households in the most exclusive residential area they can possibly afford, but they also use private schools, and sometimes even pretend a child is living at one address (perhaps that of an aunt) while actually living at another.

As Table 4.4 shows, parental concern is justified because the marks teachers give children follow the socioeconomic status gradient of the neighborhood. In schools where 30% or less of children are on meal subsidy, the first reading mark children see is generally 2.0 (C) or better. In schools where more than 30% of children are on subsidy, these marks generally are in the 1.0 to 2.0 range and in the majority of these schools, no one received a mark above C. (Those who get 1's are failing.) In the school with 88% of children on subsidy, all Beginning School Study students got a failing mark in the first quarter of first grade. Of the 11 schools with 50% or more of children on subsidy, in only two were children's average marks in reading better than 2.0 (C). Nevertheless, as we saw, children in the low socioeconomic status schools make test score gains over first grade when school is in session as large as those made by children in high socioeconomic status schools.

Children in low socioeconomic status schools are thus perceived differently and treated differently from children in high socioeconomic status schools, even though they are doing equally well. The school climates linked to socioeconomic status are not a consequence of children's actual progress because, *when school was open*, children in schools of all socioeconomic status levels gained equal amounts on standardized tests of achievement in both reading and math. The differences by socioeconomic status in marks and expectations are *not* triggered by differences in the children's actual progress in school. Children are being marked in terms of where they live rather than in terms of how they have performed in their school.

These same patterns characterize teachers' expectations. At the end of grade one when teachers were asked to predict their students' performance in grade two, in the top 10 schools, first grade teachers generally expected their pupils in the next school year to get more A's and B's than C's or below in reading, while teachers' expectations in the bottom 10 schools were for almost all children to get C's or below.

Parents' perceptions of their children's performance also differed according to the socioeconomic status of the school (see Table 4.4). Parents' expectations for their children's first marks in reading, which were ascertained either shortly before or just after school began in September of 1982, *before any report cards were issued*, show a gradient by meal subsidy level of the school. When average expectations are calculated for the top and bottom socioeconomic status schools, parents in the "top" schools expected children

Table 4.4   First Grade: Teachers' Ratings of Children's Interest/Participation, Parents' and Teachers' Mark Expectations, Students' First Quarter Marks and Retention Status by School Meal Subsidy Level

% on Meal Subsidy	Teachers' Rate Interest Participation	Parents' Expectations for Reading	Reading Mark, Q1, Gr. 1	Parents' Expectation for Math, Q1, Gr. 1	Math Mark, Q1, Gr. 1	Teachers' Expectations for Reading Q1, Gr. 2	Retention Status, End Yr. 1
11%	25.45	3.04	2.26	3.04	2.67	2.85	.07
13%	24.51	3.00	2.41	3.26	2.74	2.97	.00
14%	23.69	2.83	2.76	2.97	3.00	3.00	.00
17%	21.47	2.72	1.91	2.84	2.61	2.81	.16
30%	24.42	2.89	2.52	2.91	2.81	2.86	.12
30%	24.23	2.61	2.11	2.45	2.04	2.68	.20
33%	22.14	2.44	1.95	2.44	1.90	2.17	.10
39%	23.19	2.50	1.87	2.67	2.62	2.89	.12
43%	20.75	2.86	1.52	2.75	2.24	2.47	.14
50%	20.31	2.55	1.92	2.55	2.00	2.34	.19
52%	21.80	2.71	1.70	2.76	1.97	2.20	.17
53%	19.50	2.63	1.28	2.43	2.31	2.00	.27
68%	23.32	2.78	2.10	2.59	2.27	2.74	.16
76%	22.53	2.52	2.06	2.83	2.35	2.42	.12
77%	21.05	2.56	1.97	2.63	2.06	2.05	.05
79%	21.73	2.55	1.81	2.62	1.87	2.12	.14
82%	19.52	2.28	1.76	2.42	2.18	2.19	.16
83%	19.26	2.53	1.34	2.58	1.53	1.45	.49
88%	21.08	2.61	1.00	2.63	1.51	1.62	.35
90%	20.74	2.70	1.56	2.68	1.97	2.12	.28
Average	21.95	2.67	1.88	2.72	2.24	2.38	.17

to get 2.74 in reading, while parents in the bottom schools expected somewhat less--2.59.

Teachers' treatment of children reinforced these differential parents' expectations. In the top 10 schools, children's first reading marks averaged 2.12 (a little better than a C). In the bottom 10 schools first reading marks were only 1.62 (about 40% of the children were failing). Similarly in math in the top 10 schools the average mark (2.46) was halfway between a "C" and a "B", but "C" (2.00) in the lower 10 schools.

Beginning School Study teachers' ratings of children's classroom behavior also corresponded to the socioeconomic level of the school (Table 4.4). When first-grade teachers rated their students in terms of interest and participation in class, teachers in the school where only 11% of children were on meal subsidy rated their pupils about one standard deviation higher in interest/participation than did teachers in the school where 90% of children were on subsidy. The rank-order correlation between school meal subsidy level and teachers' average interest/participation rating of students is .71. Furthermore, in the schools with high percentages of children on subsidy, some children were literally rated as being "off the scale," i.e., 3 S.D.'s below their school's mean on interest and participation. No student was rated off the scale in the more affluent schools.

The picture becomes more disturbing the longer children are in school. Only 47% of children in the Beginning School Study who started first grade in a school where more than 90% of students were on subsidy had reached fifth grade five years later because 53% had either been retained or placed in Special Education. By contrast, 77% of those who started first grade in schools where 50% or less of the children were on subsidy were in fifth grade five years later.

Clearly, *where* children start elementary school effectively places them on a track. Children of high socioeconomic status have relatively high test scores as they begin first grade and are grouped together. Children of low socioeconomic status levels have relatively low scores when they begin first grade and they are grouped together. The same schools then report the highest and lowest scores at the end of elementary school (see Table 4.1), *despite the fact that when schools were open, children of all socioeconomic levels progressed at the same rate;* that is, children gained the same amounts on standardized tests over the school year irrespective of socioeconomic level and initial test scores in their school. Their socioeconomic status did not affect the rate at which children progressed while in school, but out-of-school, either before first grade or in summer when school was closed, socioeconomic status level did affect rates of progress. Because of these seasonal patterns, for the

Table 4.5   Overlap of First Grade and Middle School Track Placements

First Grade Placements	6th Grade English Level				6th Grade Math Level				% Taking Foreign Language (N)	Number of Low Courses (N)	Number of High Courses (N)
	% Low	% Reg	% High	(N)	% Low	% Reg	% High	(N)			
Special Education											
Yes	62	30	8	(64)	53	42	5	(64)	16 (70)	2.8 (64)	0.5 (64)
No	37	40	23	(413)	15	72	13	(417)	37 (437)	1.9 (413)	1.0 (413)
Eta[a]	.18***				.28***				.15***	.24***	.13**
Retained											
Yes	67	31	2	(88)	51	48	1	(89)	10 (94)	2.9 (88)	0.3 (88)
No	35	41	25	(389)	13	72	14	(392)	40 (413)	1.8 (389)	1.0 (389)
Eta[a]	.28***				.35***				.25***	.36***	.23***

Reading Group

Lowest	62	26	13	(78)	50	44	6	(78)	19 (83)	2.7 (78)	0.6 (78)
Intermediate	43	46	10	(153)	17	78	6	(156)	25 (167)	2.2 (153)	0.6 (153)
Highest	26	36	38	(137)	7	71	22	(137)	45 (145)	1.6 (137)	1.4 (137)
Eta^a	.33***				.38***				.23***	.35***	.30***

Number of Low Placements

0	32	43	25	(263)	9	76	15	(266)	39 (279)	1.8 (263)	1.0 (263)
1	41	41	18	(61)	28	64	8	(61)	29 (69)	2.1 (61)	0.8 (61)
2	70	22	8	(40)	50	45	5	(40)	14 (43)	2.9 (40)	0.5 (40)
3	78	22	0	(18)	78	22	0	(18)	0 (18)	3.4 (18)	0.2 (18)
Eta^a	.28***				.41***				.23***	.37***	.19**

** $p \leq .01$ level   *** $p \leq .001$ level

[a] Eta coefficient, calculated from the cross-classifications in the table, measures association analogous to a product-moment correlation.

Beginning School Study children, correlations are .41 and .55 respectively, between initial California Achievement Test scores in reading and math in the fall of first grade and scores on higher levels of the same tests at the end of elementary school. The stratified outcomes later in the educational pipeline can be forecast surprisingly well from the stratification patterns visible in first grade (see also Kerckhoff 1993; Alexander and Entwisle 1996b). These patterns, however, are a consequence of what children learn *outside* school.

The stratification patterns established in elementary school continue afterwards. Children who have the highest test scores at the end of elementary school take algebra and a foreign language in middle school, and so end up with the needed prerequisites (algebra and language skills) to move into the college preparatory program in high school, while those with low scores at the end of elementary school do not get into these high level courses (Dauber, Alexander, and Entwisle 1996). (See Table 4.5.) For example, 62% of children placed in the lowest reading group in a first grade classroom took "low level" English in sixth grade. Likewise, 51% of the children who had been retained in first grade are in "low math" in sixth grade.

Socioeconomic differentials by school match the fault lines in the larger society. Schools in high and low status neighborhoods have different marking standards and treat students differently at a time in life when rates of cognitive growth are extremely rapid. The equivalence in children's progress when schools are in session is completely obscured.

Socioeconomic Stratification and School Organization

The last section reviewed data that show teachers' and parents' perceptions of children relate to the socioeconomic status level of the school. This section takes up a different set of issues: the variation in the organizational structures of elementary schools associated with neighborhood socioeconomic status. As noted, all elementary schools are perceived as being organized along the same lines, but in fact they are not.

Grade Patterns[3]

In low socioeconomic status elementary schools, irregular grade structures are a particular hazard. Elementary schools (N=118) in Baltimore generally have grade structures that cover five or six grades plus kindergarten and perhaps pre-kindergarten, but at least 10 other organizational patterns existed when Beginning School Study students were attending these schools (K-3; PK-K; PK-2, PK-3; 3-5, 4-6, 1-5; K-8; PK-8; K-12). The problem with non-standard grade structures is that they usually require students to make "extra" transitions. For example, children in PK-2 or PK-3 schools had to transfer to another elementary school to complete grades 3, 4 and 5. The Baltimore elementary schools with non-standard grade patterns had proportionately more children on subsidy (80% versus 67%), with most having irregular grade structures (10 out of the 14) located in the poorest City neighborhoods (over 40% of residents in poverty). (See Figure 4.1 for locations of schools with non-standard grade structures.)

Making extra school transitions was thus a burden imposed more often upon low than upon high socioeconomic status children. The cost of these "extra" moves is not trivial: school transitions are difficult hurdles for children (Simmons and Blyth 1987; Alexander, Entwisle, and Dauber 1994), and among Beginning School Study students, retention rates over the first 5 years of school were significantly higher for students who did not stay in the same elementary school all the way through (50% versus 35%). Although research on school moves is thin, evidence is mounting that such moves have serious and long-term effects.

Disorderly Transitions

Another kind of transition is also more common for low than for high socioeconomic status youngsters. Low socioeconomic status families move more often, and the timing of these moves often requires children to transfer between schools at times that interfere with their schooling (McLanahan and Sandefur 1994). The serious consequences of school moves are made clear by Teachman et al.'s (1996) report that all of the benefits of attending Catholic schools for youngsters in the NELS sample can be explained by the negative relationship between family moves and attendance at parochial schools. Undoubtedly, it is not just moving or not moving that leads to this difference because families who move less are better-off, more integrated into their neighborhoods and so on, but changing schools is still hard for children. Beginning School Study children who were poorer moved more often than their better-off peers, for example. Of those who made two or more school moves in their elementary years, 88% were on meal subsidy compared to 65% of those who did not move. In addition, these moves were made *within* the school year almost twice as often as in the summer (between school years). In year 4, for example, of 92 within-system moves, 57 (62%) were within-year transfers (Table 4.6).

Moves are difficult because youngsters must adjust to a new neighborhood, new school, new teachers, new classmates, and a new physical plant with few

Figure 4.1   Percent of Persons Below Poverty Level in Baltimore City
              Neighborhoods Containing Elementary Schools with Non-
              Standard Grade Organization (1987-88)[a]

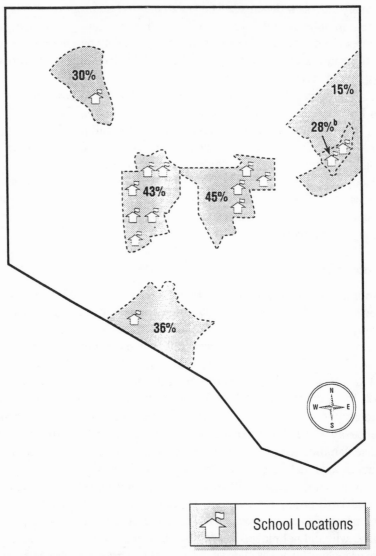

School Locations

[a] Neighborhood boundaries and percent of persons below poverty level are for
Regional Planning Districts in which Beginning School Study schools were located
(Regional Planning Council 1983).
    [b] Percent in poverty is for the Census tract where the school is located (U.S.
Bureau of the Census 1983).

Table 4.6   Number of School Moves per Year Within Baltimore Schools and Out of Baltimore Schools for Beginning School Study Sample

	Year 1	Year 2	Year 3	Year 4	Year 5
No. of BSS students in BCPS in the fall	767	745	693	631	605
Stayers (through the following fall)[a]	663	616	547	520	524
Percent Who Move[b]	13.6%	17.3%	21.1%	17.6%	13.4%
Type of Move[c]					
Within-year, within system transfers	64	68	65	57	50
Between-year (summer) within system transfers	34	31	41	35	---
Transfers outside City system	22	52	62	26	37
Total Moves	120	151	168	118	87

[a] Except in Year 5, where moves are tracked only through the spring.

[b] Percent who move in a given year is (1 - No. Stayers/No. in BCPS).

[c] Individual moves are categorized as to whether they occur (1) during the school year, or (2) over the summer, or (3) are transfers out of City system. One student may have more than one move per year, so total moves exceed number of movers.

or no institutional supports to help. Even orderly transitions like that from elementary to middle school are disruptive and challenging (Simmons and Blyth 1987), but because these moves are expected, the school and family are at least partially mobilized to smooth the student's way, with allowances made for need to readjust to new rules and a new curriculum. It is hard for teachers to accommodate students who make unscheduled moves in the middle of the school year because the curriculum and the pace at which it is covered usually differ from one school to the next (Barr and Dreeben 1983). New students not only disrupt the teaching schedule--they create a feeling of restlessness and upheaval in the classroom because they don't know the rules. With many students coming and going all year long, as happens in poverty areas, teachers find it necessary almost continuously to "reteach," "backtrack" and in other ways try to catch new students up to the class (Lash and Kirkpatrick 1990).

In the BSS, the link between meal subsidy, household moves, and deficits in school performance is clear. Students who had lower test scores and other problems moved more than others. Beginning School Study children who moved two or more times within the system *began* first grade with California Achievement Test scores from one quarter to one half of a standard deviation below those of children who did not move later on, for example. Those who moved during their first 5 years of school were absent in the fifth year 13 days compared to 10 days for children who had not changed schools. Those who moved the most also started school with other serious problems. The conduct marks at the beginning of first grade for future frequent movers (3 or more moves), for example, were very low: 45% needed improvement versus 20% of the children who did not move . Even in the first year the frequent movers were absent more (18 days compared to 12). Also, as noted, retention rates over the first five years of school were significantly higher (50% versus 35%) for those who moved.

Clearly, moving within the school system during the school year greatly compounds the problems that already plague poor children, but unlike many other aspects of poverty, schools themselves could reduce the problems that poor students face when they make disorderly transitions. Specific practices to help students weather within-year moves might include: letting students commute to their old school until the summer break; providing for them extra counseling to help them adjust in the new school; helping teachers deal with students who move; educating parents about the hazards of within-year moves; making parents aware of how to provide children with extra support when they move.

The Complexity of Poor Children's Transitions

Data concerning household moves presented so far, daunting as they are, still fail to capture the full complexity of poor children's school transitions. To get closer to that reality, Figure 4.2 displays the mobility histories of the Beginning School Study youngsters in just one school where the schools' irregular grade structure (PK-3) required that students move to a companion school after third grade to complete elementary school. Of the 69 youngsters who started first grade in this school, where the meal subsidy rate was over 90%, less than one-fifth went through their elementary years in a completely orderly way. Without tracing out every path, the reader can see that over the

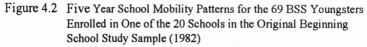

Figure 4.2 Five Year School Mobility Patterns for the 69 BSS Youngsters
Enrolled in One of the 20 Schools in the Original Beginning
School Study Sample (1982)

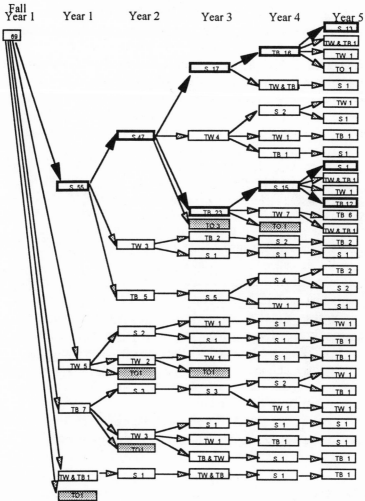

TW=school transfer within year   TO=transfer out of the City system   TB= school
transfer between years   S = remained in same school all year and into the fall of the
following year. The bolded boxes and arrows indicate most stable mobility patterns.
Shaded boxes indicate students who transferred out of the City system.

five year period, there are more than half as many distinct mobility patterns (36) as there are youngsters. (Figure 4.2 shows 30 boxes in the Year 5 column plus the 6 transfers out of system indicated by the shaded boxes.) Only 26 of the 69 students remained in their original school until they completed third grade and then moved on to a companion school to finish elementary school (patterns shown by bolded lines and boxes). Of these 26 students, only 12 completed fifth grade on time (i.e., no grade retention). Excluding the 8 students who left the City system before their fifth year, 35 students moved once, 19 moved twice, and 7 moved three or more times.

Tracks Within Schools

Within elementary schools, students are sorted in at least three ways: (1) by being held back (retained); (2) by being placed in Special Education; and (3) by being grouped for instruction within or between classrooms. Each of these administrative decisions effectively creates a "track." The last of these-- instructional grouping--is probably the most benign in terms of children's life chances, although its consequences may be more varied and pernicious than presently recognized. The tracks within schools created by retention and Special Education, however, are more problematic because these "tracks" are so far below the level of social consciousness that they are not even thought of as tracks. Yet students given these placements often end up in "odd" classrooms at a distance from the main office, their paperwork is often "lost," and they are grouped together and perceived as "different." The majority of retention and Special Education assignments are made early in children's school careers, actually in the first two years, when their full significance may not be appreciated. By the end of second grade, for example, roughly one-quarter (27%) of Beginning School Study children had either been held back or placed in Special Education. The remainder of this section takes up these tracks *within* schools.

Ability Grouping

Ability grouping for reading is found in more than 90% of first grade classrooms nation-wide (McPartland et al. 1987) and perhaps for this reason it is the structural arrangement in the primary grades to which sociologists have paid the most heed (e.g., Haller and Davis 1980; Eder 1981; Barr and Dreeben 1983; Felmlee and Eder 1983; Rowan and Miracle 1983; Hallinan and Sørensen 1987). The consensus is that grouping children by ability confers no overall advantage compared to whole-class instruction because some students do better, while others do worse (see Haller and Davis 1980; Haller 1985; Hallinan and Sørensen 1983, Sørensen and Hallinan 1984 for citations). Evidence is mounting, however, that this picture is too simplistic.

For one thing, even when different groups of children use the same basal reader, those in low groups read word-by-word, with teachers providing isolated decoding clues, so these children have little chance to apply their knowledge of spoken language or of how the world works. Those in high groups, by contrast, are required to pay attention to clauses, expressive intonation, and the emotional states of the characters in the story (see Collins 1986; Alpert 1975; Dreeben and Barr 1988). Group level also affects how group members treat one another. Other things equal, students in low groups become inattentive at more than twice the rate of students in high groups, and the longer students stay in the same group, the stronger these forces become (Felmlee and Eder 1983). Reading group rank determines how teachers assign marks, and children who get higher marks learn more (all else equal). Either because of school policy or teachers' personal convictions, often children in low groups are barred from getting A's no matter how hard they try. Also, the lower rated children in high reading groups often get lower marks than children of the same tested ability in low reading groups (Reuman 1989).

Less attention has been paid to the "institutional" effects of ability groups than to the dynamics of these groups, as summarized above. Still, educators and parents believe that grouping is a rational mechanism for sorting students, so children in high groups tend to be treated *as if* they were high performers regardless of their actual skills or competence. Evaluations of students' skills can thus be a byproduct of the symbolic meaning of their ability group placement rather than of actual performance levels. For example, Beginning School Study teachers and parents perceived children in high-ranked reading groups in first grade as being more competent in the following year than did parents of similar children in low-ranked groups. Independent of students' actual performance, and with other key variables controlled, these perceptions of greater competence led children to do better later on (Pallas et al. 1994). Such perceptions may even govern children's activities outside school, because 60% of Beginning School Study parents of children in high ability groups said that in the summer after first grade, their children went to the library compared to 49% of parents of children in low-ability groups.

Grouping by Other Characteristics. It is becoming apparent that criteria other than ability may be the *de facto* basis for "ability grouping." Kellam and his associates (1990; 1991; 1994) found that children in high-ability classrooms had low rates of aggression (5%) whereas children in low-ability classrooms had high rates (60% or more). Grouping may thus depend in part on children's non-cognitive characteristics and "concentrate" aggressive behavior even if not exacerbating it. Along similar lines, within every Beginning School Study school, whether of high or low socioeconomic status, children's reading group assignments in first grade corresponded to how the teacher ranked children's interest/participation. Compared to children in low groups, teachers saw children in high groups as being much more interested in classroom activities and also rated them higher in attention span/restlessness. (Data not shown.) There also was "concentration" by children's temperament or classroom behavior: Beginning School Study children initially placed in a high ability group also were increasingly grouped with children who had good classroom adjustment. Not many Beginning School Study children shifted reading groups during the year, but those who were shifted to a lower group were rated lower on interest participation and on attention span-restlessness than children not shifted.

Thus, grouping practices early in school could well have a different basis and more wide-ranging consequences than previously thought. The long-term sequelae of problematic classroom behavior of first grade males include dropout, teenage delinquency and violence, as well as drug, alcohol, and cigarette use (see Kellam 1994), so grouping that intensifies these behaviors is a matter of some consequence.

Problems in Forming Groups. Despite the prevalence of ability groups, children's test scores in reading at the beginning of first grade may actually be so unreliable that it is impossible for teachers to rank students accurately. The standard error for the California Achievement Test in reading comprehension, for instance, is about 25 points at the beginning of first grade (California Achievement Test 1979), which implies that the 95% confidence band *for any one child's* test score is around 100 points. In addition, the lack of variation in students' socioeconomic standing and ethnicity *within* any one elementary school worsens the problem, because the range in scores is restricted. This being the case, the "ability" groups teachers form at the beginning of first grade contain students who are quite heterogeneous in ability. Research showing little or no effect of ability grouping may thus reflect a failure to group children accurately rather than a lack of grouping effects. In 6 of the 20 Study schools, students in the lowest group on average outscored children in the middle group.

A further issue is that the "high ability" group in one school can be lower than the "low ability" group in another school. In the BSS, for example, children in the lowest reading group in one high socioeconomic status school had an average reading score of 302 at the beginning of first grade while children in the highest group in a low socioeconomic status school had an average score of 277.[4]   Given these complexities, the combined institutional and instructional effects of grouping are hard to predict.

Grade Retention

Only a rough estimate can be made of the number of children held back in school each year because there are no national data on grade retention. However, the number of children enrolled below the modal grade for their age[5] shows how many are off-time (presumably "retained"), and the number of off-time students goes up as grade level goes up (U.S. Bureau of the Census 1992b). In 1993, by age 8 (grade 3), 24% of males and 21% of females were already below the modal grade for their age, and by age 11 (grade 6) 33% of boys and 24% of girls were below modal grade (Bruno and Adams 1994). Retention rates are generally highest in large urban areas. By the sixth year, 43% of all Beginning School Study youngsters (51% of the boys and 36% of the girls) were off-time by at least one year.

Not surprisingly, enrollments below modal grade escalate rapidly as risk factors cumulate. In poverty households where the head is a dropout, about 50% of the boys and 40% of the girls are over-age for their grade (Bianchi 1984).   Likewise, among NELS-88 eighth graders, in the lowest socioeconomic status quartile over 31% were held back compared to about 8% of children in the highest quartile (National Center for Education Statistics 1990).

Retention rates vary inversely with age, being highest for first graders. For the 15 states for which data are available, first grade retention averages over 11%, and retentions are around 7% per year for grades two through six (Shepard and Smith 1989).   Grade specific rates in the 7%-8% range for elementary children are consistent with cumulative retention rates on the order of 50% in many areas of the country. Beginning School Study data reflect the same patterns: over 17% of Beginning School Study first graders were held back, a rate more than twice that for any later year, and by year 8, almost half of the Beginning School Study students still in City schools were held back at least once (Alexander, Entwisle, and Dauber 1994; see also Fine 1991).

The causes and consequences of retention are not well understood, mainly because most research on retention ignores children's pre-retention status even though students who are retained have many problems *before* retention. About 84% of the Beginning School Study first graders who were retained were on meal subsidy, for instance (Table 4.7), compared to 53% of those who were not retained through grade 7. Compared to never-retained, average

Table 4.7   Characteristics of First-Grade Retainees, All Retainees, and Never-Retained Children at Time of School Entry[a]

	Grade One Retained	Ever Retained in Any Grade	Not Retained (through 7th grade)	Total Sample
Percent male	0.57	0.57	0.43	0.49
Percent receiving meal subsidy	0.84	0.85	0.53	0.67
Average mothers' education; years	10.8	10.6	12.4	11.7
Percent in 2-parent family	0.37	0.42	0.61	0.53
Average reading mark, fall first year (1=unsatisfactory; 2= C)	1.10	1.45	2.17	1.88
Average math mark, fall first year	1.30	1.75	2.57	2.25
Average CAT score, reading comprehension, fall first year	257	267	291	281
Average CAT score, math concepts, fall first year	264	276	305	293
Average number of absences in first year	18.2	16.2	11.2	13.2
Average conduct mark (1=needs improvement; 2=satisfactory) fall, first year	1.61	1.66	1.81	1.75
Average peer popularity rated by teachers (1 to 5, with 5 high)	2.61	3.09	3.81	3.52
Average in-class interest/participation rated by teachers (5 items, each rated 1 to 6)	16.3	18.7	24.2	22.0

[a]All differences between ever retained (column 2) and never retained (column 3) groups significant at or beyond the .01 level.

reading comprehension scores of those who would be retained later that year were about one standard deviation lower when children began first grade as were scores in math concepts (Table 4.7). Compared to children never retained through grade 7, retainees were more likely to come from a one-parent than a two-parent home (58% versus 39%) and their mothers were more likely to be drop-outs rather than high school graduates (average of 10.6 years of school versus 12.4). Retainees were also absent about 50% more often, less popular with peers, less involved in classroom activity, and less well-behaved in class. The scheduling of Beginning School Study children's retentions matched the severity of their difficulties: those with the lowest California Achievement Test scores at the beginning of first grade were held back that year, those with the next lowest scores were held back in their second year, and so on (Alexander, Entwisle, and Dauber 1994; see also Shepard and Smith 1989; Reynolds 1992).

Retainees' low test scores, low marks, many absences, and disadvantaged home backgrounds all indicate that the decision to have children repeat first grade constitutes a public signal vouching for the severity of their problems. Critics sometimes assume that doing away with retention will solve children's problems, but they mistakenly ignore pre-existing conditions. The picture is very misleading because effects of retention overlap all the problems these children bring with them when they start school.

From the perspective of school organization, retention effectively creates a separate school track. (1) Retained children are separated from their age mates, moved away from their peer group. (2) Retained children are "off-time" in the rigidly age-graded system of the elementary school, usually permanently. (3) Compared to their classmates, repeaters are taller, heavier, and have fewer deciduous teeth. This size-status inconsistency is aggravated by the onset of puberty: the average Beginning School Study girl in 4th grade who was retained once, for example, was 7 lbs. heavier (about 10%) than her "on-time" classmates. (4) By taking the same grade twice retained children are exposed to a less advanced curriculum than their age-mates. Furthermore, since they are assigned to the low reading groups before being retained, they are doubly disadvantaged in reading (Alexander, Entwisle, and Legters 1995). (5) As noted earlier, retained children often have incomplete school records because they miss testing sessions and the like. Of four California Achievement Tests routinely involving Beginning School Study children in the first two years of school, 44% of retainees missed at least one compared to only 9% of the other children. Missing tests creates gaps in school records that put retained students at a further disadvantage. Gaps in themselves are a kind of "labeling."

It is worth noting that higher retention rates make schools look better because the least capable students (those who are retained) take easier tests. First grade repeaters who would take grade 2 level tests if they were on time, take grade 1 achievement tests if they have been retained, for instance. Schools also have a better looking profile on standardized tests when retained students miss tests or their tests are "lost," because then proportionately more low scores are left out of the school average.

To sum up: the largest percentage of children who will ever be retained are retained in their first and second years of school. With no national data on retention, neither the public nor policy analysts appreciate how prevalent early retention is or how misleading evaluations of its effects are.

Special Education

Special Education placement is less common than retention but still far from rare (Heller 1982; Leinhardt and Pallay 1982; Madden and Slavin 1983; on retention see Jackson 1975; Holmes 1989, Harvard Education Letter 1991; Karweit 1992). Following the passage of Public Law 94-142 in 1975, the number of children in federally funded Special Education programs jumped from about 8% of public school students to just under 12% by 1992-93 (U.S. Department of Education 1995 p.346). Children with mild learning handicaps showed the biggest jump: between 1976-77 and 1992-93 the proportion of Learning Disabled rose from 1.8% to 5.5% of the total enrollment in public schools.

Special Education children can be placed in separate classes, but the majority are mainstreamed for all but one or two hours a day. Even so, Special Education is a "track" that is obvious to students and to teachers, and the consequences of being placed in Special Education are almost as serious as the consequences of retention when it comes to middle school course-taking (see Table 4.5). Also, most children placed in Special Education tend to remain there (Walker et al. 1988; Edgar et al. 1988).

It seems that if retention was not effective in getting Beginning School Study children up to satisfactory performance levels, Special Education was often the next step taken. Of the 42 Beginning School Study first-grade retainees who remained in Baltimore schools for at least 8 years, 38 were also in Special Education for that entire period (Alexander, Entwisle, and Dauber 1994). Figure 4.3 records retention and Special Education placement for Beginning School Study children over their first 6 years of school. Again the details of the figure are presented more to convey how complex children's trajectories are rather than to convey the specifics. The bolded boxes and lines on the diagonal represent students who remained on-time throughout. Students above the diagonal were retained at least once during their first 6 years of school. Children who received only Special Education "pullout" instruction in reading and math are included in the tally for their grade level.[6] A horizontal line between boxes across two years indicates that children were retained in that year. Thus, 126 students were retained in the first year, 61 in second grade, 45 in third grade and so on.

The complexity of elementary school track assignments suggests why most studies probably underestimate or misinterpret the effects of retention and Special Education. Beginning School Study children still in City schools after 5 years were spread across four grades (see column 5 under "years"), with 8% (52) in separate Special Education classes. Of the 614 youngsters still enrolled, only 365 (59%) were in fifth grade, 171 (28%) were in fourth grade, and 22 (4% of the original cohort) were in third grade (two years off-time). The four students who had earlier skipped a grade were in 6th grade.

Multiple Placements

Researchers generally treat retention, Special Education, and ability grouping as three isolated events but ignoring children's placement in multiple tracks could easily disguise or misrepresent the effects of any one placement. For a child to be in a low reading group and then retained is a different experience from being placed only in a low reading group, for example.

The large majority of Beginning School Study children (69%) had no low placements in first grade (Entwisle and Alexander 1993; Alexander and Entwisle 1996b). Of the others, 22% were in the lowest reading group; 16% were held back at year's end, and 13% were in Special Education. Of youngsters who experienced any of these placements, more than half (55%) had only one low placement, but the rest (45%) had multiple low placements in all possible combinations.[7] For example, almost three-fourths of children in low first grade reading groups were held back, half of them in first grade. By the end of the sixth grade, 35% of those who had been in low first grade reading groups were retained a second time. In comparison, *none* of the high reading group youngsters repeated first grade and 88% did not repeat any grade. Children in low groups in first grade were also more likely than other children to be in Special Education later on: more than half the children in low reading groups in first grade were receiving Special Education services in sixth grade, compared to only 6% of children in the high group in first grade (Alexander and Entwisle 1996b).

Figure 4.3 BSS Students' Movement Through the First Six Years of School

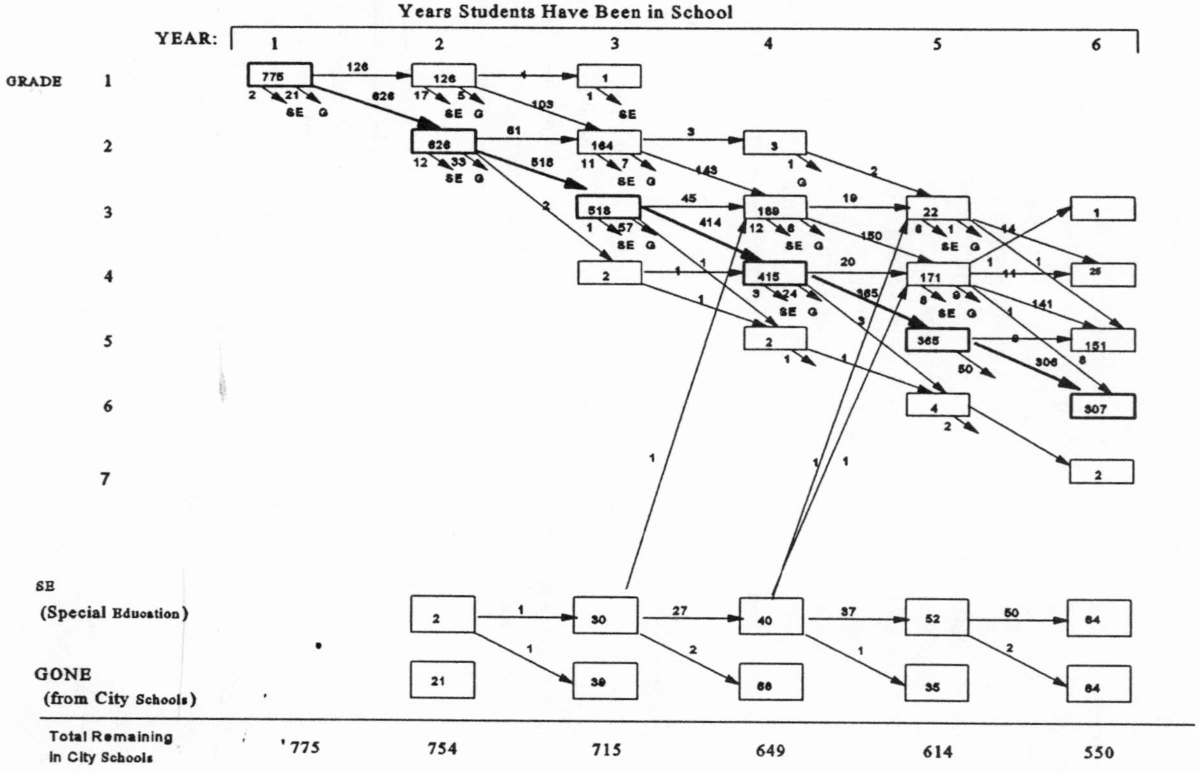

Retention and Special Education often occurred together. Three quarters of all Special Education students were first retained. Half of the first or second grade Special Education children who were not held back in first grade were held back later, compared to 23% of those not in Special Education. They also were much more likely to be held back a second time (32% vs. 10%) than children not in Special Education. First grade repeaters were also at higher risk for a second retention: 44.5% were held back a second time compared to just 6.5% of the children promoted at the end of first grade.

Some researchers emphasize the lack of mobility in reading group level from one grade to the next (see Rist 1970), but Beginning School Study children in both the lowest and highest first grade reading groups were found at all second grade reading levels. Just 45% of children remained in the same level of reading group in first and second grade with 34% predicted to stay in the same group by chance alone. Movement between years is generally downward, because 87% of first graders were in high or middle groups compared to only 69% of second graders. The lowest group enlarged the most - from 13% to 31%. The downward trend in group placement between years is partly a consequence of the high rate of retention in first grade. That is, when the least successful students are retained, the "low" group in second grade must be filled from the ranks of the children left to choose from. In this way, a high retention rate has effects on children *not* retained by consigning more of them to lower reading groups in the following years. Altogether, 37% of Beginning School Study children were in a low reading group in year one or year two, or both.

Retention and reading group level both affected Beginning School Study children's learning, *but in opposite ways* (Alexander, Entwisle, and Dauber 1994). Retention helped children do better, at least temporarily, while being in a low reading group hindered children. We think retention helped partly because in their initial first grade year, the future repeaters got very low marks, and at that time their academic self-images were lower than those of their classmates (who got higher marks). In their second year, however, when the repeaters took the same curriculum again, their marks were considerably higher (Alexander, Entwisle, and Dauber 1994), and their academic self-images improved. A rising self-image linked to higher marks is found fairly consistently (see Finlayson 1977; Reynolds 1992).

Only a few studies other than the Beginning School Study follow a single cohort of children from first grade up through the later grades (e.g. Pedersen et al. 1978; Ensminger and Slusarcick 1992; Stroup and Robins 1972), but all find evidence of long-term consequences of early tracking. *Other things equal*, Beginning School Study children's first grade reading group rank affected their standardized achievement scores in reading *and* math as well as their parents' expectations up through at least the fourth grade (see Pallas et al. 1994).[8] Children's reading group rank had larger effects on their test score gains than their reading marks did. Since teachers determined both marks and reading groups, if reading group assignment predicted only marks and not test scores we could conclude very little. Since reading group rank had some direct effects independent of marks, however, either grouping helped Beginning School Study children to learn more or there were institutional effects of reading groups (children labeled as "high" were treated as such and so learned more) or most likely both.

Beginning School Study students in high-ability reading groups also learned more mathematics than children in low groups. Possibly children "learn to learn" in high-ability groups, or perhaps placement in a high-ability reading group increased students' motivation and this carried over into other subject domains. We suspect institutional effects, however. The higher group students were probably treated as though they had more ability in math as well as in reading. Beginning School Study parents held very similar expectations for their children's performance in the two subjects: correlations between parents' expectations for their children's marks in reading and math were .62 at the beginning of the first year and .65 at the beginning of the second year. (See also Entwisle and Hayduk 1978; 1982.) The generalization of reading group effects to a completely different academic area like math lends strong support to an institutional theory of ability group effects, especially because at this age children's own expectations have negligible effects on their performance (see Table A8 in Alexander and Entwisle 1988).

Elementary School Organization Reconsidered

Age-Grading

This chapter began by pointing out that children's age is the prepotent determinant of elementary school organization in the U.S. Typically all children born within a designated 12-month period are placed in one grade-school cohort. In Baltimore, those born during 1976, like the Beginning School Study children, began first grade in September of the sixth year following their birth. Children who would turn 6 by December 31, 1982, were enrolled in September, 1982, but those born January 1, 1977 or later had to wait to enroll until September, 1983. This age rule determined that Baltimore children up to 6 years and 8 months of age began first grade with others as young as 5 years and 8 months. Later, a few children (less than 1%) were moved ahead because of superior performance, but many more, eventually 43% were "moved behind," i.e., retained over the first few years of school.

The rigid age grading of students in elementary schools goes against scientific information about how children's chronological age affects their schooling. In fact, entrance age does *not* predict children's cognitive growth in first grade (Alexander and Entwisle 1988; Jones and Mandeville 1990; Shepard and Smith 1986). Or, put another way, children's rates of learning in middle childhood are independent of their age over relatively long (1-year) time spans. If "young" Beginning School Study first-graders (those with birth dates in November-December, just before the cut-off) are compared with "old" first graders (those with birth dates in January-February, 11 or 12 months before the cut-off), the older children, on average, have higher test scores when they begin first grade than the younger ones do (Table 4.8). However, the *gains* over first grade by the "older" and "younger" Beginning School Study students are almost equivalent. It follows then that the test scores of "young" Beginning School Study first graders at the end of the school year were lower than test-scores of the "old" first-graders, but children in both age groups had gained the same number of points on standardized tests of achievement in reading and math over first grade.

Further evidence on the lack of a relationship between age and children's progress in school comes from an Israeli study of 4th, 5th, and 6th grade students in Jerusalem's state-controlled elementary schools. Cahan and Cohen (1989) compared the mean scores predicted for the youngest children in one grade with scores for the oldest children in the next lower grade. If age mattered, then the oldest child in grade 3, say, should have the same score as the youngest child in grade 4 because their ages are very close. Yet this kind of comparison showed a jump in scores between the *equally old* grade 3 and grade 4 Jerusalem children that unambiguously points to the amount of children's schooling rather than their age as the key factor explaining growth.

Evidence from natural experiments also suggests that *time spent in school* rather than age explains how much children know.[9] Ceci (1991) estimates that children's IQ scores drop between 0.25 and 6 points per year when schools are shut down. He notes that when the public schools in Prince Edward County, Virginia were closed between 1959 and 1964 to avoid integration, most African American children received no formal education. On average, their IQ's dropped by about 6 points per year for every year they missed school, with children of all ages affected (Green et al. 1964). For another example, when World War II forced Holland's schools to close, the IQ scores of children whose schooling was delayed dropped by about 7 points (DeGroot 1951).

Table 4.8   Beginning California Achievement Test (CAT) Scores and First Year Test Score Gains For "Young" and "Old" Beginning School Study (BSS) First Graders [a]

	"Young"	t-tests[b]	"Old"
Beginning Year 1 CAT Score			
Reading	270	*	282
Math	278	*	301
Year 1 Test Score Gains			
Reading	64.7		68.7
Math	54.0		49.4

$*p \leq .05$

[a] "Young" BSS first graders are defined as those whose birthdays fall in November or December, just before the cut-off date for entering first graders. "Old" is defined as those with birthdays in January or February, 11 or 12 months before the cut-off date.

[b] t-tests compare means of "young" and "old" BSS students.

Other facts are consistent with the importance of school attendance rather than age for young children's cognitive growth. The number of hours of schooling children receive correlates with their scores on verbal and math aptitude tests (Wiley and Harnischfeger 1974), and the number of children's absences is inversely related to their test score gains (Heyns 1978; Karweit 1973; Bond and Dykstra 1967; Alexander and Entwisle 1988). Most persuasively, as noted earlier, all children's achievement scores in the spring exceed their scores in the preceding fall, but some children's growth slows down or stops when school is closed for the summer. All children get 3 months older in summer but only those whose families are well enough off to provide sufficient resources can continue to make achievement test gains over the summer (see Ceci 1991; Heyns 1978; Entwisle and Alexander 1992; 1994).[10]

The intent here is not to assemble exhaustive evidence about chronological age in relation to cognitive growth, but rather to make clear that children's chronological age may not be the best or only criterion to use in organizing elementary schools. For children who come from low socioeconomic status homes, it may be highly profitable to start school as early as possible.

Age and the Schooling Process

A serious question but one rarely considered is whether the *process* of schooling is the same at every age. Do the same structural models portray the schooling process at ages 6, 7, 8? That is, do the same variables affect schooling in the same way for children of different ages? If different variables explain children's achievement at different ages, school programs should be fashioned accordingly. First grade seems to be the time when students' non-cognitive characteristics have their greatest effects,[11] for example, so special attention should be paid to the "fit" of the student in the first grade classroom. Physical arrangements of classrooms could matter most in first grade and need to be different from those in later grades. Changes in how classrooms are laid out or changes in scheduling might make it easier for some first graders to pay attention or to participate in class. Also various versions of the first grade curriculum may be required to stimulate different children's interest and participation. If some kinds of development occur at a rapid pace early in children's school careers and then slow down, the resources to support that development should be allocated early so as to exert the greatest effect. An analysis of the learning process could suggest logical ways to re-shape elementary school organization so as to enhance children's achievement.

Although research with secondary school students (8th grade and up) assumes that the resources related to school achievement (family background, student ability, teacher expectations and so on) *are* the same in the eighth grade as in the twelfth, this assumption has yet to be seriously tested. For Beginning School Study children, some variables affected cognitive growth differently from one year to the next. For instance, variables related to temperament and personality directly affected schooling *early*--in first grade-- and had only negligible direct effects in later grades. Also, even by the second year of school, boys' reading marks had slipped compared to girls' (Alexander and Entwisle 1988).

Some effects of schools also carry over from one elementary year to the next (Alexander and Entwisle 1988), while others do not. Parents' expectations for children's performance at the beginning of grade one, for example, directly affected performance in that first year, and their children's performance in grade one affected performance in grade two. The indirect effects of grade one parents' expectations added on to the direct effects of parents' expectations in grade two (Alexander and Entwisle 1988; Pallas et al. 1994). Changing parents' grade one expectation could, therefore, affect performance indirectly for several years after first grade.

As shown earlier, children's growth rates also vary throughout the year (see

Heyns 1978; also Entwisle and Alexander 1992; 1994). In winter, when all children grow at much the same pace, family background and neighborhood quality have very small effects. In summer when school is closed, however, rates of learning vary markedly according to the socioeconomic status of family and neighborhood. How could resources be marshaled to support children's cognitive growth when school is closed? The calendar now in place, with schools shut down for the summer, exacts a heavier penalty on poor than on better-off children.

Changes in school practices within the school year are not likely to close the gap in achievement between poor and well-off children because poor children are already gaining at the same rate as better-off children when school is open. Rather, resources must be supplied in summer to supplant those that the school supplies in winter. This order is not easy to fill because traditional "summer schools" so far have not done the job. (See Chapter 3; also Heyns 1987; Entwisle and Alexander 1992; Entwisle and Alexander 1997.) The topic of summer school is beyond the scope of this chapter but fruitful ways for children to use their time over the summer months are badly needed.

Implications

Socioeconomic Tracking

The major thesis of this chapter is that children in U.S. elementary schools are rigidly tracked by socioeconomic status, and this tracking produces school contexts that foster inequality. When they are open, schools are nevertheless *very* effective in making up for shortfalls of resources in poor youngsters' homes (Chapter 3). Children who are not so well-off actually learn as much or more than their better-off classmates do when school is open, *but they are not treated that way.* Children in one elementary school are treated as "high ability" (because on average they have "high" test scores when they start first grade) and children in another elementary school are treated as "low ability" (because on average they have "low" test scores when they start first grade). These disparities in treatment can be seen as soon as children begin school or even before, even though all children make equal progress once they start first grade. Over first grade, children in the top ten Beginning School Study schools gained 62 points on California Achievement Test tests in reading, almost exactly the same as the average number of points children in the lowest ten Beginning School Study schools gained--60 points. Even so, the first-grade reading instructional level for children in the Beginning School Study school located in the most advantaged neighborhood was halfway between average (pre-primer which is considered at grade level) and above average (primer), while the reading instructional level of children in the school located in the poorest neighborhood was below the pre-primer level. The myth that elementary schools share the same curriculum is thus false because the type of instruction provided for students varies by socioeconomic status of the school. Furthermore, when schools are closed students in more prosperous neighborhoods have the resources to learn even more. The "neighborhood school" has a friendly ring to it, and of course 6-year-olds are more comfortable going to school close to home with other children they know than traveling to some other neighborhood, but the long-term costs of neighborhood schools are high.

The lack of good preschools for 3 and 4-year-olds is an important issue related to tracking that is beyond the scope of this chapter. Still, it must contribute to the differences between better-off and poor children's achievement levels when they start school. Headstart reaches about 40% of eligible 4-year-olds and under 20% of eligible 3-year-olds (Stewart 1993). Even with nursery school, Headstart, and all other center-based programs combined, however, only about 60% of 4-year-olds with family incomes under $15,000 were enrolled in center-based programs in 1991, with high school drop-outs and/or teenage parents the least likely to enroll their children (U.S. Department of Education 1994b). The lack of preschool facilities for disadvantaged youngsters prior to kindergarten is a major way that differential tracking by family income takes an early hold upon children from disadvantaged backgrounds. A few extra test points conferred by attending a good preschool could be enough to protect economically disadvantaged youngsters against low placements or retention in the first couple of grades. (See Entwisle 1995.)

Presently socioeconomic status patterns *across* elementary schools are virtually ignored, yet this kind of tracking probably explains all or most curricular tracking in high school. Fifth year test scores effectively determine course-taking patterns in middle school, and the middle school patterns in turn determine high school placements (Dauber, Alexander and Entwisle 1996). Early tracking must also have serious and long-lasting consequences for children's socioemotional development, but so far these have been barely hinted at.

Transitions

The matter of student age when children begin school demands review. Almost everywhere in the U.S., chronological age alone dictates when children begin first grade. If all goes well, children march in lockstep with their age mates up the grade ladder. If all does not go well, however, children end up "off-time," which in and of itself can have deleterious effects. The rigid structure of American elementary schools in terms of children's age is not warranted by the facts about children's school learning because within a rather wide age range children learn at about the same rate. Grouping children by wider age bands should be considered because (1) it would help reduce the number of off-time students and (2) it would also reduce the number of between-grade transitions young children have to make. Much more research is needed, but multigrade classes appear to be as effective as single grade classes in terms of both cognitive and non-cognitive outcomes (Veenman 1995).

Children's level of development when they move into first grade is a key issue for elementary school organization. Only a few studies besides the BSS, however, address the "settling in" and "transition" issues that face children starting school (Entwisle and Hayduk 1978; 1982; Reynolds 1989; 1991; 1992; Barr and Dreeben 1983). The fact that children's test scores vary by socioeconomic status when they start school is widely accepted, but that variation could be considerably reduced by Headstart (Consortium 1983), or by full-day kindergarten attendance (Entwisle et al. 1987) and no doubt by other means as well. The beginning school transition is probably the most important school transition because it sets the stage for all that follows.

One way to ease the first grade transition is for children to attend full-time kindergarten. Because kindergarten is not compulsory, a surprisingly large number of children do not attend or do not attend full-time. About 8% of 5-year-old children nationally are not in school (U.S. Department of Education 1995) and in Maryland in 1994, 3.3% of first graders had not previously attended kindergarten. In Baltimore City, however, which is one of the poorest districts in Maryland, 10% of the children did not attend kindergarten. Also time spent in kindergarten varies widely even within the same district. The large majority of Beginning School Study children in Baltimore attended half-day programs. Not surprisingly, Beginning School Study children from the least advantaged home backgrounds more often were enrolled in the half-day than the full-day programs: of Beginning School Study children who attended half-day kindergarten, 77% were on meal subsidy compared to 32% of those who attended full days. The benefits of full day as compared to half-day kindergartens were striking. With family background and many other variables controlled, first grade children who had attended full day kindergarten were absent less, were less often retained, and got higher academic marks and test scores than those who attended half days (Entwisle et al. 1987). Kindergartens are now almost universally available in the U.S.

but they are underutilized. Half-day programs should be replaced by full-day programs, especially in poorer areas.

Disorderly transitions between grades are a separate issue, and we suspect that in many large school systems besides Baltimore, the irregular grade structures that force children to make extra transitions are found mostly in the poorer neighborhoods. These transitions reduce children's school success and quality of life. If unusual patterns of grade structure are indeed required, these should not be imposed mainly upon students who are already at a disadvantage. The negative consequences of extra transitions could probably be reduced if parents and schools were made aware of how seriously they affect young children's schooling, however.

Notes

1. In 1990-91 mean enrollment in Baltimore City public elementary schools was 529, in middle schools 888, and in high schools 1078.

2. The examples here of the variation between schools in Baltimore City is a "minimal" picture because all these schools are in one of the poorest school districts in Maryland. If schools were contrasted between districts as well, the variation across elementary schools would be much greater. In 1991-92, the average expenditure per pupil in Baltimore was $4,947, which was about 85% of the state average ($5,815) at the time, but only 65% of the average ($7,591) for Montgomery County, the wealthiest district. Furthermore, in Baltimore 67% of children were on meal subsidy compared to 17% in Montgomery County (Maryland State Department of Education 1992). Baltimore City children were thus allotted only two-thirds as much money for education as were children in a nearby school district where families were much better off.

3. Data refer to Baltimore schools in 1987-88.

4. Low reliability of tests is less of a problem for group averages than for individual students because the variance of the mean scores decreases as a function of the number in the group. For example, the variance in the means of groups of 10 students is only one-tenth of the variance in individual scores.

5. An 8 year-old who is in third grade is "in modal grade for age" while a 9 year-old in third grade is "below modal grade for age." Those above the modal age could have been held back, *or* could be behind for many other reasons, including starting first grade at a later age. For this reason, modal age data are less than ideal for estimating trends in grade retention.

6. The total number of retainees in these years is slightly higher because students assigned to Special Education in the spring of the year, *before* being retained, are added to the Special Education category at the bottom of the chart. Their grade placement following that assignment is not displayed in the Chart, so figures in the upper section of the Chart slightly undercount retentions. The complete tally of

retainees is as follows: 1st grade - 127, 2nd grade - 68, 3rd grade - 47, 4th grade - 21, 5th grade - 10.

7. A maximum of about half the cohort could have placed low in one of the three areas (16% retained + 13% in Special Education + 22% in low reading groups = 51%). The actual figure is 24% (or 31% looking at just those with data in all three measures.)

8. Controls include race, socioeconomic status, sex, family type, parent expectation level, marks and test scores when children started first grade.

9. See Karweit (1976) for a discussion of time spent in school in relation to achievement.

10. The evidence as to how various kinds of cognitive growth depend on formal schooling is burgeoning, but patterns at present are not altogether clear. Over kindergarten or first grade, schooling affects language, spatial perceptions, a combined test of language and spatial concepts, but not associative memory (Huttenlocher et al. 1997). From the beginning of kindergarten to the end of first grade (two years), Morrison, Griffith, and Williamson (1993) found differences in growth in mathematics and cultural knowledge between children enrolled in school and those not enrolled, but not differences in their reading or receptive vocabulary, probably because children practice reading and vocabulary skills outside of school, while math and cultural knowledge are topics less widely available. In other studies, grade-one schooling enhanced short-term memory and mental arithmetic with no evidence that age played a role, but phonological segmentation depended on both age and schooling (Morrison, Smith, and Dow-Ehrensberger 1995). By contrast, conservation of number depended only on age (Bisanz, Morrison, and Dunn 1995) and instruction does not seem to help children acquire general principles of conservation.

11. See Alexander and Entwisle 1988. Such effects are not found for high school youngsters, or if found, are extremely small (e.g., Bachman, O'Malley, and Johnston 1978; Gottfredson 1982; Mueser 1979; Olneck and Bills 1980).

5

Family Configuration

We know

Children growing up in the United States today have different family experiences from those of their parents. Between 1970 and 1993, for example, the proportion of children maintained by their mothers jumped from 11% to 23% (U.S. Bureau of the Census 1994), so that by 1993 more than 19 million children lived in families that did not contain two parents. Single parenting is the mode for African Americans; in 1993 only a minority (36%) resided in homes with two parents (U.S. Bureau of the Census 1994). Also, over the past two decades an increasing number of "single parents" are fathers: the number of families in which children lived with never-married fathers increased 15-fold (from 22,000 to 345,000) between 1970 and 1990 (U.S. Bureau of the Census 1990a). By 1990 about 14% of single-parent families were "father-only."

Family configuration overlaps economic disadvantage. Children in husband-wife families fare best. In 1992 their average income was about two and one-half times as great as that in mother-only homes (about $47,000 compared to $18,000) (U.S. Bureau of the Census 1992a), while their poverty rate (10%) was only one-fifth the rate for children in female-headed households (53%) (U.S. Bureau of the Census 1992a). One reason the number of mother-only families has swelled is because of the upswing in non-marital births. In 1970 less than 6% of white births were non-marital, but by 1991 this figure had more than tripled (22%). Parallel figures for African Americans are over three times those for whites (U.S. Bureau of the Census 1992b): about 38% in 1970 and 68% in 1991. Children of these never-married mothers are the worst off. Their poverty rate exceeded 66% in 1992 (U.S. Bureau of the Census 1992a), in part because only 27% of their mothers had child support awards (U.S. Bureau of the Census 1995).

It is becoming increasingly clear that children growing up in single-parent families do not do as well in school as their counterparts in two-parent

99

families. What is not so clear is why family structure affects schooling, or, put another way, exactly what causes the schooling deficits of children in single-parent families. This chapter reconsiders how and why family configuration affects children's elementary schooling. To do this it draws extensively upon data pertaining to Beginning School Study parents. In addition to their marital histories and their children's school performance, there are data on family life events (job loss, illness, and the like), parent's occupation and education, size of family, living arrangements, as well as parent's attitudes and activities related to children's schooling.

Study findings in this chapter supplement, enrich, or modify similar information from other sources. This chapter mainly covers the elementary school period, but occasionally refers to longer term outcomes that link back to those early years. Details of most analyses are omitted for reasons of space but citations are given to the full analyses elsewhere.

School Outcomes for Children in One- and Two-Parent Families

Compared to children in two-parent families, those being raised in single parent families have lower IQ and achievement test scores (Zill 1996; McLanahan and Sandefur 1994), more often repeat a grade (Dawson 1991), more often drop out (Coleman 1988; McLanahan and Bumpass 1988b), and less often go to college (Zill 1996). In fact, living in a single-parent family substantially increases the likelihood of being a high school drop-out and diminishes the likelihood of attending college, even when current family income and mother's education are held constant (McLanahan and Bumpass 1988a; Zill 1996).

Living in a single-parent family is also problematic for students' classroom behavior and adjustment (Garfinkel and McLanahan 1986; Zill 1996). Children's academic success depends partly on their social and emotional adjustment but the overlap between children's cognitive and affective growth has prompted little large-scale research. Still, whether children attend school regularly and are well-behaved can matter a great deal for their long-term academic prospects, especially in first grade, because their adjustment to the student role has large and lasting effects on their test scores and marks. These "adjustment" effects can be as large or larger than effects associated with their initial standardized test scores (Alexander and Entwisle 1988).

Allowing for differences in family economic background and ethnicity, children in single-mother families are over 2.5 times as likely to be suspended or expelled between grades 6 and 12 as are those in mother-father families, and children of single mothers are more often tardy or truant (Zill 1996).

These children also display more disruptive behavior in class, receive more problem referrals, and rate lower in social skills, "personality," homework completion and study habits than do children in two-parent homes (see Epstein 1984; Garfinkel and McLanahan 1986; Hetherington, Camara, and Featherman 1983; McLanahan and Sandefur 1994; Santrock and Tracy 1978).

Beginning School Study youngsters who were growing up in single parent families displayed many of the same problematic patterns as those just summarized. At the time they started first grade, they showed relatively small but significant deficits in their scores on standardized tests of reading and math compared to children in two-parent families (a little less than one-quarter of a standard deviation), but these deficits increased as time passed. After five years in school, those in one-parent families were behind children in two-parent families by more than one third of a standard deviation in both reading and math.

Beginning School Study children from single-parent families also performed less satisfactorily than those in two-parent families in terms of non-academic criteria. They were absent only a little more often in first grade (14 versus 12 days), but they were late twice as often (8 versus 4 days). At the end of first grade, teachers rated 39% of the boys being raised in one-parent homes as needing improvement in conduct versus about 19% of the boys in homes where two parents were present. Differences in girls' conduct associated with family type were less marked, but also favored those in two-parent homes (20% versus 9% needed improvement). When adjusted for family background characteristics and parental expectations, many of the differences listed above are no longer significant but, even with such controls taken into account, children from homes of single mothers who did not share a residence with other adults did not improve in conduct over the first school year whereas all other children did (Thompson et al. 1992).

Beginning School Study teachers rated first grade children's classroom behavior on scales of attention span-restlessness, cooperation-compliance, and interest-participation. On each of these scales, children from two-parent homes scored significantly above those in one-parent homes, by about one-quarter of a standard deviation. A one standard deviation increase in a child's interest/participation *or* attention span-restlessness rating in first grade was associated with improved reading marks (more than one-third of a unit in that year, and by one-fifth of a unit even at the end of grade 4). Better participation and attention ratings also led to substantial increases in standardized tests: 15-20 points in both reading and math at the end of first grade, with smaller but significant effects still visible in grade 4 (Alexander, Entwisle, and Dauber 1993). In fact, the interest/participation and attention span-restlessness scales each predict children's gains on standardized achievement tests in reading comprehension better than do scores on the same tests obtained when children began first grade (Alexander, Entwisle, and Dauber 1993). Teachers' ratings of students' "adjustment" in first grade thus matter a great deal.

Differences Among Single Parents

Before considering what could hamper the school performance of children from single-parent families, a word is needed about differences among single parents. Until fairly recently, most research on single parenting and youngsters' schooling centered on children who live with separated or divorced single mothers (see Garfinkel and McLanahan 1986; Kurdek and Sinclair 1988; McLanahan and Sandefur 1994). In the past decade, however, it has become clear that school outcomes like test scores and drop-out differ not only between children from one- and two-parent families but also among children whose single mothers are widowed, never-married, divorced or separated (Moore 1995).

In 1970 73% of children living with one parent were in a home where the parent was divorced or separated, another 20% were living with a widowed parent, and only 7% were living with a never-married parent. Two decades later, 31% of children living with one parent were in a home with a never-married parent. In 1990 over half (52%) of African American children in single-parent homes were living with a never-married parent compared to only 14% in 1970 (U.S. Bureau of the Census 1991b).

Children of never married mothers show much more severe schooling deficits than do children of divorced or separated mothers. Almost 20% of the children of never-married mothers repeat a grade compared to 16% of children of other single mothers, and compared to children in biological two-parent families, twice as many children of never-married mothers have been the focus of a parent-teacher conference (26% versus 13%) (Dawson 1991).

Children of never-married mothers are also by far the poorest. They are spared the trauma of marital break-up, but the financial resources available to them are far less than the resources available to children in other single-mother homes. In 1992, for example, the average income for never-married mothers ($14,802) was about two-thirds that of divorced mothers ($21,880). Never-married mothers also have distinctly lower levels of education than other mothers: 59% are high school graduates compared to 82% of divorced mothers (U.S. Bureau of the Census 1992a). A key distinction between never-married mothers and other single mothers is that they are more likely to have given birth as teenagers, and a mother's age at her child's birth appears to have some effect on the child's scores on standardized tests, retention in grade, and other teacher evaluations of performance, even after associated factors such as mother's income, education, and the like, are taken into account (Hofferth 1987; Grissmer et al. 1994). Roughly 70% of unmarried parents are teenagers (Elster, Ketterlinus, and Lamb 1990), and among adolescents age 15 through 19 who became mothers in 1975-1979 (the same 5-year period in which the Beginning School Study children were born), about 32% of white and 80% of African American births were non-marital (O'Connell and Rogers 1980).

To make the picture even more problematic, the social ties of never-married mothers are limited. They spend more hours at home with their children than divorced mothers do, but they are less likely than divorced mothers to participate in a variety of family activities and to provide an intellectually stimulating home environment for their children (Zill and Rogers 1988).

The contrasts among Beginning School Study children of never-married and other parents are less marked than the contrasts drawn from Census data because Beginning School Study mothers as a group are more disadvantaged than mothers in national samples. Still, never-married Study mothers had finished only 11.2 years of school, while divorced or separated Study mothers had finished 11.7 years of school; also as first graders, 91% of Study children with never-married mothers qualified for meal subsidy compared to 72% of children of divorced or separated mothers. Beginning School Study mothers in two-parent families and the divorced or separated mothers were considerably older than the never-married mothers (25.1 and 24.8 years versus 20.8 years). About 46% of those who became mothers under age 20 were not married when the study child was born versus 16% of mothers 20 and over.

In terms of school outcomes, about 21% of Beginning School Study children of never-married mothers were retained in first grade vs. 18% of children from other single-mother homes, and by the end of elementary school retention rates for children of never-married mothers reached 49% versus 41% for other single mothers (Table 5.1). Over elementary school, compared to those from other single parent families, children of never-married mothers consistently received lower marks in reading and math, got lower scores on standardized tests and were more often absent or late. By the end of the fifth year of school, their reading comprehension scores were almost one-half of a standard deviation below those of children in other single-mother homes. Absences in the early grades are a particular concern because they affect the later school performance mainly of children whose home backgrounds are weak (Douglas and Ross 1965). Beginning School Study children of never-married mothers were absent 16 days in first grade compared to 10 days for children of other single mothers.

Table 5.1   Beginning School Study Students' Characteristics, Early Elementary Performance Measures, and Parental Expectations by Family Type and Mother's Marital Status

	Family Type[a]				Single Mother's Marital Status[a]		
	Mother Alone	Mother-Other Adults	t-test[b]	Mother-Father	Never Married	t-tests[c]	Divorced/Separated
Proportion African American	.67	.73	*	.43	.86	*	.49
Proportion Female	.45	.53		.52	.53		.50
Mother's Age at Student's Birth	23.53	20.94	*	25.14	20.82	*	24.84
Number of Siblings	1.43	1.04	*	1.60	1.02	*	1.52
Proportion on Meal Subsidy	.82	.86	*	.53	.91	*	.72
Parent's Education	11.38	11.57	*	12.26	11.16		11.66
California Achievement Test: Reading Comprehension							
Fall Year 1	280	277	*	286	280		286
Spring Year 1	328	338	*	346	331		342
Spring Year 2	377	381	*	400	373	*	390
Spring Year 5	462	475	*	495	463	*	495
California Achievement Test: Math Concepts							
Fall Year 1	289	289	*	297	287	*	297
Spring Year 1	336	336	*	346	329	*	344
Spring Year 2	374	378	*	391	371	*	383
Spring Year 5	458	469	*	487	460	*	480
Report Card Marks							
Reading-Fall Year 1	1.72	1.84	*	1.99	1.67	*	2.00
Reading-Spring Year 1	2.06	2.09	*	2.46	1.97	*	2.37
Reading-Spring Year 2	2.20	2.21	*	2.50	2.06		2.39
Reading-Spring Year 5	2.26	2.21	*	2.51	2.17		2.29

	Mother-only	Mother-Other Adults		Mother-Father	Never married		Divorced/Separated
Report Card Marks							
Math-Fall Year 1	2.09	2.11	*	2.36	2.03	*	2.33
Math-Spring Year 1	2.37	2.49	*	2.66	2.32	+	2.58
Math-Spring Year 2	2.37	2.42	*	2.65	2.29	*	2.54
Math-Spring Year 5	2.17	2.41	*	2.59	2.29		2.44
Conduct-Fall Year 1	1.67	1.68	*	1.81	1.70		1.73
Conduct-Spring Year 1	1.68	1.73	*	1.86	1.73		1.74
Conduct-Spring Year 2	1.70	1.68	*	1.80	1.69		1.62
Conduct-Spring Year 5	1.61	1.65	*	1.72	1.61		1.65
Proportion Retained in Grade 1	.25	.20	*	.12	.21		.18
Proportion Retained, Grades 1-5	.51	.47	*	.39	.49		.41
Total Days Absent, Year 1	14.29	13.62	+	12.24	16.28	*	10.53
Total Days Late, Year 1	7.76	7.73	*	3.85	10.14	*	4.12
Work Habits, Spring Year 1	8.43	8.71	*	9.01	8.57		8.87
Parent's Expectations for Student Marks							
Reading-Fall Year 1	2.54	2.56	*	2.77	2.55		2.60
Math-Fall Year 1	2.64	2.71		2.75	2.68		2.65

* $p \leq .05$

+ $p \leq .10$

[a] Sample sizes vary because coverage varies for different variables. Ranges in sample size are: Mother-only, N=103-148; Mother-other adults, N=102-156; Mother-father, N=247-422; Never married, N= 100-135; Divorced/Separated, N=69-92. Marital status is not available for all single mothers.

[b] Reported significant differences are for t-tests comparing means of Single Mothers ("Mother-Alone," "Mother-Other Adults") with "Mother-Father" families.

[c] Reported significant differences are for t-tests comparing means of "Never married" and "Divorced/Separated" mothers.

Possible Mediators of Single Parenting Effects

Single parenting could have negative effects on children's schooling for many reasons: (1) The relative dearth of economic resources in single parent homes; (2) the greater difficulty that single parents have in socializing children for school; (3) mother's age at the child's birth, because more single mothers have given birth as teenagers; (4) the number of children in the family, which differs between one and two parent homes; and (5) the family's living arrangements, because many single mothers share residences. In what follows, each of these reasons will be discussed in turn, first in terms of evidence in the literature and then in terms of Beginning School Study findings.

Economic Resources

Using four national data sets, McLanahan and Sandefur (1994) estimated that about half of the "single parent" decrement in children's schooling stems from economic deprivation, and other researchers agree (e.g. Bianchi and McArthur 1991; Schneider and Coleman 1993). Beginning School Study children's gains on standardized tests over the first two years of school likewise show family economic standing is a major reason that children's achievement gains over the first grade transition differ between those in one-parent and two-parent homes (Entwisle and Alexander 1995; 1996b). With family size, mother's age, and other relevant variables held constant but allowing economic resources to vary, Beginning School Study children from two-parent homes gained 26 more points (more than half a standard deviation) on standardized tests in both reading and math over the first two years of school than did children in single-parent homes. However, when economic resources were controlled, the difference favoring children in two-parent households dropped enough (about a quarter of a standard deviation in reading and math, respectively) so that the performance differences among children from the various family types were no longer significant.

The Beginning School Study evidence on seasonal differences in learning bears on the financial aspects of single parenting: children in homes with few economic resources fell behind children in homes with more resources mainly in summers, but the *summer deficits were the same irrespective of whether or not two parents were in the home* (Entwisle and Alexander 1995). That is, the gains that children in high and low socioeconomic status families made on standardized tests were virtually the same in winter, but those who were more economically advantaged made relatively greater gains in summer. In summer, however, children in two-parent homes gained about the same number of points as those in one-parent homes, once economic status was taken into account. Deficits in children's cognitive growth thus matched the cutting off of resources provided by the school rather than the presence or absence of two parents in the home.

Consistent with this conclusion, Salzman's (1987) meta-analysis of 137 studies of effects of father absence on children's school performance shows no clear trends, and nationally representative samples also show that frequent father contact has no detectable benefits on children's school performance (McLanahan and Sandefur 1994, p. 98). In sum, although the ideal of an intact family is prominent in the schooling literature and in policy-makers' thinking, research indicates that family economic status far overshadows the number of resident parents as an influence on children's schooling.

Socialization for School

Another reason why children from one-parent families do not do as well as those in two-parent families is that one-parent families are less effective in socializing their children for school (Garfinkel and McLanahan 1986). Single parents, for instance, are less likely than those in two-parent families to monitor their children's school work (Astone and McLanahan 1989; 1991) and to supervise them at home (Dornbusch et al. 1985). Parent supervision matters for children's academic performance because well-monitored children get higher grades and better conduct ratings than other children do (Crouter et al. 1990). The benefits conferred by home supervision are also borne out by the superior performance of children who live in extended families, where single mothers share a residence with grandparents or other adults. These children have higher preschool cognitive scores (Furstenberg, Brooks-Gunn, and Morgan 1987) and less difficulty in adjusting to school than do children who live with mothers only (Furstenberg 1976; Kellam, Ensminger, and Turner 1977).

In the Beginning School Study, socialization effects of extended families look to be important because African American children whose mothers shared residences with other relatives improved significantly in conduct over their first year of school whereas those in solo-mother homes did not (Thompson et al. 1992). Also, Beginning School Study children whose mothers shared a residence with additional relatives earned better reading marks in first grade than either children in other single-parent homes *or* those in two-parent homes, controlling for the usual background factors plus mother's age and sibship size (Entwisle and Alexander 1996a). These latter factors are usually not controlled in studies of co-residence, but could cloud the picture because mothers who live with other relatives tend to be considerably younger and have fewer children than single mothers who live on their own. Still, the image of the "happy grandmother" family is probably exaggerated or even untrue, as other costs attached to living in multi-generational families can be high (Chase-Lansdale et al. 1994). More research is needed on how patterns of co-residence affect single mothers and their children, but the presence of other adults living with single mothers may help children in making the first-grade transition, as discussed more fully later.

Maternal Age at the Child's Birth

Why a mother's age at her child's birth should affect that child's school performance is unclear, because age itself does not seem to affect the quality of parenting. Nevertheless, a whole constellation of other factors covary with the small effects of maternal age on children's schooling (Chase-Lansdale et al. 1994). Teen mothers are more likely than other adolescents to have had problems in school--suspension, truancy, drug use, fighting, or even drop-out (Elster, Ketterlinus, and Lamb 1990). The fact that teen parents have had more problems in school than other teenagers could handicap their children in adjusting to school because parents who had school problems themselves may be unable to coach children about how to behave in school or even be confrontational in dealing with teachers. To our knowledge, how parents' own school problems affect their children's schooling has not been examined over a wide range of parents' age, but children of drop-outs do have more school problems than other children do (see Furstenberg et al. 1987).

Compared to older Beginning School Study mothers, those who gave birth under age 20 were just as likely to be living alone (19% versus 18%), but the younger mothers lived less often with children's fathers (40% versus 64%). Also, many more of the children of the younger than the older mothers were eligible for meal subsidy (86% versus 58%). Even with family structure, maternal schooling, and economic standing held constant, however, children of Beginning School Study teen mothers still gained about 5 points less over the first two years of school on standardized tests in math (nearly one-fifth of a S.D.) than did children of mothers who were 20 or over when the child was born (Entwisle and Alexander 1996b).

The deficits in the school performance of Beginning School Study children of teen mothers could be related to their psychological resources. Compared to older mothers, the Beginning School Study teen mothers were marginally more depressed, significantly lower on the Rotter locus of control scale, and they saw their children as significantly more restless and less attentive in school. The teen mothers also had significantly lower expectations for their children's first marks in reading and math (by about one-quarter of a grade point), and did not expect them to attend college. Older Beginning School Study mothers, on average, expected their children to go to college for at least 1 or 2 years. For all these reasons, teen mothers may be less well equipped psychologically than older mothers to socialize their children for school.

Family Size

Children's school performance is negatively correlated with family size both in intact and non-intact families (Mercy and Steelman 1982; Blake 1989; Lloyd and Miner 1993). The number of siblings tends to be larger in two-parent than in one-parent families (Blake 1981; 1989), but how family size and parent configuration *together* affect young children's school performance is not clear. Single parenting has negative effects, but the relatively smaller size of single-parent families could help compensate. Also the negative effects of large family size on school performance are based on populations that included families of very large size (7 or more children) (Mercy and Steelman 1982). Both family size and the variance in family size have decreased sharply in recent years, so effects of family size may now be considerably attenuated.

By the time Beginning School Study children entered school, those in two-parent households had more siblings (1.6) than those in single-mother households (1.2), but Beginning School Study single mothers who lived alone had more children (1.4) than those who lived in extended arrangements (1.0). With family type controlled, Beginning School Study children with more sibs got better conduct marks when they started first grade than did those with fewer sibs (Thompson et al. 1992). However, the benefits of having sibs are confined to children who have *one* sib as compared to children with no sibs; those with two or more sibs did worse. It is possible that differences favoring two-child families over one-child families, like those observed for Beginning School Study children starting school, could have been present all along but overlooked.

Why would children with no sibs have difficulty settling into school? For one reason, only children receive more parental help and nurturance than other children do (Sutton-Smith and Rosenberg 1970), so "onlies" may have trouble adjusting to a classroom group. In addition, onlies are more likely to come from a broken family and to have had health problems as infants (Blake 1989). They have fewer social ties than other children because they belong to fewer organizations, have fewer friends, and visit friends less often (Falbo 1982).

Living Arrangements of Single Parents

Living arrangements for children in single-parent families vary considerably. About the same *percentage* of African American (39%) as white (40%) children of single mothers live in families with other adults (U.S. Bureau of the Census 1992a), but because about 58% of African American families are headed by single mothers compared to about 18% of white families, the likelihood that an African American child will live in an extended family arrangement is much greater (U.S. Bureau of the Census 1992a). The stereotype is that the African American single mother lives with other adults because it helps in managing scarce economic resources (Stack 1974; Staples and Mirande 1980), but this pattern occurs irrespective of financial pressures because even with income controlled, extended family arrangements are twice as likely for African Americans as for whites (Farley and Allen 1987).

Research on whether the school performance of children of single mothers who live alone differs from that of children who live in extended arrangements is thin, but two studies cited earlier show that African American children of single mothers who lived in extended families adjusted better to first grade than did children of mothers who lived alone (Furstenberg 1976; Kellam et al. 1977). McLanahan and Sandefur (1994) found that having a grandmother in the house increased parental supervision whereas having a male partner did not, but that overall the average child raised by a mother and grandmother did about the same in school as the average child raised only by a single mother.

Residential patterns for Beginning School Study mothers are consistent with national trends: 12% of the white mothers and 28% of the African American mothers were living in extended arrangements, and most mothers in both groups who lived in extended arrangements shared a residence with "other relatives" (for 40%, this was a grandmother). In both groups also, single mothers who lived alone had more children and were about 3 years older than those who lived in mother-other adult families.

Beginning School Study children who lived in mother-other arrangements did consistently better in school than children of single mothers living alone. Although differences are not statistically significant, their test scores and marks over the first five years of school are noticeably higher (Table 5.1). Furthermore, if we take into account children's test scores when they began first grade, the gains made by children in mother-other families were 198 points in reading comprehension by the end of year 5 compared to 182 points by children in mother-alone families and 210 points by children in mother-father families. In other words, allowing for where children started, those in mother-other homes came closer to those in mother-father homes than to those in other one-parent homes. Also the first reading mark and initial work habits scores of children who lived in mother-other homes were significantly higher than those in mother-alone *or* mother-father homes with family background and all other variables controlled (Entwisle and Alexander 1996b; in preparation).

Mother-Grandmother Families

An important question is whether some subset of the mother-other families has a distinct profile in terms of children's school performance. The beginning test scores in reading comprehension of children whose families fell in the mother-grandmother subset were higher (marginally significant) than the test scores of children falling in the remainder of that group (284 versus 272). Significant differences also separate the work habits scores and first reading marks of children in the mother-grandmother families from children in the rest of the mother-other group when they began first grade (Table 5.2). Children raised in mother-grandmother families thus had an advantage in terms of their socialization for school, because when they began first grade, compared to their counterparts in homes where the "other-adult" was not a grandmother, they had better work habits, and were even a little better in work habits than children in mother-father settings. Still, by year 5 this difference had faded because children in mother-grandmother and mother-other adult families then scored about the same in work habits. Also children in the mother-grandmother group did *not* gain significantly more over the whole 5-year period on standardized tests than did children of other single parents who shared a residence with other adults (Table 5.2); after the first year, those in the mother-grandmother families and those in different mother-other arrangements did about the same. The work habits and reading mark advantages of the children in mother-grandmother families were assets that gave children a boost over the first-grade transition, however.

The significant reading mark advantage is extremely important because Beginning School Study youngsters given 1's in reading in first grade (unsatisfactory) were always retained. Thus, a big difference in first-year retention status separates children in mother-grandmother families from the remainder of the mother-other group (0% retained versus 28% retained). By the end of year 5, still only 27% of the children in mother-grandmother families had been retained compared to 50% of the other children, *because of the advantage in first reading mark.* From the second year on, their retention rates look about the same as other children's. In sum, children of single mothers in mother-grandmother families did better making the transition into

Table 5.2   Comparison of Mother-Other Families with and Without Grandmothers Present[a]

	Mother-Grandmother		Mother-Other Adult
	Mean	t-test[b]	Mean
Parent and Family Measures			
Propor. on Meal Subsidy	.97		.89
Mother's Years School	11.5		11.3
Mother's Age	20.9		20.7
Proportion Teenage Mothers	.55		.51
Parent's Expectations for Student's Readg Mk, Fall Yr 1	2.65		2.59
Parent's Ability Est, Begin Yr 1	3.77		3.65
Parent's Expectation for Child's Education, Yr 1	3.16		3.10
Parent's Depression Scale, Year 6	12.5	+	13.9
Parent's Locus of Control (Rotter) Yr 6	9.78		10.1
Children's School Outcomes			
CAT Reading Comprehension			
Beginning Yr 1	284		272
End Yr 5	487		480
Reading Mark, Begin Yr 1	2.13	*	1.67
Propor. Retained, End Yr 1	.00	*	.28
Propor. Retained, End Yr 5	.27	*	.50
Non-Cognitive Outcomes			
Total Days Absent, Yr 1	10.1	*	14.7
Total Days Late, Yr 1	5.45	+	10.5
Work Habits, Begin Yr 1	8.87	*	7.71
Work Habits, End Yr 5	8.52		8.66
Propor. Parent-Teachr Conf., Yr 1	.23	*	.47

*$p \leq .05$ +$p \leq .10$

[a] Data is for the sample used in the regression model reported in Entwisle and Alexander (in preparation). In this sample, mother-grandmother category contained 31 cases and mother-other adult, 49 cases.

[b] t-tests compare means of mother-grandmother and mother-other-adult families.

first grade than did children of all other single mothers (whether they lived alone or shared a residence with a non-grandmother). Probably most important, children in mother-grandmother families were retained much less often in first grade.

What explains why children in mother-grandmother families did better over the transition? Two possible answers are that (1) mothers who share a residence with their own mother are a select group compared to mothers living with other relatives, or (2) grandmothers help socialize children so they settle into the student role better. As to selection, the two groups of mothers look quite similar whether they share a residence with the grandmother or with some other relative. Mothers who do or do not live with grandmothers are closely matched in age (20.9 versus 20.7 years), years of schooling (11.5 versus 11.3), parent depression (12.5 versus 13.9) parent locus of control (9.8 versus 10.1) and whether or not they are employed (30% versus 33%). "Selection" does not appear important. But the mother-grandmother children started school with marginally higher reading scores and (284 versus 272, p=.102), and also with a work habits and a reading mark advantage. The evidence in Table 5.2 seems to favor the more effective socialization of children for school over maternal selection in explaining why children in mother-grandmother families do better in first grade.

Resources for Parenting

Probably the most important parental resource is the parent's capacity to have "developmentally sensitive interaction with a child...that satisfies the child's need to grow socially, psychologically, and cognitively" (Bronfenbrenner 1991). This capacity is not necessarily tied to any single mediator among those we have considered, whether income, age, living arrangements, or anything else. Parents' reduced capacity to act in ways that support their children's schooling, however, is an increasingly persuasive reason to explain why children from single-parent families do not do as well in school as those from two-parent families (Schneider and Coleman 1993; McLanahan and Sandefur 1994; Entwisle and Alexander 1996b; Zill 1996). A cluster of parents attitudes and behaviors (parental involvement in school, parental supervision, and parents' aspirations) account for over half the difference in the rate of high school drop-out between children from single-parent and two-parent families, for example, and account for all of the difference in boys' idleness (not working or not in school) (McLanahan and Sandefur 1994, p. 109). A key component of parents' psychological resources to support schooling seems to be the level of their expectations and aspirations for the child, and in national data sets, two-parent families' aspirations for their children are consistently higher than those of one-parent families (McLanahan and Sandefur 1994, p. 106).

Parents' Expectations

In line with these national trends, single parents in the Beginning School Study had lower expectations for their children's school performance all through elementary school than other parents did.   Compared to mothers in two-parent families, single mothers expected their children to get lower marks on the first report card and the gradient in parents' expectations by family type maps directly onto the gradient in Beginning School Study first graders' reading marks--children of single mothers who lived alone got 1.72 (below a C), children in mother-extended families were slightly higher (1.84), but children in two-parent families got solid C's (1.99).   Thus, parents' expectations, measured in the fall of first grade before children's first report cards, were higher than the marks their children received on those report cards, but by the spring of first grade, Beginning School Study children's marks in reading went up by almost half a grade point and were closer to parents' expectations.

Single parents' expectations for how far their children would go in school were also lower than those of other parents (37% of single parents expected their children to finish college versus 44% of parents from 2-parent families). Expectations that parents held for how far their first-graders would go in school, furthermore, tended to persist--they correlate .50 with parent expectations for the same child in year 8.

Most large-scale research on single parenting does not explicitly consider parents' expectations for children's school performance, yet parents' opinions and attitudes have extremely powerful and long-lasting effects on young children's school performance (Seginer 1983). Entwisle and Hayduk (1988), for instance, found that parents' forecasts of their children's ability to do schoolwork in the primary grades had large and significant effects on the children's California Achievement Test and Iowa Test of Basic Skills scores 4 to 9 years later, *with later cognitive ability test scores controlled.* Stevenson and Newman (1986) likewise found that in grade 10 youngsters' self-concept and academic attitude were predicted by their mothers' ratings of their ability in grade 5 and earlier. (See also Parsons and Ruble 1977; Parsons, Adler, and Kaczala 1982; Entwisle and Hayduk 1982; Hess et al. 1984; Alexander and Entwisle 1988; Alexander, Entwisle, and Dauber 1994). The efficacy of parent involvement in school (Zill 1996) or of parents' visiting school (Lareau 1987) may stem largely from the overlap between parent involvement and parent expectations: parents who expect their children to do well in school are more likely to take steps to encourage this outcome such as attending parent-teacher meetings and providing resources at home to help their children do well in school.[1]

Why would parents' expectations for their children's school performance differ by family structure? Probably because parents are acutely aware of their own life situations and draw upon that knowledge when they form expectations for their children's schooling. The realities are that, compared to married parents, single parents have fewer financial resources, more demands on their time, and many more daily hassles. Also, single parents themselves have less schooling than other parents do, and because of this have fewer of the academic and personal resources that help children "work the system." All of these circumstances could contribute to single parents setting lower goals for their children's school performance.

Social Ties

Single-parent families not only have less income and fewer psychological resources than two-parent families, they also are involved in fewer social relationships and organizations (Coleman 1988). The major social tie for children, of course, is the parent-child bond and this tie potentially is stronger if parent and child live in the same household. A co-resident father is available on a daily basis to tell stories, answer questions, help with homework, or monitor the child's activities, and having more than one parent helps in the communication of family rules and discipline (Kellam et al. 1975; Weiss 1979). Two parents also often possess different interests and skills, so that the male parent may follow professional sports and teach children about batting averages, game rules, and the like, as well as share activities involving home and yard care, while the female parent may ensure that the child learns about family history and rituals and share activities related to family care and meal preparation (Bryant and Zick 1996). Parents also tend to differ in their interaction styles. Male parents tend to engage youngsters in rough, unconventional and physical play (Parke et al. 1980), while female parents interact with children less vigorously, more as caretakers than as play partners.

Having only one parent living with children also leads to fewer social connections outside the family, for example, with the absent parent's relatives, co-workers, and friends, and also to fewer connections between home and school (see Booth and Dunn 1996). One parent has less time to visit school and take part in school activities than two do.

Completely aside from skills or social connections, two parents who reside in the same home can help each other maintain the psychic stamina required to provide steady and consistent discipline of children. Perhaps the most challenging aspect of parenting is its unremitting nature: not just infants, but children of all ages require monitoring 24 hours a day and 7 days a week. Two parents are much better able to meet this challenge than one is.

Helpful versus Harmful Resources

However, having two parents in the same home can lead to one parent's expectations offsetting or undermining the other's. Likewise, two parents could support each other in monitoring children, as suggested above, but in some families the parents disagree or even undercut one another's discipline of the children. For these reasons we think it important to emphasize the *quality* of social relationships, irrespective of family configuration. Single parents have fewer social ties, and, on average they also have lower expectations. Still, some single parents have expectations as high or higher than married parents do and manage to provide a home environment where children feel secure and supported. These resources help their children do well in school.

The psychological adjustment of the resident parent is another kind of psychological resource that affects children's well-being (Zill 1994). The psychological adjustment of Beginning School Study mothers who became parents as teenagers, mentioned earlier--more depression, less positive views of their children's personal qualities--is less optimal than that of older parents, and such limitations subtract from the resources available to support children's schooling. This lack could increase any deficit specifically created by the lower income and reduced number of social ties possessed by single parents.

Family relationships can carry many other kinds of negative valences that could well affect schooling. For example, psychological resources contributed by the father could be negative if he is not only physically absent but avoids visiting or supporting the child, or if present he abuses the child. Also, parents can be depressed, or levy psychic costs on children in other ways, such as by being inconsistent or harsh in their discipline.

Economic hardship reduces parents' psychological resources. Job loss undercuts fathers' mental and physical well-being and often strains relationships with their children (McLoyd 1989): in other words, it can contribute negatively to a father's psychological resources. Likewise, for single divorced mothers, financial stress predicts increased maternal demands and childrearing restrictions (Colletta 1983) that have more deleterious results for boys than for girls. Or, to take a different example, if single mothers reside in homes with grandmothers who resent the extra financial burdens imposed by taking in mother and child, and who do not relish the idea of raising a young child, the bottom line may be negative even though Beginning School Study data indicate that *on average* children in mother-grandmother arrangements do better over the first-grade transition. In some families the psychological relationship between grandparent (or parent) and child could have a negative rather than a positive valence. On the other hand, an unmarried teenage mother who lives alone may have few social ties, but she can provide psychological stimulation and the emotional security that help children do well in school (Moore and Snyder 1991).

Overview

The full consequences of variations in family structure for elementary children's schooling still need to be spelled out, but the Beginning School Study and other research over the past decade fill in some pieces of what turns out to be a complicated picture. A serious hindrance to research on how single parenting affects schooling is that the phenomenon of schooling itself is extremely complex. Cognitive status as measured by scores on standardized tests is often used as the exclusive benchmark to evaluate children's schooling, but *gains* on standardized tests are a more suitable indicator of schooling effects. Also, children's marks, retention, dropout, social adjustment, psychological well-being, and other outcomes of schooling can respond differently or more strongly to various family arrangements. For example, for Beginning School Study children the differences in first-year retention rates favoring children in mother-grandmother families were striking. Avoiding retention in first grade is extremely important for children's long term school success, but without data on retention rates, this outcome favoring children in mother-grandmother families would have been missed.

The conclusion from earlier studies that children raised in two-parent or one-parent families do about the same on standardized tests (Ferri 1976; Hetherington, Camara, and Featherman 1983; Garfinkel and McLanahan 1986) is called into question. More recent analyses, including those in this chapter, show test scores of children in single-parent families to be consistently lower than those of children in two-parent families (Entwisle and Alexander 1992; Zill 1996; McLanahan and Sandefur 1994), and these deficits in test scores are linked to the lower economic status and lower expectations of single parents (McLanahan and Sandefur 1994; Entwisle and Alexander 1996b). But, as this chapter points up, single parents are not a homogeneous group. More work is needed to distinguish among outcomes for children in different kinds of single-parent families, and what mediates those outcomes.

Still another issue is the lack of attention to contextual effects. Teachers have more negative perceptions of children from single-parent homes than of children from two-parent homes (Epstein 1984), and they rate children from divorced homes more negatively on happiness, adjustment, and ability to cope with stress (Santrock and Tracy 1978). If a child is labeled as coming from a divorced family, schoolmates also rate a child lower in academic, social, and emotional functioning (Guttmann, Geva, and Gefen 1988). On the one hand, these effects may be fading as the number of divorced parents increases. On the other hand, contextual effects could be even more severe for children of teen or never-married mothers.

Given findings now at hand, it seems unlikely that alterations in family structure are the root cause of school failure, or that academic achievement has declined over time only because of the increased prevalence of marital disruption and parenthood outside marriage (see Zill 1996). Still, national data for children over a wide age range are consistent with Zill's assertion that divorce and single parenthood have *some* negative effects on children's school achievement, and Beginning School Study data point to a significant deficit for children of never-married mothers.

Also, the Beginning School Study emphasizes the key role of children's ability to negotiate the first grade transition, a topic so far not emphasized in national studies. The Beginning School Study points up the importance of parents' expectations and the potent role they play in young children's achievement after test scores are controlled (Seginer 1983; Hess et al. 1984; Stevenson and Newman 1986; Entwisle and Hayduk 1988). Parents' expectations are not included in most large-scale analyses of single-parent effects (see Zill 1994), but parents' expectations vary across family type, and when they are taken into account, differences across family type can disappear (Entwisle and Alexander 1996b). Put differently, Beginning School Study data show that a very considerable portion of family structure effects are mediated by effects of parents' psychological resources. Too, effects of parents' expectations and the attitudes related to these expectations add on to effects of economic resources, at least in the Beginning School Study (Entwisle and Alexander 1995; 1996b). Parents' expectations covary with parental warmth and with a whole range of other psychological characteristics and specific actions that parents can take. Beginning School Study parents who expected their children to do well in school were more likely than others to provide books and academic games, for example, or to read to the child, take the child to the library, and so on. These kinds of activities, at least for young children, are almost as available to parents of limited means as they are to more affluent parents.

An important caveat: this chapter mainly considers schooling in the elementary grades while most other studies of single parenting and schooling focus more on older students. Family configuration effects could differ because of differences in children's age. The dearth of economic resources in single-parent families may affect adolescents more if only because being older, they have experienced this lack for a longer time. Also elementary school children are more cloistered--their classmates tend to be much like them and they play mainly with neighbors and relatives who live nearby. For these reasons, poor elementary children could feel less relative deprivation than do poor secondary youngsters whose schools contain classmates from a much wider band of economic backgrounds. The peer pressures that adolescents experience in terms of clothes, cars and the like, and their needs for expensive equipment like computers and software could be less of a problem for younger children.

The two basic questions pertaining to family structure and children's schooling are whether differences associated with structure are large and consistent, and what the mediating factors are. Not surprisingly, the answers are not simple. Children in two-parent homes do better than those in one-parent homes, but children live in many kinds of "one-parent" homes, including many not discussed in this chapter. As for mediating factors, to the extent they can be separated, the dearth of economic and psychological resources in single-parent families is critical, but effects of contexts, including the living arrangements of single parents, can be dramatic. More research is needed on contextual effects.

Notes

1. Ho and Willms (1996) found that of four factors in parent involvement, home discussion of school related activities was the most potent in affecting students' academic achievement.

6

The Pluses and Minuses of Being Male

Social institutions are organized along lines that reflect both common sense and society's values. Boys and girls, therefore, generally attend school together because having children of the two sexes in one school is more economical and this practice also matches social norms of gender egalitarianism. Still, children of the two sexes perform differently in school and these differences persist despite efforts, legislative and otherwise, to make school truly equal for all. At some times it has seemed that boys are better served by schools than girls, but at other times girls seem better served. Reflecting society's changing opinions about which sex is better served, researchers have focused alternately on the school problems of one sex, and then the other.

From the turn of the century to about 1970, the relatively poorer performance of boys in language and reading prompted research into elementary school practices that might have negative effects on boys (Brophy 1985). By 1980, however, and not because boys' school problems were solved, but because of publicity about women's labor market disabilities, the pendulum began to swing in the other direction. As women increasingly left the home for the workplace, their deficits in higher level math skills prevented them from competing with men for the highest paying jobs (Sorenson 1991). A shower of studies then began to examine how girls' experiences in school contributed to the relatively poorer performance of females in math (e.g. Parsons, Adler, and Kaczala 1982).

The gender gap in math is not going away (Feingold 1988) and is still not fully understood, but the pendulum now seems to be swinging back in the other direction, toward boys, probably for two reasons. One is middle class parents' growing awareness that boys are more likely to have difficulty in first grade than girls are (see Bellisimo et al. 1995; Cameron and Wilson 1990). Parents now often delay their sons' entrance into kindergarten or first grade, especially for boys born very late in the year. Thus a boy with a November or December birthday will be held out until the following year instead of being enrolled the preceding September. Parents "redshirt" boys--that is, hold them back from starting school for an extra year--because of their conviction that boys who start school later will do better than boys who start earlier.

   The second and more compelling reason for the pendulum to swing back to boys' schooling problems is that men with low levels of education are increasingly disadvantaged in the labor market. The real wages of men between 20 and 24 with a high school education or less declined by over 42% between 1973 and 1986 (W.T. Grant Foundation 1988). An even starker comparison is that between employment rates for men with various levels of education. In 1994, 72% of men with less than a high school education were employed compared to 90% of men with 1 to 3 years of college (U.S. Bureau of the Census 1995). As the nation's economy more and more takes on the shape of an hourglass, well-educated workers are making higher and higher incomes and poorly-educated workers are falling farther and farther behind. The labor market disadvantage of poorly educated men warrants a careful look at boys' early schooling to identify the root causes of poor performance at that stage, because boys who do not do well early in school tend to leave school sooner than those who do better (Ensminger and Slusarcick 1992).

Boys' Poorer Performance

   In elementary school, boys typically get lower marks than girls in reading and deportment (Averch et al. 1972; Dwyer 1973; Entwisle and Hayduk 1982; Alexander and Entwisle 1988). Also many more boys than girls fail a grade. In 1990, by the end of elementary school, roughly one out of three white boys versus one of four white girls were behind in school by at least one year (U.S. Bureau of the Census 1992). African American and Hispanic boys also were more often behind in school than their female age-mates. Not surprisingly, grade failure is highest for children with multiple risks. Bianchi (1984) cites failure rates of about 50% for boys whose parents are high school drop-outs and live in poverty, compared to 40% for similarly disadvantaged girls. Irrespective of geographic location, the rate of failure is uniformly highest in the first grade for both sexes (Chapter 4). Rates then drop gradually each year so that over the elementary years failure rates average 7% to 8% per year (see Shepard and Smith 1989; Alexander, Entwisle, and Dauber 1994). The poor school performance of boys in elementary school has serious long-term consequences. Boys who get marks below a B in first grade, for example, are twice as likely to drop out of school as are boys who get better marks, *even when they begin school with the same initial test scores* (Ensminger and Slusarcick 1992), and the link between early retention and dropping out is strong (Cairns, Cairns, and Neckerman 1989; Lloyd 78; Stroup and Robins 1972). One national study shows a dropout rate of about 40% among those who had failed a grade, compared to only 10% among those who were never held back (Bachman, Green, and Wirtanen 1971). (See also Tuck 1989; Fine 1991.) Young people who drop out of high school have lifetime earnings far below those of youngsters who continue (McDill, Natriello, and Pallas 1986), and retention undercuts other kinds of success after high school as well. For example, Royce, Darlington, and Murray (1983) report that, compared with similar students who had not repeated a grade, repeaters were more likely later to be unemployed or not seeking work, to be living on public assistance, or to be in prison.

The Role of Marks

Marks are understood by parents, classmates, and students of all socioeconomic levels, and schools issue them often, usually at least four times a year. Although researchers favor test scores over marks as barometers of school performance, for several reasons marks and not test scores drive the schooling process.

(1) Marks serve as *reinforcements*, either positive or negative, and by that means directly influence the amounts children learn. Beginning School Study children who received an "A" in reading on their first report card, for example, gained on average at least a half a standard deviation more in reading comprehension over the first 2 years of school than did children who got a "C," *when other factors were equalized* (i.e., equivalent home background and the same standardized test scores at the beginning of first grade) (Entwisle and Alexander 1996).

(2) Marks are strong determinants of children's *academic self-image, which in turn affects how much children learn.* When marks improve, children's self-images rise. For example, Beginning School Study youngsters who were retained in first grade got very low marks (1.0 in reading, 1.3 in math) their first time through the grade, and their academic self-images were significantly lower (about two-thirds of a standard deviation) than those of their promoted

classmates who got much higher marks (2.7 in reading and 3.0 in math). When these youngsters repeated first grade, however, their marks rose (to 1.9 in reading and 2.2 in math) and their academic self-images jumped about one-third of a standard deviation even though they earlier had been held back. The gap in academic self-esteem between retained and promoted youngsters at the end of the first year thus narrowed significantly by the end of second year, *after* retainees had repeated first grade. This responsiveness of children's self-image to their marks, which persists with demographic factors and test scores controlled, is rather convincing evidence that children's marks can affect their self-image.

(3) Marks set the level at which parents and other people peg their *expectations*. If children get a "C" in reading rather than a "B," parents' expectations are more likely to be for a C rather than a B on the next report card, and parents' expectations for marks have strong effects on young children's school performance (Entwisle and Alexander 1996; Sundius 1996). In fact, parents' expectations at the beginning of year 4 are more powerful predictors of marks later in that year than are children's California Achievement Test scores or family economic status (Pallas et al. 1994).

(4) Marks provide children with *feedback* as to how they are doing. Feedback itself promotes learning, as teachers well know. In a randomized experiment, for example, in which the papers of over 2,000 youngsters were handed back either with neutral comments by teachers or without any comments, students who received comments did significantly better on the next test than did those who did not (Page 1958).

(5) Finally, marks also convey *teachers' expectations*. Marks have rarely been studied in connection with teachers' expectations, but marks and expectations overlap considerably (see Entwisle and Hayduk 1982).

Why marks are so seldom included in research studies is perplexing, but one explanation is that ignoring marks is the path of least resistance. Marking standards differ from teacher to teacher and even more from school to school, so researchers fear that including marks as variables in their studies would greatly complicate or even prevent a proper analysis. Standardized test scores, by contrast, are relatively easy to use because they are scaled in comparable units from school to school and are widely available from school records. Also test scores are "objective"--teachers are not involved in them--so they seem more "dependable" or "reliable" than marks. Because young children and many parents do not understand test scores or have comparative information on other children's scores, however, those scores cannot function in the schooling process in the fundamental way that marks do. Marks are to some degree subjective, but because children and parents see them repeatedly and know what they mean, they are central to the schooling process in ways that test scores cannot be.

Gender Differences in Marks

Deportment Marks

Deportment marks in elementary school generally favor girls. On average, boys misbehave more often and more intensively than girls do (Brophy 1985), so much of teachers' contact with boys tends to be negative and disciplinary in nature (see Bossert 1981; Huston 1983). But more negative contact occurs with boys even when they are not misbehaving (Eccles and Blumenfeld 1985), and whether this "negative contact" translates into marks is not clear from reading the literature. Beginning School Study teachers, however, consistently rated boys' general conduct, effort, attention, and other aspects of their performance as students lower than girls' (Table 6.1). First grade teachers rated 29% of boys versus 14% of girls as "needing improvement" in conduct; they gave 50% of the boys at least one bad mark in some area of deportment compared to 38% of the girls; and they gave almost twice as many boys as girls bad marks in all five areas of deportment (11% versus 6%).

The lopsided picture favoring girls' marks in classroom behavior the first year grew worse in the second. The percentages of boys who needed improvement in conduct, effort, paying attention, completing assignments, and class participation *went up*, while the percentages of girls thought to need improvement in these areas declined (Table 6.1). As time passed, then, teachers did not perceive boys as adjusting to the demands of school and mastering the student role, but instead saw them as moving in the opposite direction.

All of the imbalance in conduct marks between the two sexes cannot be laid to parents' having higher expectations for girls than boys or to other home background factors, because Beginning School Study girls' marks in conduct were significantly higher than boys' even after allowing for family structure, parent education, kindergarten attendance, parent performance expectations and inter-school variability (Thompson et al. 1992). Furthermore, teachers in nearly every one of the Study schools favored girls over boys in their conduct ratings.

Do conduct marks early in school matter? To answer this question, an earlier Baltimore study traced the consequences for about 1500 children of receiving low conduct marks in the first three grades. It found that negative conduct ratings were linked to the low marks in both reading and math, and by using

Table 6.1   Students with Deportment Marks That "Need Improvement"
               at the End of the School Year

	Year 1		Year 2	
	Male (%)	Female (%)	Male (%)	Female (%)
Conduct	29	14	35	17
Effort	24	17	27	15
Attention	31	20	35	19
Class Participation	20	14	21	14
Completes Assignments	30	20	32	17
Works Independently	38	26	38	24

structural equation models with reciprocal causal paths, it determined that poor conduct ratings *led to* poor academic marks more than the reverse (Entwisle and Hayduk 1982). That is, poor marks in reading and math were not a consequence of children being bored with academics and then engaging in misbehavior but rather, when teachers rated children's conduct as needing improvement, their academic marks also went down. Low conduct ratings also led parents to expect their children to get poor marks and these lowered expectations increased the likelihood that children *would* get poorer conduct marks later on. Boys' lower conduct ratings could thus affect their early progress in school by two routes: directly by interfering with their learning, and indirectly by lowering their parents' expectations. The impact of poor conduct marks on academic progress was greatest in the first year, next greatest in the second year, and so on.

How do conduct marks affect Beginning School Study students' feelings about the teacher? The large majority of Beginning School Study children of both sexes started school liking their teachers "a lot," but before long, boys' low conduct ratings were associated with negative feelings for the teacher. Although 76% of boys and 81% of girls liked their teacher "a lot" at the beginning of first grade, by the end of first grade girls had not changed their opinions but fewer boys liked their teacher a lot (70%) (Table 6.2). By the end of fourth year, 70% of girls still liked their teacher "a lot," but only about half the boys (52%) did. A large majority of the children of both sexes were thus positively disposed toward the teacher when they started school, but boys' liking fell off faster than girls'.

Table 6.2   Students Who "Like Teacher a Lot," Years 1-4

	Male (%)	Female (%)
Beginning Year 1	76	81
End Year 1	70	81
Beginning Year 2	68	78
End Year 2	71	82
Beginning Year 4	64	81
End Year 4	52	70

Does liking the teacher matter? The answer seems to be "yes." At the beginning of year 1, only 23% of boys who said they did not like their teacher received a satisfactory mark in conduct compared to 68% of those who liked the teacher "a lot." A similar but less pronounced pattern emerged for the girls. Fewer of the of girls who said they did not like their teacher in year 1 received a satisfactory mark in conduct compared to those who liked the teacher "a lot" (67% versus 85%). These patterns intensified in the second year: only 42% of the children of either sex who said they did not like their teacher received a satisfactory conduct mark. In fact, controlling for sex, race, initial test score, family configuration, family socioeconomic status and parental expectations, children's liking their teacher "a lot" versus "not liking" or rating the teacher as "just OK" almost doubled the odds of their receiving a satisfactory conduct mark.

Beginning School Study teachers also assessed students on three other scales (National Survey of Children 1976): classroom interest/participation, attention span/restlessness, and cooperation/compliance. They rated girls significantly higher than boys by about half a standard deviation in terms of attention-span/restlessness or cooperation/compliance in both the first and second years. (See Appendix C for definition of scales.)

Children's success early in school thus seems to be partly a consequence of the interpersonal dynamics between teacher and student. Six-year-olds can be noisy and inattentive, but most do not misbehave deliberately. On this account, it is worrisome that gender, a non-academic characteristic, can have such serious correlates. When as many boys as girls say they like the teacher "a lot" as they begin school, but their teachers then rate a third or more of the boys as inattentive in first grade and see them as becoming more inattentive the longer they are in school, questions arise as to how or why this occurs.

Reading Marks

As we said, generally girls get better marks in reading than boys do (Averch et al. 1972; Dwyer 1973; Entwisle and Hayduk 1982) even if their standardized test scores are equalized (Brophy and Good 1970; Rehberg and Rosenthal 1978; Alexander and Eckland 1980; McCandless, Roberts and Stannes 1972; Alexander and Entwisle 1988; Prawat and Jarvis 1980), and even if they are fraternal twins (Doma 1969). Consistent with these reports, in every Study school, boys on average received consistently lower reading marks than girls did even though boys' test scores in reading were the same as girls' when they started first grade.[1] In each quarter of first grade, girls' reading marks were slightly better than boys' and over the second year, the gender spread between marks enlarged. By the end of the second year, teachers rated girls at 2.49 in reading and boys at 2.21, which is a significant difference with initial test scores, family background, and many other variables held constant (see also Table A6 in Alexander and Entwisle 1988). In short, Beginning School Study girls' reading marks exceeded boys', even when standardized test scores are equalized.

How these gender differences in marks look from the students' perspective is a key question. The gender imbalance in Beginning School Study children's marks noted above could play out in an average second grade classroom so that about half the girls would get a B or better in reading compared to about one-fifth of the boys. That is, if 30 children in a class were equally divided by sex, one possible pattern to produce the average differences we see is for 12 boys to get C's and 3 to get B's, while 8 girls would get B's and 7 would get C's. A small difference in average marks (2.5 versus 2.2) could thus cause almost three times as many girls as boys to get B's. Children and parents seeing mark distributions like these--and marks are highly public for children at this age--get a clear message that the boys are not doing as well as the girls.

As we said, relationships between gender and reading marks cannot be explained by differences in Beginning School Study children's standardized test scores when they started school because California Achievement Test scores in reading comprehension were the same for children of the two sexes. Rather, the gender imbalance in children's academic marks probably came about because those marks were based to a considerable extent on *non-cognitive* criteria, such as boys' less satisfactory deportment and their less satisfactory attention in class as perceived by the teacher. This supposition seems the more likely because secondary school students' work habits (homework completion, class participation, effort and the like) count for twice as much as course mastery does in determining teachers' marks, and males are rated lower than females on work habits and disruptiveness (see Farkas et al. 1990). As Hinshaw (1992) suggests, gender differences in marks might also stem from gender bias that varies from one teacher to another, an hypothesis that is taken up in the next section.

Teacher Favoritism

Most studies of teacher bias in marking practices focus on social class or race, or both (see Alexander et al. 1987). The underlying notion is that social distance between teacher and student leads to teacher disaffection or disparate standards of performance. The margin in conduct marks favoring girls over boys appeared in almost every Beginning School Study school, even though schools ranged widely in ethnicity and social class, however, suggesting that negative teacher bias toward young males may be less a consequence of pervasive social structural factors like class, than of a teacher's individual response to disruption or boisterousness in class.

If gender differences in marks do reflect teacher bias, and if that bias springs from personal rather than social structural sources, then we would expect gender favoritism to vary from teacher to teacher. Following this lead, we found that in grade one, about a third of Beginning School Study teachers (16 out of 46) did *not* favor either sex in their marking practices, and of the remainder, 14 favored girls and 16 favored boys (Table 6.3). Data for the second year show that 33 out of 52 teachers did not favor either sex but of the remainder, 14 favored girls and 5 favored boys.

Gender bias in ratings of student's classroom behavioral adjustment was likewise characteristic of some teachers but not others. In the first year, 52% of teachers favored girls on interest/participation; 74% favored girls on attention span/restlessness, and 87% favored girls on cooperation/compliance. These biases declined a little in the second year but continued to favor girls (50%, 67%, and 82%, respectively).

Teacher differences by gender in their ratings of children's classroom behavior covaried with students' performance. Over the first year, gains on standardized tests and improvement in marks were both greater for children of the sex favored by the teacher's interest-participation ratings. That is, among students of teachers who favored boys, boys showed greater test score gains and more improvement in marks than girls did, and among students of teachers who favored girls, girls did better. (Table 6.4.) Other things equal, children of one sex or the other did significantly better on standardized tests of reading and math according to whether the teacher favored members of their

Table 6.3   Correspondence Between Teacher Gender Bias in Mark
               Assignment and Gender Bias in Personal Maturity Ratings
               in Year 1

	Teacher Mark Bias			Teacher Personal Maturity Bias
	Favors Girls	Neutral	Favors Boys	
Interest-Participation				
Favors Girls	14	6	4	24
Neutral	0	0	0	0
Favors Boys	0	10	12	22
Attention Span-Restlessness				
Favors Girls	14	11	9	34
Neutral	0	0	0	0
Favors Boys	0	5	7	12
Cooperation-Compliance				
Favors Girls	14	14	12	40
Neutral	0	0	2	2
Favors Boys	0	2	2	4
Teacher Mark Bias	14	16	16	46

sex in terms of interest/participation in class.[2]   Still, and with other things equal, children who rate higher in interest/participation generally gain more on standardized tests (Alexander and Entwisle 1988) and the "excess" gains by "favored" girls or "favored" boys could represent the impact of *veridical* ratings by teachers.   Perhaps this attribute of children rather than teachers' favoritism could be responsible for the gender difference in Table 6.4.   The other possibility is that some teachers actually foster more interest-participation in one sex than the other because they prefer that sex.   We cannot tell from Table 6.4 which of these possibilities is correct.

In Year 4, however, teachers indicated whether they preferred children of one sex or the other to carry out non-academic tasks.   This measure of gender preference is relatively independent of characteristics that would directly affect achievement gains, and teachers' opinions of children's ability to carry out school chores were also imbalanced by gender.   In year 4, when Beginning School Study teachers named three students they "could or would rely on to help" with tasks that seem gender-neutral, such as taking notes to the office,

Table 6.4   Gender Difference in Year 1 California Achievement Test Score Gains and End of Year 1 Marks by Teacher Gender Bias in Interest-Participation Ratings[a,b]

| | Teacher Gender Bias in Interest-Participation Ratings | | |
	Bias Toward Boys[c]	Interaction[c]	Bias Toward Girls[c]
CAT Reading Comprehension, End Year 1	-5.31	+	6.74
Reading Mark, End Year 1	-0.09		0.06
N	209		264
CAT Math Concepts/ Applications, End Year 1	-6.56+	*	4.46
Math Mark, End Year 1	-0.12	*	.17*
N	219		266

+ $p \le .10$
* $p \le .05$

[a] All regressions control for beginning Year 1 CAT score in Reading Comprehension or Math Concepts/Applications, race, student meal subsidy status, parent education level, parent estimate of student ability, parent mark expectations, family configuration, school segregation status, and school level parent education. Regressions predicting CAT score gains also include beginning Year 1 marks.

[b] A 2-level HLM model was also devised to examine possible effects of teacher bias on gender differences in test score gains. The number of students per teacher proved too small to reliably estimate parameters in the level-1 analysis, and the level-2 model did not converge.

[c] Columns 1 and 3 report metric coefficients for sex of student (coded 0 for boys, 1 for girls) in regression analyses estimated separately by teachers' gender bias on the Interest-Participation ratings. Thus a negative coefficient indicates a gender effect that favors boys and a positive coefficient favors girls. Column 2 reports whether or not the interaction term (sex by Teacher Rating Bias) for the pooled sample was significant. A significant interaction term means the sex coefficient is different for students with teachers biased towards boys and those with teachers biased towards girls.

passing out papers or cleaning blackboards, helping with a T.V. or other equipment, and the like, the vast majority of teachers (72%) selected more girl than boy helpers, while 2% selected an equal number of boy and girl helpers and 26% selected more boy helpers. When children's standardized test scores (CAT) in reading comprehension at the end of year 4 are regressed on scores at the beginning of that year for students whose teachers prefer girl helpers, the female students of those teachers gained 38 points over the year and the male students gained 31 points. This differences is marginally significant (p=.086). For students whose teacher preferred boy helpers, the difference favors males but is not large enough to be significant.

There are a few other relevant clues. *All* teachers who favored girls in terms of marks in first grade also favored girls in all three classroom behavior ratings (see Table 6.3). Teachers who were gender-neutral or biased toward boys in their marks look gender-neutral in their other ratings as well, except for cooperation/compliance, in which girls are favored. If teachers are biased toward girls, this pattern tends to be pervasive, while teachers who are gender-neutral or who favor males are more selective, favoring girls in some areas, boys in others. In the second year, teachers who favored girls in terms of marks also consistently favored girls in other ratings, while other teachers again were less consistent.

We suspect that when teachers favor one sex over the other, their expectations favor one sex over the other so they act in ways that encourage achievement of children of that sex. Curiously, although teachers' expectations have been studied for almost 30 years (Rosenthal 1968), how their expectations relate to the marks they give students has been disregarded. Even so, teachers' marks and expectations are highly correlated: Entwisle and Hayduk (1982, p. 134) found, for instance, that teachers' expectations (guesses for the child's mark in the subsequent school year) were usually within a quarter of a grade point of the child's marks in the *current* year, and these expectations predicted the child's marks in the following year (with a new teacher) just as well as marks awarded in the current year did. Teachers' expectations and marks in any one year were thus *interchangeable* as predictors of children's performance in the following year.

Teachers' expectations are conveyed by their actions--smiling at students, ignoring them, pressing them for answers, and the like. By contrast, marks are conveyed in written form directly to children, parents, and others: they are unambiguous, and children and parents know what they mean. We suspect that teachers' expectations are strongly conveyed by the marks they give and because marks are issued often and understood even in families of limited circumstances, they affect the schooling process in all the ways listed earlier.

Table 6.5   First Grade Marks as Predictors of the Odds of Being Placed in Middle School Advanced Level English and Math Courses[a]

	Advanced Courses English/Math [b]			
	Year 6/7		Year 8	
Reading Marks				
Year 1, Quarter 1	1.28	.68	2.08*	1.20
Year 1, Quarter 4		2.67*		2.28*
Math Marks				
Year 1, Quarter 1	3.47*	2.76*	3.76*	2.54*
Year 1, Quarter 4		1.67		2.41*

*$p \leq .05$

[a] Coefficients are odds ratios representing the effect of a unit change in marks on the odds of placement in advanced level courses. Parameter estimates come from logistic regressions that control for fall grade 1 California Achievement Test scores in Reading Comprehension or Math Concepts/Applications, sex, race, student meal subsidy status, parent education level, parent estimate of student ability, parent mark expectations, family configuration, school segregation status, and school level parent education.

[b] Reading marks are predictors for middle school English placement and math marks for math placement.

The patterns in Beginning School Study data strongly suggest that teachers assess boys' non-academic qualities lower than girls', and this contributes to boys' poorer reading performance in elementary school. Do children's early marks make much difference in the long run? They certainly do, because Beginning School Study children's earliest marks persisted strongly thereafter. For one example, reading marks at the end of first grade correlate .59 with marks at the end of second grade (two different teachers), and these year-to-year correlations increased over elementary school--the correlation between fourth and fifth year reading marks is .65. For another example, Beginning School Study children's marks in first grade predicted advanced level placements in middle school. Children whose first marks in math were A's rather than B's were almost four times as likely to be in advanced math classes in year 8 (see Table 6.5). Better reading marks in first grade also greatly improved the odds (2:1) of advanced placement in English in middle school.

Gender Differences in Retention

Next to dropout, grade failure is probably the most ubiquitous and vexing issue facing school people today. As noted at the outset, many more boys than girls fail a grade in elementary school, but why boys are held back more often than girls is not fully understood. Even so, the decision to retain children in first grade depends to a great extent on the marks children get, especially in reading (Dauber et al. 1993).

We have seen that boys get lower reading marks and are rated lower than girls in non-academic criteria like deportment as well. Two explanations are popular for boys' lower marks. One is that boys mature more slowly than girls, especially in verbal skills, and therefore do not do as well as girls in early reading. The other is that girls do better because they find the student role more compatible than boys do. While we cannot securely confirm either hypothesis, our findings for Beginning School Study children over the first two grades support the second explanation more than the first.

At 6 years of age when Beginning School Study children began first grade, the two sexes had virtually identical California Achievement Test scores in reading comprehension (averages of 280 for boys and 282 for girls). These scores suggest that children of the two sexes were equally mature in reading skills when they began first grade. However, boys' marks in reading were significantly lower than girls by the end of the second year (see Tables A6, A8 in Alexander and Entwisle 1988). The first explanation--that boys are less mature--would require that equally mature children at the start of first grade show divergent growth rates thereafter. The second explanation would require that the two sexes be perceived differently.

While we cannot directly observe maturity rates, we can infer that boys and girls were perceived differently by teachers because they rated boys lower than girls in all aspects of deportment and classroom behavior, especially retained boys. (See Table 6.6.) At the beginning of year 1, for example, composite deportment scores were lower for promoted boys (8.41) than for promoted girls (8.78), and the gender discrepancy was even greater among retained students (6.20 for boys and 6.81 for girls). Both reading marks and the ratings teachers gave students for classroom behavior also show girls generally higher than boys whether or not they were retained.

All marks, including those in conduct, are among the criteria teachers used to make promotion decisions (Dauber, Alexander, and Entwisle 1993), so teachers' tendencies to rate boys lower in non-cognitive characteristics and in reading could explain much of the higher retention rate for Beginning School Study boys, especially since boys' conduct marks were significantly more

Table 6.6   Average Performance by Retention Status and Gender[a]

	Not Retained in Grade 1		Retained in Grade 1	
	Male (N=281)	Female (N=307)	Male (N=59)	Female (N=47)
California Achievement Test Reading Comprehension Scores, Fall Year 1	286	286	257	256
Reading Marks				
Fall Year 1	2.05	2.00	1.10	1.11
End Year 1	2.50	2.52	1.00	2.08
Fall Year 2	2.19	2.38	1.88	2.15
End Year 2	2.29	2.54	1.74	1.79
Conduct Marks, Fall Year 1	1.69	1.86	1.47	1.79
Work Habits Ratings, Fall Year 1				
Effort	1.69	1.77	1.25	1.34
Attention	1.61	1.76	1.27	1.43
Class Participation	1.80	1.78	1.29	1.45
Completes Assignments	1.72	1.81	1.19	1.26
Works Independently	1.59	1.67	1.20	1.34
Composite Work Habits	8.41	8.78	6.20	6.81
Composite Work Habits Scale, Spring Year 1	9.03	9.37	6.28	7.00
Personal Maturity Scales, Ratings by Teacher, Spring Year 1				
Interest Participation	23	23	16	17
Cooperation-Compliance	20	22	18	19
Attention-Restlessness	21	22	15	17
Proportion in Low Reading Groups				
Fall Year 1	.22	.17	.75	.83
Spring Year 1	.12	.12	.75	.81

[a] Sample sizes are for students with data on marks and work habits ratings from the quarter 1, year 1 report card (N=694). Sample sizes are somewhat lower for personal maturity scales (N=650) and first grade reading group placement (N=582).

important in making retention decisions than girls' were. The probability of being retained in first grade, given an unsatisfactory conduct rating, is 27% for boys versus 18% for girls.

Early tracking patterns also show gender differences that could contribute to boys' higher retention rates as well. Despite gender parity in standardized reading scores when children began school, more Beginning School Study boys than girls were placed in low reading groups at the beginning of first grade (30% versus 26%), and more boys than girls were placed at a low instructional level in reading (24% versus 21%). By the end of first grade, boys were still over-represented in low reading groups (23% versus 20%). Altogether 53% of Beginning School Study students (57% of boys and 49% of girls) who were placed in low reading groups in the spring of first grade were retained that year. Moreover, these placement trends continued throughout the first 5 years of school. By year 5, 28% of boys and 18% of girls were at a low instructional level in reading, and by the end of elementary school, 40% of boys compared to 27% of the girls had been held back at least once.[3]

Low marks in the early grades eventually contribute to drop-out. As noted earlier, Ensminger and Slusarcick (1992) found that males who received A's or B's in first grade were twice as likely to graduate from high school as males who received C's or D's, and females were about 1.5 times as likely, although children of the two sexes did not differ in standardized test performance in first grade. In national data the drop-out rate for 16 to 24 year olds is about 10% for those who had never repeated a grade, but almost double that for those who had repeated (Smith et al. 1994, p. 31).

Early Schooling and Gender

Society "expects" gender differences in young children's reading marks and classroom behavior that favor girls. "Deportment," "work habits," and the like are categorized as "non-cognitive," so they are not defined as the school's major responsibility even though inattentive children or those who participate less in class do not learn as much as their more attentive or active peers. It is dangerous, however, to link the *non-cognitive* characteristics of any group with their ascriptive characteristics. Laypersons and policy-makers alike would properly object if ethnicity (an ascriptive characteristic) were taken as the *root cause* of low marks. Likewise, to observe that boys get lower marks, and then to conclude that gender (a non-cognitive characteristic) is the basic reason why boys consistently make less progress than girls in elementary school is dangerous. The parallel between school inequity linked to gender and school inequity linked to minority-group membership is obvious: boys do get lower marks in elementary school but being male does not itself "produce" those low marks. Children's adaptation to the classroom, teachers' views of children, the structure of the curriculum, the physical layout of the classroom, the lack of male role models in the classroom, and many other factors probably contribute to boys' poorer performance.

Gender differences in elementary school prejudicial to males have no doubt been downplayed until lately because of the prevailing zeitgeist. In earlier times, men with minimal educations could obtain high-paying jobs in mines, factories, construction, and the skilled trades so their difficulties in school did not prove an impediment to some kinds of labor market success. In the last two decades, however, men's lack of educational credentials has begun to undermine their earning capacity. For this reason, gender differences in early schooling that lead to reductions in men's long-term earnings should generate more interest. It is clear that boys' lower marks in the early grades have a serious prognosis for their earning trajectories over the long term.

In discussing gender patterns favoring females in high school performance, Farkas et al. (1990) see two possible mechanisms behind teachers' bias in assigning high school marks--the first perceptual and the second involving a self-fulfilling prophecy. In "perceptual bias," teachers perceive lower levels of performance when evaluating boys, even though their actual performance does not differ from that of girls. A self-fulfilling prophecy would involve setting up a feedback loop: teachers' lower expectations lead students to reduce effort, which in turn prompts teachers to demand less, and so eventually children's achievement declines. These two explanations are not mutually exclusive, of course, because any initial perceptions which prompted teachers to give boys lower ratings could also initiate a self-fulfilling prophecy.

A third explanation could account for the gender bias that Farkas et al. (1990) observe in high school, however. Gender differences favoring females in marks and conduct established in the early grades probably remain in high school. By this reasoning, high school performance differences between the two sexes could be a consequence of youngsters' experiences earlier in school, rather than a consequence of teacher bias at the high school level.

Family Socialization

Teachers are not the only ones who treat young boys differently from young girls. Families also treat children of the two sexes differently, and their gender-related actions also can have consequences for schooling. Beside holding different expectations for the school performance of the two sexes, parents supervise girls more closely and keep them closer to home than young boys. Compared to girls, boys spend more time out in neighborhoods, move about the community more on their own, and much more often play organized sports or games. Boys then learn how to find their own way about the community, and how to interact with neighborhood children and adults. They also have more opportunity to develop skills related to sports and games.

Research on how the freedom parents give young sons affects boys' cognitive development is not extensive, but the more freedom that families give children the more they seem to learn. In one early study, for example, Strodtbeck (1958) asked New Haven parents the age at which they expected their young sons to know how to get around the city, to make their own friends, and to do well in competition with other children. Jewish parents expected their sons to have mastered these skills when they were just over 6, while Italian Catholic parents expected their sons to acquire these skills later, after age 8. When he observed more rapid cognitive growth of the Jewish as compared to the Catholic boys, Strodtbeck attributed it to the greater freedom and independence given the Jewish boys. Along similar lines, Bing (1963) saw that mothers gave their sons more freedom to explore than they gave their daughters in preschool and in fifth grade; later on the boys' spatial and numerical abilities varied directly with the freedom their parents allowed.

Beginning School Study families granted their young sons more independence than their daughters: starting in grade one, boys were allowed to spend more time away from home and were monitored less closely than girls. In the summer after first grade (age 7), Beginning School Study boys more often played with friends than girls did, while girls played more with siblings or other relatives; at this age boys also were more often cared for outside their homes than girls were. In the summer after second grade (age 8), boys were more likely than girls to go to recreation centers, play organized sports, or to play in the street, while girls played in the house. At age 9, boys were more likely than girls to have after-school care away from home and/or to be supervised by a non-relative, or even be left by themselves. The independence accorded Beginning School Study boys over their elementary years, as just summarized, continued into middle school because then the after-school supervision of boys was also less home-based than that of girls, or even absent.

Patterns of supervision for Beginning School Study children square well with information about sex differences in the freedom parents grant children elsewhere in the country. Among sixth-graders from 20 Oakland working-class neighborhoods, for instance, boys were more likely than girls to take part in activities out of doors, to visit cultural or recreational sites *on their own*, and to ride the bus alone at least once a week (Medrich, Roizen, Rubin, and Buckley 1982, pp. 74, 84). Similarly, in Atlanta, both African American and white boys from families of all economic levels were permitted a broader range of independent activities than girls were (Heyns 1978, p. 147): they took more trips alone, were subject to adult supervision more sporadically, were more likely to have a bicycle, and attended camps more often and typically for longer periods than girls. In Connecticut the picture is the same, with middle-class urban and suburban fifth-grade boys spending more time in outdoor play than girls (Lever 1976). Generally, then, it seems that young boys have much greater freedom to explore the neighborhood than young girls do, perhaps because parents are likely to value independent initiative more in their sons than in their daughters (see Kohn 1977), and/or because parents see girls as requiring more protection than boys.

Parents' motives aside, for several reasons playing outside in neighborhoods could help boys develop their problem-solving and mathematical skills. For one thing, by traveling about on their own, boys learn the spatial arrangements of streets and buildings, and also must figure out how to pay bus fare, make change, and keep track of time. Even more important, boys' activities out in the neighborhood often involve organized sports and other complex forms of play, the more so the higher their family's socioeconomic status level. Lever (1976) and Sleet (1985) both found that boys participated more in neighborhood sports and games than girls did, also that boys more often played games at high levels of complexity than girls did. Beginning School Study boys were involved three times as often in organized sports and games as girls, and boys attended sporting events more than twice as often as girls. Moreover, these neighborhood resources are more available in high socioeconomic status neighborhoods. When Beginning School Study parents of boys (age 8) were asked whether their child had participated in organized sports over the preceding summer, 45% of those in higher socioeconomic status neighborhoods (fewer than 10% of families below poverty level) said their sons had participated in organized teams while only 24% of parents in lower socioeconomic status neighborhoods (more than 20% of families below poverty level) reported their sons had participated. This difference is significant beyond the 5% level.

Games are more complex if they require players to (1) take different roles, (2) work collectively toward a common, explicit goal, and (3) follow specific rules that are constant from one game to the next. Thus baseball is more complex than hopscotch because it involves two teams of nine players, all with different roles, while in hopscotch players take turns at the same role. Hopscotch involves simply repeating a set of physical maneuvers while saying aloud rhymes matched to hops and jumps. Baseball involves every player in several different roles: running, hitting, catching, fielding, and pitching as players on one side cooperate to prevent opponents from reaching a base before the ball does. Complex games provide experiences that could help children develop their math-related skills. For example, complex games require children to do arithmetic: add up the score, keep time, note the size and weight of players, and maintain records involving the number of home runs per season or consecutive games played. But complex games also require more complicated mental activities. For example, determining when one rule applies in a game and not another, or whether several rules apply, is similar to constructing a proof. (In baseball, a pitch the batter misses *or* has hit out of bounds is a strike. However, if the batter already has two prior strikes called, any ball that is swung at and missed is a strike, but a ball hit out of bounds is a foul, any number of which can be racked up.) Choosing up sides to play a game is like ensuring the equivalence of two sets. (Team captains alternate their choices, so players on the two teams are equally matched.) Understanding how to apply the scoring and precedence rules in a game is similar to exercises in syllogistic logic. (A football kicked through the goal posts after a touchdown is worth one point (or two points depending on the league,) but the same act is worth 3 points if no touchdown precedes.) In addition, playing sandlot baseball or hoops generates children's interest in professional sports, and the media track many statistics on players and teams: batting averages, earned run averages, rebound percentages, odds of winning or losing, the proportion of complete forward passes, and the like.

To see whether being out in neighborhoods and playing complex games did affect Beginning School Study children's cognitive development, we examined boys' and girls' test scores in math. In agreement with earlier research (Aiken 1971; Hyde, Fennema, and Lamon 1990), boys' and girls' *average* test scores in math concepts/reasoning (Table 6.7) did not differ significantly in the elementary or middle school years: at the beginning of first grade, scores for the two sexes were 5 points apart, and stayed close through the eighth year. The *variances* of boys' test scores did increase between the first and eighth years, however. In first grade, the standard deviations of boys' and girls' scores were similar (33 and 31, respectively), but by the eighth year, the standard deviation of boys' scores was almost 25 percent larger than the girls'. Why did this happen?

A hierarchial linear analysis (see Entwisle, Alexander, and Olson 1994) of Beginning School Study children's gains in math over the first two years of

Table 6.7   California Achievement Test (CAT) Math Concepts/Applications
Scores, 1982 to 1990 (Standard Deviations)

		Mean CAT Math Score		
Year	N	Females	Males	Total
Fall 1982, Year 1	455	292	297	294
		(31)	(33)	(32)
Spring 1983, Year 1	447	343	346	344
		(35)	(36)	(36)
Fall 1983, Year 2	421	342	345	343
		(34)	(39)	(37)
Spring 1984, Year 2	416	385	387	386
		(36)	(39)	(38)
Fall 1984, Year 3	455	380	382	381
		(37)	(46)	(41)
Spring 1990, Year 8	399	545	540	543
		(65)	(78)	(71)

school revealed that boys who lived in neighborhoods where resources were most plentiful had higher math scores than boys who lived in less affluent neighborhoods, other factors held constant.   There was no relationship between girls' math scores and neighborhood quality, however. We suspect that boys' math skills responded to the resources in their neighborhoods, especially to organized sports, and that sensitivity to resources in neighborhoods is the reason for boys' score variances to exceed girls'.

The variance of boys' math scores exceeds the variance in girls' scores in many other studies also (see Flanagan et al. 1964; Feingold 1988) and this greater variance of boys' scores could explain the deficit that has repeatedly been found in females' higher level math skills (see Feingold 1988 for citations). The explanation goes as follows.   In eighth grade, of the 399 Beginning School Study students who had been enrolled continuously in City schools since grade one, 31 boys and 38 girls scored over one standard deviation above their respective means. The Beginning School Study boys and girls who were high scorers did not have similar means, however. In these selected "high" groups, the boys' average California Achievement Test score was 23 points higher than the girls' (Table 6.8), a difference significant beyond the 1% level. Put simply, we suspect that as Beginning School Study boys and

Table 6.8   Means and Standard Deviations of California Achievement Test
(CAT) Math Concepts/Application Scores for High and Non-
High Scoring Beginning School Study Students in Year 8, Spring
1990 (Standard Deviations)

	Boys		Girls	
Year 8 Students	Mean	N	Mean	N
High Scoring Students[a] (1 or more S.D.'s above mean)	660 (39)	31	637 (30)	38
Non-High Scoring Students	516 (60)	154	525 (52)	176
Total	540 (78)	185	545 (65)	214

[a] The sex difference in the means of high scorers is 23 points (t=2.70; $d.f.$=67; $p \leq .01$).

girls progressed up through the grades, boys who came from better-off
families profited from their neighborhood's resources in ways that promoted
their math skills. Poorer boys, on the other hand, could not profit from time
spent in neighborhoods because their neighborhoods lacked resources, and in
addition the boys may have been kept at home to avoid the hazards in poor
neighborhoods. Girls did not benefit from neighborhood resources because
they spent their time at home, irrespective of the type of neighborhood they
lived in.

Most explanations for boys' superiority in higher level math skills have
centered on sex-role socialization: the relative lack of appropriate female
models for young girls to emulate (Parsons, Adler, and Kaczala 1982);
parents' expectations that boys will do better in math than girls, even when
their school performance is equal (Entwisle and Baker 1983); parents' beliefs
that math is more difficult for girls than for boys (Eccles [Parsons] 1982);
teachers' encouraging males in math more than they do females (Fox, Tobin,
and Brody 1979); girls' views of math as a "male" domain that conflicts with
their sex-role identity (Fennema and Sherman 1977); parents' purchase of
more toys and games encouraging math skills for their sons than for their
daughters (Hilton and Berglund 1974); and girls' perceptions that math is
"less useful" to them than it is to boys (Fox, Brody, and Tobin 1980).

These prior explanations to account for the gender gap in math all
emphasize *individual-level-factors* (parent's actions, children's expectations
and/or perhaps genetic factors, see Benbow and Stanley 1980). Our
explanation, by contrast, invokes differences in the freedom that families grant

boys as compared to girls. This freedom could provide experiences outside the home relevant to math-related skills that young boys take advantage of, while girls cannot. This experience starts early in life so it could gradually lay the foundation for the gender difference favoring boys in math that emerges in adolescence.

Family socialization practices could thus be a subtle but important factor in producing gender differences in children's development by regulating how much time children of the two sexes spend in neighborhoods, or more generally, spend outside the circle of family supervision. In neighborhoods where middle class role models are mixed with poorer residents, the poorer children seem to benefit (see Chapter 3; Jarrett 1995). In ghetto neighborhoods, however, sheltering children from neighborhood contact and monitoring them closely may be the better strategy.

Neighborhood quality could relate to the development of many other kinds of gender differences, such as males' greater affinity for risk taking, males' use of language, and males' lower rates of depressive symptoms, among other things. How families mediate neighborhood influence, and how neighborhood resources affect children's development are topics deserving much broader study, especially in terms of the positive contributions that neighborhoods can make to development.

Overview

This chapter points up school practices that favor girls' educational careers and family practices that favor boys'. In both instances, the favored sex eventually has a marked advantage in the labor market, and in both cases also the trends are subtle and the long-term consequences serious.

The route toward achieving greater gender equality in teachers' or parents' treatment of young children are not easy to specify. Schools as presently organized seem better matched to young girls' needs than to young boys', if only because of the predominance of female teachers, while society more generally and neighborhoods in particular seem better matched to the needs of young males, for example the predominance of males in organized sports, from the major leagues on down. In short, strong patterns in social institutions underlie the gender differences in how children of the two sexes are perceived and treated. Still, as with other social problems, recognizing that gender inequity exists is the first step, particularly in the case of teacher ratings, and in the matter of how classrooms and curriculum are organized. As to parents' treatment of boys versus girls, change seems more difficult because part of this problem is the growing decay in urban neighborhoods. At the same time, the increasing prevalence of sports like soccer and softball for girls is a trend that can be further encouraged, and the need for supervised sports in poor communities can be further justified.

Notes

1. Girls averaged 282 on the California Achievement Test subtest in reading comprehension in the fall of first grade, boys averaged 280.

2. Pedersen, Faucher, and Eaton (1978) likewise found that in a class where all boys were placed at the back of the room and all girls placed at the front, boys' IQ scores declined over the year while girls' scores increased.

3. These figures on reading instructional level and cumulative retention rate come from the sample of students with complete data on reading instructional level through grade 5 (N=343). The retention rate for all Beginning School Study students still in Baltimore City Public Schools at the end of year 5 shows and even larger disparity by gender (51% boys and 36% girls, N=548).

7

The Overall Picture

The purpose of this book is to clarify how children's socioeconomic status, family structure, age, and gender, as well as the social organization of their elementary schools affect their development over the first few years of school. We chose to study these particular topics because they represent key ways that social inequality impinges on young children's development, and because the Beginning School Study archive has produced something new or useful to say about each topic. Concerning gender, for example, we have seen that Beginning School Study girls got better reading marks than boys did in the early grades despite equivalent standardized test scores for the two sexes when children began first grade. Teachers saw boys as conforming to the student role less well than girls, and these differences in teachers' judgements in first and second grade, while not large, are probably sufficient to produce much of the observed gender gap in reading performance. This deficit in boys' early reading marks then feeds into the considerable gender gap in rates of grade retention favoring girls.

Hopefully, this book begins to fill important gaps in the literature, as the beginning school period thus far has been relatively overlooked as a critical period for children's development. On the one hand, knowledge about children's schooling in the early grades is scarce because sociologists have had much less interest in how children develop in middle childhood (roughly ages 6 to 12) than in how they develop over adolescence. But on the other hand, knowledge is also scarce because developmentalists have paid more attention to children's personal characteristics than to the social contexts that surround youth. A life course approach like that taken in this book begins to remedy both of these deficiencies because it emphasizes middle childhood as a key life

stage in explaining the genesis of social stratification more generally, and it
emphasizes the environmental settings in which children develop.

A life course perspective (or even common sense) suggests that children's
success in secondary school must depend to some degree on their experience
in elementary school. Students attend high schools that draw from large
catchment areas, *after* elementary school. At the elementary level, however,
the boundaries of school catchment areas follow the contours of
neighborhoods. Where children live dictates the school they attend. For these
reasons, elementary schools are the logical place to look for evidence about
how inequity maps onto schooling. In fact, it appears that social disadvantage
maps onto social inequities in schooling most tightly at the start because
children's relative standing when they begin school is replicated when they
finish. To wait until high school to determine how social disadvantage affects
youngsters' schooling, or how to counter it, is to wait too long.

A longitudinal approach also reveals differences in the rate of children's
development as they age, and this provides another reason to focus on
elementary schooling. If development is most rapid when children begin
school, then this life period is a strategic one to investigate in order to
understand the process of schooling. From ages 4 to 8, children are especially
responsive to schooling for both developmental/cognitive and
social/contextual reasons. In these years they are launched into achievement
trajectories, they start to construct their academic self-images, and they
necessarily build school dossiers that then shadow them through all the rest of
their school days and beyond. Still, the organizational imperatives that so
effectively track students over this early period get little notice. These include
the limited access to preschools or kindergarten for 3 to 5 year olds; the social
homogeneity within elementary schools coupled with the heterogeneity
between them; and the triage-like sorting of students, especially in the first and
second grade, by grade retention, ability grouping, and Special Education.

Throughout this book, data from the Beginning School Study are used to
supplement knowledge about schooling derived from other sources. The
Beginning School Study directly questioned parents and teachers as well as
children, and collected a broad range of information from schools in an effort
to clarify a complicated picture. This approach produced many insights. For
example, Beginning School Study boys growing up in a home where a single
mother shared a residence with other adults improved their conduct marks
over first grade, while boys from other homes did not. This finding (and
others like it) sounds simple, but actually is not. First, it represents *change* in
one group of youngsters as compared with another when performance in both
groups is equated statistically at the start of school. Second, it compares boys

with and without resident fathers taking family *economic resources* into account. Comparing changes in marks over first grade across subgroups of boys who reside in different types of families provides a much clearer picture of how family structure affects schooling than could data taken at a single point in time. Also the breadth of the Beginning School Study archive allows us to take into account multiple contextual resources--not only family structure, but the socioeconomic level and ethnic composition of the school, and even the neighborhood.

The reader by now should be aware that this book is *not* an account only of the Beginning School Study, nor does it completely describe that project by any means. For example, we do not say much about race/ethnicity. This choice was made, not because we doubt the importance of race/ethnicity, but because of the need to keep this book within limits. Also much of our previously published work has dealt directly with this topic.

Schooling and Human Development

A major source of social inequity is that elementary schools are exceedingly homogeneous in terms of their students' socioeconomic background. As a consequence, these schools function along lines dictated by the socioeconomic characteristics of the neighborhoods in which they are located rather than along lines determined by the school's own educational goals. The boundaries of U.S. neighborhoods faithfully mirror the fault lines in the larger society. Children who live in good neighborhoods effectively land on a fast academic track because their parents and teachers perceive them and treat them as "high ability" children, while children who live in poor neighborhoods land on a slow academic track because they are perceived and treated as "low ability" children. The myth that elementary schools share the same curriculum is false. Even when schools use the same lesson plans and textbooks, as in Baltimore, the socioeconomic status of the neighborhood determines the way instruction proceeds and the "quality of life" children experience in their classrooms.

Ironically, socioeconomic status is generally supposed to affect how much children learn, but it does not affect how much children learn *in school*. When schools are in session, all children move ahead at the same pace. Only when schools are not in session do children whose families are better off move ahead of those whose families are poor. Small gaps in achievement levels correlated with family socioeconomic status are present when children start first grade because up to that time their development depends mainly on family resources, and some families have been able to provide more resources than others. Then, after formal schooling begins, the better-off children pull farther ahead each summer because they have the resources to continue learning outside school. By the end of elementary school, the average achievement gaps between better-off and poor children have increased, even though all children have learned equivalent amounts when schools were open. Economic disability in the parent's generation thereby leads to educational disability in the children's generation via unequal achievement growth in summer (and before school starts).

A key theme of this book is that elementary schools to a considerable extent counteract economic disability, because Beginning School Study children from all socioeconomic backgrounds gained *on average* the same amounts during the school year, no matter the school they attended. Those from the poorest backgrounds even tended to make up ground when schools were open. As a group, however, children in low socioeconomic status schools were nevertheless treated as though they were "low ability." In effect, they were treated as less capable than other children *because* their home background was of relatively low socioeconomic status. It is hard to imagine a clearer case of social inequity.

Inequity in schooling gets worse as economic inequality becomes more pronounced. In 1970, about 14% of children were living in poverty, but by 1993 official figures show the rate at 22%, and some estimates are as high as 33%. With proportionately more children attending schools in poverty areas, probably one-third of U.S. children are now attending schools that effectively track them as "low level" from the start.

The good news in this book is that despite widespread poverty and family disruption, young children's ability to learn in elementary school seems little affected. The bad news is that the quality of poor children's lives suffers while they are in school. Besides being inappropriately treated because they are assumed to be of "low ability," the atmosphere and facilities of schools in poorer neighborhoods are inferior to those in better neighborhoods. In Baltimore, even the brand-new elementary schools that enroll mainly poor children are set in the midst of old rowhouses and tenements surviving from the nineteenth century, with bars and liquor stores in close proximity. The schools that enroll economically advantaged children are set on expanses of grass, among single-family houses with well-kept lawns and shrubbery, generally removed from commercial activity. Even when they share the same school district, as in Baltimore City then, the elementary schools in an urban ghetto are far different social institutions from the elementary schools in well-to-do neighborhoods. The hidden tracks *between* elementary schools lead to a quality of life within schools that is distinctive, and this stratification across schools undermines their effectiveness as social equalizers despite their remarkable but unrecognized success at promoting *all* children's cognitive growth.

Beginning School Study and other children start school with positive views of themselves. At age 6 it is hard to measure what would correspond to a child's self-image, but in first grade Beginning School Study children's academic self-images were unrelated to their parents' economic resources. This seeming sturdiness of young children's self-images, however, is soon tested by school organizational patterns. Children's marks, instructional level, and first grade placements like retention all reflect the socioeconomic status of their school. More children are held back in schools of low socioeconomic status and marks are lower on average. Eventually marks and other school evaluations affect students' self-image: Beginning School Study children retained in first grade, for instance, had less favorable self-images than non-retained children did by middle school. (Alexander, Entwisle, and Dauber 1994; Alexander and Entwisle, in preparation).

The first grade transition, a key life stage for understanding schooling, has to be a bumpy ride for children at the low end of the socioeconomic scale. Their seasonal growth rates are markedly uneven, and society confuses their uneven growth trajectories with a reduced ability to grow. Even though Beginning School Study children of all socioeconomic levels advanced at the same rate when school was in session, parents and teachers of children in low socioeconomic status schools had lower expectations for those children, and those children got much lower marks than did their counterparts in higher socioeconomic status schools. Many more of them were also held back. Small wonder that their academic self-images spiral downward over the course of their schooling.

Resolution of Some Paradoxes

Findings from the Beginning School Study , when added to knowledge from other sources, produce a more coherent picture of schooling than has been possible heretofore. In particular, the faucet theory of schooling presented in this book makes sense out of a number of well-established facts that previously seemed to be at odds with one another, listed below.

(1) The consistent finding, starting with the Coleman Report in 1966, of *less variance in children's achievement across than within schools*. Data for elementary schools and middle schools (Heyns 1978) show that winter gains are much the same for children of various family backgrounds and further, that disadvantaged children gain at the same rate as the advantaged when school is in session. Poorer children appear to be "behind" other children at the end

of first grade, however, because they started school a little "behind." The shortfall in poorer children's scores at the end of first grade compared to better-off children's is not attributable to the school, however. Rather, it is attributable to home background. Thus the paradox of large within-school variance and small between-school-variance is explained.

(2) The disappointing observation that *pouring resources into schools, altering their curricula, and reducing class size, makes so little difference in children's achievement levels*. When school is in session, all children gain about the same amounts, but the times when children are not in school are the times when poorer children fall behind.

(3) The repeated demonstrations *that attending summer school does not benefit disadvantaged students*. So far summer school attendance or special summer programs have not boosted the achievement scores of disadvantaged children (see Heyns' 1987 review). As we said, most of these programs have been short (6 weeks or less), not well-designed academically, and aimed mainly at "problem" students. Still, in the largest effort to date, the national Sustaining Effects Study (Klibanoff and Haggart 1981; Carter 1983; 1984), which was thoughtfully designed and carefully executed, summer school attendance did not accomplish the desired goal of helping poorer students catch up. In fact, Heyns' (1987, p.1155) reanalysis of some of these data shows that in the Sustaining Effects Study the racial gap actually increased during the summer.

Why has summer school proved ineffective in boosting scores of disadvantaged children? We earlier suggested two possible answers (Chapter 3). One is that summer programs have been inappropriately timed. If reading achievement moves up twice as fast in year one as year three, as is true for Beginning School Study children, then the optimum time to intervene would be in the summer after (or before) grade one. The other reason is the nature of the program provided. Summer activities should afford children a different set of experiences to learn from than those provided in the school year.

(4) Mistakenly, schools that enroll children whose scores are somewhat above average credit themselves with producing children who excel, and society takes this view as well. But higher socioeconomic status children *appear* to do better than poorer children because when they start school they have higher scores. This starting point depends on their *access to resources outside school*, not on what the school provides. Children from resource-poor home environments, if anything, gain relatively more from school than do children from resource-rich home environments. Schools are thus blamed unjustly for the lower achievement levels of poor children.

Smith (1972, p. 265) makes the same points somewhat differently. He notes that the relationship between background variables and achievement is initially strong in first grade: first, because the early years of life prepare the child for school, and second, because the *selection* and *assignment* practices carried out by schools probably exacerbate the relationship between social class and achievement in the early grades. We would emphasize that "assignments" are across schools and since characteristics of home and school are usually matched at the elementary level, the gradient across schools follows the gradient across neighborhoods (Chapters 3 and 4).

Schooling Models Re-Specified

Children from less advantaged backgrounds are as capable of learning the basics of reading and arithmetic as are more advantaged children, because all children do so when school is open. Moreover, children of various ages learn at much the same rate as long as they are in school. A key requisite for achieving equity in schooling, then, is to bring poorer children up to speed before they start school. We already know that less advantaged children can be brought up to speed (e.g. the Headstart evaluations by Lazar and Darlington 1982 or the Consortium 1983; see also Barnett 1996). Attending-preschool away from home helps children before they start first grade (Barnett 1996). The original Headstart programs were exceedingly variable even in the ages of the children they enrolled, but, as pointed out earlier, for this very reason, the benefits derived from Headstart are strong testimony to the importance of school attendance per se rather than the details of programs or settings. Less advantaged Beginning School Study children who spent full days rather than half days in kindergarten also did better when they started first grade--again, attending school is the answer.

The legacy of an agricultural society is that U.S. schools are organized around the calendar. They are open in winter (about 9 months) but closed in summer (about 3 months). The episodic nature of schooling creates a strategic advantage for studying the process of children's cognitive growth: the opening and closing of schools produces a "natural experiment"--it turns the resource faucet on and off. Schools provide resources for children in winter but not in summer, and the intermittent character of schooling clarifies how the resources provided by homes, neighborhoods, and schools dovetail in support of cognitive growth. The Coleman report (1966) and many subsequent large-scale studies concluded that home influences were far more important than school influences for determining *differences* in children's achievement. This conclusion is absolutely true. Even so, when students are evaluated in cross-sectional studies or in longitudinal studies once a year the exact role of home resources in producing differences in children's learning is necessarily obscured. During the school year, schools foster by far the largest portion of children's annual achievement gains and poor children, on average, do as well or better than anyone else. Only in summer do poor children fall behind. The equality of school-year gains for children of all family backgrounds is strong evidence that home resources do not interact with school resources, but instead supplant them.

Children's growth rates have been incorrectly assumed to be linear. It has been assumed that home background influences children's achievement all year round, but this assumption is false because a number of studies now show that children from poorer homes advance much more slowly in summer than do their better-off peers, if they advance at all. At least through elementary school and into middle school (Heyns 1978), the achievement levels of children from poor socioeconomic backgrounds increase on a par with those from favored economic backgrounds *when school is open*. Schools mitigate effects of home disadvantage because children's cognitive growth in winter depends almost wholly on going to school, not on home resources. As we have seen, on average Beginning School Study children attending the ten most disadvantaged schools gained as much as children attending the ten most advantaged schools. This finding and research on how age affects schooling are strong testimony to the equalizing power of schools.

A strategic advantage comes from taking advantage of the school calendar to isolate schooling effects. If we divide the year into periods when school is or is not open, we can show that home resources matter little when school is open, at least in this sample. Serious attention in the future needs to be given to the complementary issue--do schools as well as families have effects on cognitive growth in summer? We show that neighborhoods have effects in summer that supplement family effects. Can some (or any) of these neighborhood effects be lagged school effects? This issue is one we are currently investigating.

Missing Variables

Another pitfall in model specification is omission of key variables. The Beginning School Study included measures of parents' psychological resources in models of children's school achievement, although such measures (other than college plans) had not been prominent in status attainment research with high school students. Parents' economic standing undergirds schooling in part because, compared to the not-so-well-off, better-off parents tend to value education more, have higher expectations for their children's school performance, know better how the educational system works, and have the time and resources to interact with their children in "developmentally sensitive ways." Over and over the potency of parents' expectations in determining young children's school performance has been brought home, especially for youngsters in the early grades. Parent involvement, the topic of a flurry of recent research (e.g., Booth and Dunn 1996), may, in fact, be a proxy for parents' psychological resources.

Perhaps the major contribution so far made by the Beginning School Study is the finding that parents' expectations and other psychological resources, which are higher or more plentiful in families of higher socioeconomic status, bear fruit mainly in summer when school is closed. The "psychological capital" of the family, which can be independent of its social or financial capital, is a key parental resource for children's achievement. Most succinctly, it is the ability of parents to interact with their children in ways that prompt cognitive growth.

Debate in the past has centered on whether poverty affects children's schooling through parents' altered norms and "tastes" for non-normative behavior (e.g., welfare dependence, chronic joblessness, and the like), or whether poverty affects children for structural reasons, through continuing social and economic disadvantage (see Tienda 1991). This dichotomy is something of a fiction, however, if the faucet theory is taken seriously, because that theory holds that the resources furnished by schools are sufficient to prompt growth in children of all socioeconomic status levels when schools are open (schools as social organizations are not biased), but parents and teachers *see* children in terms of their origin rather than their potential. Parents' joblessness and the like lead to norms (ways of viewing children) that do not augment achievement. Differences in achievement levels arise when schools are closed, before first grade or in summers, when children depend entirely on resources in neighborhoods and families. These out-of-school resources appear to be mainly *psychological* resources that can mediate economic resources, but to a considerable degree these psychological resources can be independent of economic resources, especially for young children. Some low socioeconomic status families have high expectations for their children and provide summer activities that support learning. Certainly the social stratification of families by neighborhoods is a key element in school inequity--the larger social structure does matter--but most of the impact of this stratification is transmitted by a lack of or a diminution in parents' psychological resources.

Selective Bias

Models can be mis-specified in several ways, as just discussed, but even models correctly specified can be poorly estimated because of problems in sampling or selective bias. Sampling problems have undercut past research on elementary schooling in an especially insidious way, because most research samples are chosen by grade level. These grade samples appear to be representative but actually they tend to miss relatively more of the children with the worst problems--those who are absent more, those who move more, those in Special Education who are in separate classrooms, and often those who have been retained. The grade populations are defined by the schools not the investigator. Furthermore, most studies start at grade 3 or higher, but by third grade much of the sorting of children by retention and Special Education has already occurred, and children's rate of cognitive growth begins to tail off.

Selective bias is another serious problem. A life course perspective on schooling helps because it encourages research on cohorts, that is, on persons bound together at some common time point by an event like birth (Furstenberg et al. 1987), or by an event like starting first grade, as in the Beginning School Study. A prospective strategy pushes researchers away from falling prey to selective bias because it leads them to examine how a whole cohort fares, i.e., those who succeed as well as those who fail. All too often a retrospective strategy has prevailed: a group of "problem" individuals like teen mothers or school dropouts is sampled *after* their problems have become manifest, and then their life histories are scrutinized in hope of finding clues to what prompted problems to occur. The catch is that such individuals constitute a selectively biased group. A prime example of the fatal flaw in a retrospective design is that virtually all adult criminals have been delinquents as juveniles, but only a very small percentage of juvenile delinquents grow up to be adult criminals (Sampson 1992). In a sample of adult criminals, the correlation between adult criminality and juvenile delinquency looking backward over the life course appears perfect, but following a group of juveniles prospectively produces a far different picture. Only a few juvenile delinquents become criminals--most do not--so the correlation then between delinquency and adult criminality is actually very weak.

Left censoring is present in the Beginning School Study, of course, in that it began when children started formal schooling at age 6. These children obviously had experiences in the first six years of life that could shape school outcomes at age 6 and afterward. In an effort to overcome part of this difficulty, we inquired about kindergarten attendance, but reliable information about prior preschool attendance (ages 4 and below) could not be secured. As a consequence, variables acting before age 5 may have more or different influences from what we believe.

Notwithstanding, a particular strength of the Beginning School Study related to left censoring is that children's test scores and much other data were secured at the very *beginning* of first grade, at the time when schooling began. Securing test scores in both fall and spring has allowed study not only of children's relative standing when they started first grade, but their seasonal growth patterns. The Beginning School Study remains the only study, to our knowledge, that has semi-annual test scores on youngsters that cover the entire elementary period.

Elementary Schools as Institutions

Developmental theorists have focused much more intently on changes within the child than on changes in the child's surroundings. Research on schooling helps redress this imbalance, because children's achievement does not occur in a social vacuum: the minority-group child often attends a low socioeconomic status school, or the boy has a teacher who tends to favor girls, or family moves force the poor child to make "extra" school transitions. Powerful social forces envelop the child whatever his or her own characteristics. For example, "ability groups" in first grade are organized in part along lines of children's socioemotional characteristics and these characteristics as well as "ability" could shape children's achievement in first grade. Or, the school climate varies by neighborhood location, so the nature of the "school context" is mainly determined by conditions outside the school. Or, elementary schools are not organized so as to facilitate their own goals or needs, rather they are organized by external forces that serve goals unrelated to schooling.

Overlap with Other Contexts

Most educational research conceptualizes family resources as *potentiating* school resources. For example, parents' school involvement supposedly helps students do better in school because parents will be more likely to check homework or will consult teachers when problems arise. The assumption has been that family resources act year round, in winter as well as in summer. But because family resources matter mainly--or only--when schools are closed, as we have repeatedly said, they do not interact with school resources in underwriting children's achievement. Rather, family resources promote cognitive growth in summer that adds on to the growth children make during the school year.

Similarly, research on neighborhoods assumes that they affect children's school performance on a continuous basis. Whether neighborhood effects interact with or add on to school effects is an issue yet to be settled, but so far Beginning School Study research suggests that neighborhood resources, like home resources, matter mainly in summer. They appear to be redundant with school resources when schools are open.[1] Neighborhood resources may not be redundant with home resources, however, because neighborhoods affect Beginning School Study children *after* allowing for family background effects. This issue needs much further study using hierarchial modeling techniques.

The seasonal action of neighborhood resources coupled with the seasonal action of family resources strengthens the argument that effects of the school context are relatively independent of other contextual effects. Still, it is important to examine *how* poor neighborhoods contribute to schooling deficits like drop-out. Neighborhood-school links thus need to be approached from the standpoint of how resources in one domain could *replace* resources in the other. If resources in neighborhoods add on to family resources in summer, as we suspect, then providing neighborhood centers and community activities in summer could boost children's achievement independent of family status. This conclusion fits in well with our hypothesis that organized sports and games are an important resource supporting boys' math development (Entwisle, Alexander, and Olson 1994).

Long-Term Effects

Evidence is burgeoning that children's life chances are affected strongly by their elementary schooling, especially by events and experiences in first grade or just before. Studies cited throughout this book show that repeating a grade or getting poor marks in elementary school increases the likelihood that students will drop out. The other side of the coin is that attending preschools or kindergarten can improve reading and math achievement in elementary school (Lazar and Darlington 1982; Entwisle et al. 1987; Barnett 1996), and long-term follow-ups of preschooling show that attending preschool apparently has some effects into adulthood (Consortium 1983).

Findings from the Beginning School Study have enriched this picture by showing more specifically how and when such effects are transmitted (Table 7.1). For example, the *amount* of Beginning School Study children's kindergarten experience (full-day versus half-day) by itself improved a child's chances of avoiding retention in first grade by almost 2 to 1 (with initial test scores and other key variables controlled). Also, children living in a single-parent family that included a grandmother in the preschool period had better work habits at the beginning of first grade than other children of single parents. Superior work habits helped children avoid retention in first grade. For still another example, if Beginning School Study children's very first marks were high, those marks could pump up test scores over first grade by as much as half a standard deviation, other things equal. The first-grade teachers' opinion of the child's classroom adjustment added still another layer: children whom teachers perceived as interested or attentive gained significantly more on standardized tests in reading and math over grade one, other things equal, and these teachers' perceptions forecast children's year-end test scores better than did children's initial test scores. Another key observation is that test scores and marks both persist strongly from grade one on up--Beginning School Study children's grade one scores correlate .58 and .66 with scores at the end of year 5 in reading and math, respectively. (See also Alexander, Entwisle, and Dauber 1994.)

Studies by other investigators add to the larger picture by tracing long-term effects of schooling before first grade and by showing that effects persist over longer periods after elementary school than is so far possible for Beginning School Study students (Table 7.2). Several studies in both the U.S. and the U.K. that used designs with children assigned randomly to preschool and non-preschool groups show that preschooling leads to better verbal and reading skills in elementary and secondary school, lower rates of retention and/or less Special Education placement--even to superior adjustment in early adulthood. Long-term studies on drop-out show that absences, retention, low reading levels, low marks in the early grades, or early behavioral problems in school increase the likelihood that students will leave before graduation.

Table 7.1   Long-Term Effects: Beginning School Study Research

Citation	Early School Measure	Outcome
Entwisle, Alexander, Cadigan, and Pallas 1987	Amount of kindergarten	First grade absence Beginning CAT scores Beginning marks in reading, math
Dauber, Alexander, and Entwisle 1993	Beginning marks Grade 1 math CAT score	Retention in Yrs 1-4

(continues)

Citation	Early School Measure	Outcome
(continued) Alexander, Entwisle, and Dauber 1993	Teacher behavioral ratings in Grade 1	School performance in Yr 4: -reading, math marks -reading, math CAT scores
Alexander, Entwisle, and Dauber 1994	Grade 1 retention	Academic self-image, Yr 8 Student mark expectations, Yr 8 Reading, math marks, grade 6, 7 CAT reading, math, grade 6, 7
Pallas, Entwisle, Alexander, and Stluka 1994	Grade 1 reading group assignment	Yr 4 CAT scores, reading marks, parent and teacher expectations
Alexander and Entwisle 1996b	Grade 1 reading groups Grade 1 tracking (reading groups, Special Education, retention)	Retention in elementary school Grade 6 course placements
Alexander, Entwisle, and Horsey 1997	Grade 1 CAT reading & math scores; grade 1 reading & math marks; grade 1 retention	High school dropout
Unpublished	Grade 1 parent educ. expectation for student; Grade 1 marks in reading and math	Middle school placement in advanced course tracks
Unpublished	Amount of kindergarten	Retention in Yr 1
Unpublished	Work habits grade 1; Number of school moves	Retention in Yr 1 Test scores in Yr 5

Table 7.2   Long-Term Effects: Other Investigators' Research

Study	Early Schooling	Lasting Effect
Bloom 1964	By grade 3	At least 50% of the general achievement pattern at age 18 has been developed
Husen 1969 (N =1116) Sweden	Grade 3 marks (GPA) Teacher ability rating in grade 3	Attendance at secondary school Future ed. success (completion of post-secondary study)
Fitzsimmons, Cheever, Leonard, and Macunovich 1969 (N=270)	Achievement test scores in reading and math, grades 1-3	Performance in high school
Stroup and Robins 1972 (N=223; African-American urban males)	Absences and grade repetition in elementary school	High school dropout
Kraus 1973 (N=274)	Grade 3 reading achievement tests	Reading and math marks General academic performance in high school
Lloyd 1978 (N=1562)	Grade 3 marks and CAT reading score	High school graduation
Pedersen, Faucher,and Eaton 1978 (N=59; urban disadvantaged)	Exceptional first grade teacher	Achievement of high adult status Completion of at least 10 years of school
Pope, Lehrer, and Stevens 1980 (N = 545)	Kindergarten achievement (Wide Range Achievement Test)	Reading achievement in grade 5 ($r = .50$)
Lazar and Darlington 1982 (N=2008)	Participation in Headstart preschool programs	Reading achievement (grade 3), Math achievement (grades 3-5) Lower rates of retention and Special Education

(continues)

Study	Early Schooling	Lasting Effect
(continued) Richman, Stevenson, and Graham 1982 (N=705; United Kingdom)	Preschool attendance	Higher IQ-adjusted reading at age 8
Palmer 1983 (N=240)	One-to-one preschool instruction at ages 2-3 for 8 months	Higher reading and math achievement at grades 5 and 7 Lower rates of retention
Royce, Darlington, and Murray 1983 (N=1104)	Preschool attendance	Achievement in reading (grade 3) and math (grade 5) Lower rates of Special Education and retention High school graduation
Schweinhart and Weikart 1983 (N=123)	Preschool attendance (Perry Preschool)	Higher CAT scores at ages 7-14 Lower rates of Special Education placement and delinquent behavior
Meyer 1984 (N=165; economically disadvantaged)	Kindergarten-grade 3 participation in Distar curriculum with increased allocation of time to basic skills	Higher grade 9 CAT reading achievement Lower retention rates Higher rates of high school graduation, application and acceptance to college
Berrueta-Clement, Schweinhart, Barnett, Epstein, and Weikart 1984 (N=123)	High quality preschool program (Perry Preschool)	Higher GPA in high school; Lower rates of Special Ed; Positive outcomes at age 19: -high school grad -postsecondary ed -employed -lower rates of crime, delinquency -lower rates of pregnancy

(continues)

Study	Early Schooling	Lasting Effect
Hess, Holloway, Dickson, and Price 1984 (N=47)	Maternal expectations for achievement in preschool	Grade 6 ITBS scores, vocabulary and math
Butler, Marsh, Sheppard, and Sheppard 1985 (N = 286)	Battery of tests in kindergarten Grade 1 reading achievement	Reading achievement tests in grade 6
Stevenson and Newman 1986 (N=105)	Pre-kindergarten cognitive measures Elementary achievement Mother's and teacher's ratings in grades 2-5	Gr 10 test scores in reading and math Gr 10 self-concept and expectancy for success in reading
Wadsworth 1986 (N=1675; U.K.)	Preschool attendance	Higher verbal skills at age 8
Entwisle and Hayduk 1988 (N=654)	Parent's estimate of child's ability in grade 3 Teacher's mark expectations in grades 1 and 2	English and math achievement tests 4-9 years later, current ability level controlled
Cairns, Cairns, and Neckerman 1989(N=475)	Elementary school retention	High school dropout
Barrington and Hendericks 1989 (N=214)	Grade 3 ITBS achievement test scores	High school dropout
Morris, Ehren, Lenz, and Keith 1991(N=785)	Grade 4 reading achievement scores	High school dropout
Simner and Barnes 1991 (N=193)	Grade 1 reading and math marks	High school dropout
Ensminger and Slusarcick 1992 (N=917; African-American, urban)	Grade 1 math mark Grade 1 aggressive behavior (especially for males)	High school dropout
Weller, Schnittjer, and Tuten 1992 (N = 415)	Metropolitan Reading Readiness, beginning of grade 1 Received remediation (Chapter 1) in grade 3	CTBS reading and math scores, grade 10 ($r = .57$) CTBS reading and math scores. Yr 10 ($r =.56$)

(continues)

Study	Early Schooling	Lasting Effect
(continued) Brooks-Gunn, Guo, and Furstenberg 1993 (N=254; African-American)	Pre-school attendance Pre-school cognitive ability No elementary grade retention	High school graduation Post-secondary education
Roderick 1993 (N=757)	Grade 4 academic marks Grade retention, K-grade 3	High school dropout
Reynolds 1994 (N=1106; African-American, low-income)	Follow-on intervention in grades 1-3 (school-based comprehensive service program providing instructional support and parental involvement)	ITBS reading and math, grade 5 Cumulative grade retention, grade 5

Schools and Childhood

Most books about inequality and schooling aim to explain how social stratification comes about and then what makes it persist. This book's mission is different. Its aim is to understand how social structure affects human development in middle childhood, in particular how children's development proceeds as they go through elementary school. Childhood is a life period that lasts for many years, 25% of the life span or more. It is a period of primary importance in and of itself, quite apart from any effects it has on the subsequent life course. Our question is not only how early schooling dovetails with stratification, but what children's lives are like in school. A contest-mobility (or meritocratic) system may cause children to come closer to developing their full potential than a sponsored-mobility system does, but not necessarily, and both systems concentrate on the end product rather than on quality of life in childhood. While we are far, far from knowing the optimum mix of childhood experiences, the ideal of equal opportunity is still a primary guide. The most important outcome of the Beginning School Study, in our eyes, is establishing that family resources and *not* school resources presently lead to violation of the equal-opportunity ideal.

This book concludes that the variation across test scores by socioeconomic status when children begin first grade is mainly explained by family resources and related factors. It also concludes that despite the school's remarkable capability to prompt equal growth in children whatever their socioeconomic backgrounds, family and neighborhood resources that act in periods when children are not in school prompt children from more advantaged backgrounds to gain ground. This book, then, like many others, points to family socioeconomic status as a major factor in predicting children's achievement, but this fact is hardly news. What is news is that family background affects achievement *only* in summer and that living in a poor neighborhood likewise hinders achievement because it does not support cognitive growth in periods when school is closed. These findings point to a new path to take in the efforts to improve the overall achievement of poor children.

Summer School

It has been very perplexing that when poor students attend summer school it adds little or nothing to their achievement levels. As noted, Heyns (1987) concluded from a careful analysis of a wide spectrum of summer programs that summer school has not been effective in reducing differences in children's achievement associated with social inequality. This conclusion remains true today. What no summer program has addressed so far, however, is the *unique contribution* that parents and neighborhoods make when school is cut off. We found that better-off Beginning School Study children went on more trips, more often went to the library in summer, and also that children who lived in better neighborhoods played more organized sports in summer. Without at all implying that these activities are the only or even the main ones that matter, these activities are not the same as classroom activities. One obvious need, then, is for intense ethnographic study of the home environments that children experience in summer. The physical possessions of better-off families—computers, books and the like—may be of some importance in producing the "summer advantage," but parents who view themselves as partners in the learning process and who possess the other kinds of psychological resources that support learning probably explain most of the "summer advantage." Parents also contribute to the ambience of the neighborhood, even by selecting themselves into it in the first place. Poor children suffer from the dearth of resources in their neighborhoods as well as in their families. The inverse correlation between neighborhood quality and children's growth when school is in session supports the idea that schools probably overcome to some extent shortfalls in neighborhood resources as well as shortfalls in family resources. A lack of resources in both families and neighborhoods is a double burden for poor children.

Transitions

To date research on school transitions deals mainly with the move from elementary to middle or junior high (see Eccles, Midgeley, and Adler 1984).

Research on this transition closely examines socio-emotional or affective outcomes along with cognitive outcomes because adolescence is the life period when youngsters' developing sense of identity and self-worth occupy center stage. Generally a drop in self-image accompanies the junior high transition, but susceptibility to that decline in psychological well-being depends on youngsters' own characteristics (Simmons and Blyth 1987), on family characteristics (Rosenberg and Simmons 1971), and on social structural characteristics of schools like peer group membership (Eccles et al. 1984), as well as upon the interactions among these variables.

In light of the remarkable pay-offs from research on the junior high transition, the dearth of research on the first-grade transition is startling. As far as we know, except for Reynolds (1992) who focused on African American disadvantaged youth, the Beginning School Study is the first large-scale attempt to examine how children's transition into full-time schooling influences their development over the subsequent life course. At age 6, children's cognitive development is proceeding at a fast pace, much faster than it proceeds two or three years later. Beginning School Study data also show convincingly that children's relative standing when they start school forecasts where they will be at later points in their school careers. School helps all children gain the same amounts, so those who start ahead tend to stay ahead even though those who start behind profit just as much from school as their more fortunate classmates. Both this fact and the importance of early schooling for establishing the path of children's long-term educational trajectories make it imperative to focus more sociological research on the pre- and primary school periods.

Policy Implications

Of the many ways to improve the school climate in poor neighborhoods, the main one is to correct the mistaken public perception that elementary schools are falling down on the job. Children's families and the public at large need to be made aware that the deficits in school performance of poor children are not the fault of the school. By our analyses, elementary schools are doing a much better job than they have been credited with. The importance of this belief is hard to overstate because schools have become the target to blame for most of society's intractable problems. Think how much more pleasant schools would be if they were deservedly credited with being good at what they are doing and if poor children were credited with their actual progress in school, *which matches that of better-off children*. Children, too, would be happier in school if they sensed an aura of respect and community enthusiasm for their work and for the school. This suggestion is not fanciful because most parents and students have positive feelings about schools and teachers when children start first grade and this attitude could be preserved.

Getting the facts out could also help in dealing with boys' poorer performance in reading in elementary school. To a considerable extent, teachers' difficulty in dealing with young boys in classrooms probably is an organizational problem. Various remedies suggest themselves. The day's schedule could be modified to allow more physical activity and moving about. Ways could be found to intersperse physical activity with seat work. A mid-morning break with some food is common in kindergarten, and a similar morning break might help children in first grade.

The issue of redshirting could also be addressed immediately by disseminating information. Parents and teachers should be aware that time spent in school rather than children's age governs how much they achieve, and that younger children *gain* as much as older children do once they start school. The grade structure could be modified so as to increase the age ranges of children in a class, and also to reduce the number of early transitions.

Retention

The thorny issue of retention is treated extensively in our book *On the Success of Failure*. (See Alexander, Entwisle, and Dauber 1994.) Here we have added some new information about how retention patterns differ by gender and by family structure, and also emphasized that retention is an internal track in elementary schools that overlaps other tracks like "ability" grouping.

Still, the issue of equity in schooling calls for a few additional words about retention. Many people are negatively disposed toward retention, because they do not fully understand that retained children have serious problems long before they are retained. Retention signals these pre-existing problems. Abolishing retention will not erase the problems that lead schools to practice it, and to the extent that it helps children do better, it seems preferable to social promotion. But if we understood better how it works and when it is necessary, repeating *part* of a grade or even just *one* subject area could be one way to help children who get off to a shaky start to get back on track without shunting them off the main line.

Another way to reduce retention is to make strong efforts to get all children up to speed at the beginning of first grade. In effect, the developmental level of all children needs to be brought up to that of better-off children by the time they start first grade and *we know how to do this*. Beginning School Study research points to work habits as a priority area to be developed as children start first grade, or preferably before. Our analysis indicates that focusing on this topic would pay large dividends. The rate of retention in first grade for Beginning School Study children raised in "grandmother" homes is far below the rate for children in other single-parent families. What exactly is the "grandmother curriculum?" Is it in effect a home-based "preschool" in that children are held to reasonable standards of behavior and rewarded by someone else besides the parent for doing so? Or is it provision of care in a single place by the same adult? Or is it a diffuse effect produced by replacing the absent father with a pseudo-parent?

Our major suggestion with respect to retention is to provide more preschool for economically disadvantaged children, especially boys--the goal of original Headstart programs in the 1960s. The Consortium's (1983) central finding is that attending preschool led to a reduction in retention rates, and this finding has been replicated many times (Barnett 1996). As we said (Chapter 4), the lack of good preschools for poor 3 and 4-year-olds is an important means by which social inequality undercuts schooling, and high school drop-outs and/or teenage parents are the least likely to enroll their children in center-based programs (U.S. Department of Education 1994b). The lack of facilities for schooling of disadvantaged youngsters prior to kindergarten as well as their tendency *not* to take full advantage of public kindergarten and available preschools is a major way that differential tracking by income levels takes an early hold upon children. A few extra test points conferred by preschool or kindergarten attendance could be enough to protect economically disadvantaged youngsters against low placements or retention in the first couple of grades. (See Entwisle 1995.) In other words, the cognitive boost children get from preschool is one way to ease the first grade transition. A giant step would be taken if children whose backgrounds are problematic could be helped to improve their skills before the time they began first grade. With kindergarten so widely available, the means are there. All children must be encouraged (required?) to attend full-day kindergartens, preferably in the same schools where they will start first grade.

A Short List of Suggestions

Even without further research, the suggestions below could be implemented.

(1) Keep school transitions to a minimum, including those between kindergarten and first grade. Avoid school organizational patterns that create

"extra" transitions, especially for children who are in the poorest neighborhoods.

(2) Introduce practices that would make the social climate and quality of life in all schools more like that in the best schools. For example, in some Baltimore schools, the principal shakes hands and greets students by name when they come through the front door in the morning.

(3) Educate parents about the negative impact of household moves.

(4) Make kindergarten programs compulsory and extend them to full-day and full-year.

(5) Improve the activities available to children in poor neighborhoods in summer, especially organized sports for both sexes.

Schooling and Social Equity

This book began by pointing to its roots in three intellectual traditions: ecological studies in mainstream child development, status attainment research in sociology and a growing body of findings from investigators who take a life course perspective. The mainstream studies established that social variables far outweigh biological or medical variables in explaining young children's learning problems and school deficits. In particular, they identified family economic status and parent configuration as key variables for understanding young children's ability to profit from school. Status attainment research contributed techniques to clarify the structure and estimation of models to explain schooling, and thereby led to the discovery of the strong seasonal variations in school achievement. The life course approach suggested focusing intensively on the early grades, and on the overlapping social contexts in which children develop. A life course approach joined the mainstream child development and status attainment traditions, and enriched both.

A fascination with inequality in society is part of the human condition and along with it goes a fascination for how social inequality is perpetuated (Kerckhoff 1993). The imagery is strong that a set of occupational slots at the top of the school ladder is ready for people to move into. This image to us seems to be upside down. Seeing society as a set of occupational pigeon holes is not useful. High schools reflect the stratification patterns in the larger society, but this book sees the critical sorting processes at the *beginning* rather than near the end of children's school careers.

A focus on the first grade transition reveals that elementary schools are layered according to the population's economic resources, and this layering stems from stratification *between* neighborhoods. Families sort themselves by socioeconomic status into neighborhoods that then determine the kind of schooling their children receive. This early sorting is a kind of "sponsoring," *but not in terms of demands of the larger society* (i.e. that certain slots must be filled by certain types of people), but rather in terms of parents' power to enhance the development of their own children. Choice of neighborhood is far more important than choice of school, and most of what defines a neighborhood are the *differences that separate it from other neighborhoods*.

Organizational theorists visualize the internal structure of schools as vertical or horizontal because they assume that organizational structure is determined by the needs of an organization. This approach may be rational for some organizations but does not work for schools because the internal structure of schools, or of school systems, depends on the structure of the society in which they sit rather than on their own "production goals." When elementary schools became common at the beginning of the 19th century, they fulfilled the need to prepare youth (boys) to function as citizens in a participatory democracy, but they also occupied children's time in winter months when farms lay dormant. Later in the 19th century, when the steady flow of immigrants from abroad led to an oversupply of labor, schools kept children from competing for jobs in factories. Thus, social forces largely unrelated to children or their needs dictated both when schools became universal and how long children stayed there. Schools' internal organizational structure is still being driven by economic and social pressures. Parents try to maximize their own and their family's social status, which leads them to place their children on what they perceive to be the most effective paths to compete successfully in the markets of 20th or 21st century life. Parents struggle to send their children to ivy league schools, or even the preschools that lead up to the ivy, not so much because they are deeply committed to their children's intellectual development or to what their children might learn, but because of their perception that adult success draws mainly on social capital rather than on human capital once school is over. Also they themselves draw prestige from the quality of the child's college or preparatory school. Schools are institutions that serve to perpetuate the social status quo, but we believe the engine that drives the system is located mainly in the individual family and in its elementary schools, rather than later in its secondary schools.

Elementary schools also tend to maximize social homogeneity and this distribution does not serve children well. As we have repeatedly said, however, schools are not the problem. The distribution of resources across families and neighborhoods is the problem. Problems in families and neighborhoods cannot be solved only by tinkering with schools.

Notes

1. The observation that in low-income countries the effects of schools on achievement in primary school is comparatively greater than in high-income countries is also consistent with our ideas about home versus school learning (Heyneman and Loxley 1983).

Appendixes:
The Beginning School Study

The Beginning School Study (BSS) is a prospective longitudinal study of children's academic and social development beginning in first grade and continuing through high school graduation and beyond. Data collection began in 1982 and is ongoing. In June 1994 the panel of youngsters completed their twelfth year of schooling. This book focuses mainly on the elementary years.

The Beginning School Study archive includes a wide array of measures covering students from the time they entered first grade through high school and beyond. The measures listed in the Appendixes are those most relevant to the central themes of this book. Because some youngsters are retained in grade each year, throughout the book "years" are used to indicate the chronology of children's schooling rather than "grade." Thus children who were held back in first grade in their second year of schooling would be in "year 2" not "grade 1."

Appendix A:
Study Design

Characteristics of Beginning School Study Sample

In 1982 a two-stage random sample of youngsters beginning first grade in the Baltimore City Public Schools (BCPS) was selected for study. First, a sample of 20 schools, stratified by racial mix (6 predominantly African-American, 6 white, 8 integrated) and by socioeconomic status (14 inner-city or working class and 6 middle class) was selected. (See Figure A.1 for geographical location of schools within Baltimore.) The percentage of African-American students averaged 99.5% in the six African-American schools, 6% in the white schools, and 48% in the eight integrated schools (range 17% to 87%). (See Table B.2 for further information on individual schools.) Second, within each school, students were randomly sampled from every first-grade classroom (at least 2, usually 3) using kindergarten lists from the previous spring supplemented by class rosters after school began in the fall. Three percent of parents refused to have their youngsters participate.

The final sample consisted of 790 students beginning first grade for the first time (non-repeaters) in the fall of 1982. While the city public school system as a whole enrolled about 77% African Americans (U.S. Bureau of the Census, 1983), the Beginning School Study oversampled whites so 55% of students in the Beginning School Study were African American. (The 1980 Census found Baltimore City was 55% African-American.) Parents' educational levels ranged from less than eighth grade to graduate and professional school degrees, averaging just under 12 years (11.9), with a standard deviation of 2.59. African-American parents had a slightly higher mean level of education than whites (12.1 years versus 11.7). More white than African-American parents had completed four or more years of college (14.7% versus 10.3%), but whites were represented much more heavily among those with the least education. Over a third (35.3%) of whites had completed ten or fewer years of school compared to 17.2% of African-Americans. School records indicated that 67% of Beginning School Study families qualified for free or reduced price meals at school, 77% of African Americans and 53% of whites. Overall, about 56% of Beginning School Study youngsters resided in two-parent households at the beginning of first grade, 70% of whites and 44% of African Americans. (See Table A.1)

Figure A.1   Location of Original 20 Beginning School Study Schools

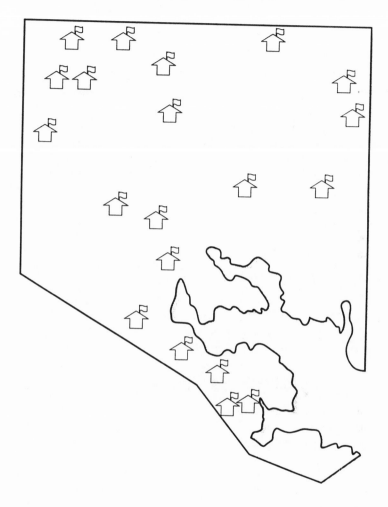

School Locations

Table A.1   Characteristics of Sample by Ethnic Group

	Whites			African Americans			Group Total		
	Mean	S.D.	N	Mean	S.D.	N	Mean	S.D.	N
California Achievement Test Scores									
Reading, fall Year 1	282	43.0	294	280	39.4	381	281	41.0	675
Reading, fall Year 3	398	58.8	243	378	51.9	346	386	55.7	589
Math, fall Year 1	297	35.7	310	290	28.2	383	293	32.0	693
Math, fall Year 3	388	43.8	244	373	39.1	346	380	41.7	590
Reading grade, Year 1, Q 1	2.02	.67	322	1.77	.72	380	1.88	.71	702
Math grade, Year 1, Q 1	2.42	.82	322	2.10	.83	380	2.24	.84	702
Proportion Female	.51	.50	358	.50	.50	432	.51	.50	790
Proportion mother alone[a]	.14	.35	345	.24	.43	409	.20	.40	754
Proportion two parents[a]	.70	.46	345	.44	.50	409	.56	.50	754
Proportion mother and other adults[a]	.12	.33	345	.28	.45	409	.21	.41	754
Proportion meal subsidy, Year 3	.53	.50	296	.77	.42	405	.67	.47	701
Occupational prestige scores									
Mother's job	33.5	16.6	261	30.7	15.2	349	31.9	15.8	610
Father's job	37.6	19.8	266	28.8	14.9	252	33.3	18.1	518
Parent's education (yrs.)	11.67	2.87	346	12.09	2.32	407	11.89	2.59	753
Parent's ability estimate, Year 1	3.50	.80	345	3.78	.86	409	3.65	.84	754
Parent's expectation for student's marks									
Reading, Year 1	2.64	.80	345	2.70	.72	406	2.67	.76	751
Math, Year 1	2.70	.77	343	2.73	.67	406	2.72	.72	749

[a]In 4% of cases mother was absent. Among single mothers, 25% had never been married at the time students began first grade (1982). Of these, 86% were African American and 14% were white.

Note: Ethnicity was determined from school records. In 1982, Year 1 of the BSS, 54.7% of children were African American, and 44.4% were white. The few (7) of other ethnicities were 4 Asians, 2 Native American, and 1 Hispanic.

Data Collection Procedures

Beginning in the summer and fall of 1982, data were collected by face-to-face interviews with students and parents. Teachers responded to questionnaires, and school records were examined for data on marks, test scores, and the like. In later years, most of the parent questionnaires were answered by mail or by phone.

A full data collection schedule is shown in Chart A.1, and Figure A.2 summarizes the yearly schedule of data collection through year 9. Parents were surveyed in the summer or early fall of each year beginning in 1982. Fall interviews always took place before the end of the first marking period and spring interviews took place between the third and fourth (final) marking periods. The timing of student and parent questionnaires ensured measurement of parents' and children's mark expectations before receipt of report cards (see Figure A.2).

Students were interviewed in the fall of 1982 before the end of the first marking period, again in the spring of 1983, and fall and spring of the following year (1983-84). Then they were interviewed twice in their fourth and sixth years (1985-86, 1987-88). In year 6 students began to enter middle school. In year 7 only those who were making the elementary to middle school transition were interviewed twice. Mainly these students were retainees, but some were youngsters enrolled in elementary schools that still covered grades 1 to 6. For all other students, in year 7 only height and weight were measured in the fall, and an abbreviated interview was conducted in the spring. In the third and fifth years there were no student interviews or questionnaires, but height and weight were measured in year 5, and data from school records were collected every year, including years 3 and 5. Only parents were interviewed in year 3.

Teachers filled out three questionnaires in the first two years of the Beginning School Study. In the other years when students were interviewed (fourth and sixth years), teachers filled out one questionnaire per year.

Chart A.2 lists the major categories of information available in the Beginning School Study archive for the elementary years.

Sample Attrition

Students in the Baltimore City Public Schools are highly mobile. Data on school moves, both within-year and between-year transfers, were obtained from BCPS records. By the end of the fifth year of the Beginning School Study, children enrolled in the original 20 schools had dispersed to 112 schools within the system as well as to an unknown number of schools outside the system.

Over the period of the Study, follow-up practices changed. During the first three years of the study, resource limitations allowed only students who remained in the original 20 schools to be followed. Beginning in year 4, however, all Study students who remained in City schools were followed. Also, students who had transferred out of the original 20 schools during the first three years of the study were located and re-enrolled in the study, backfilling data available from school records or other sources.

176

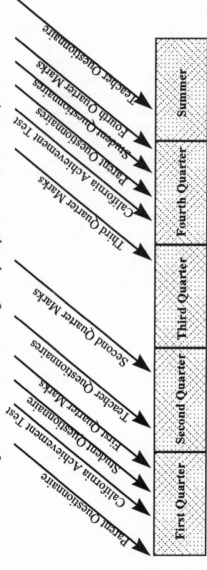

Figure A.2 Timeline Showing Yearly Sequence of Data Collection, Years 1-9

Note: This timeline represents the relative time placement of all possible instruments and data collected, and not all data were obtained each year. During 1984-85 and 1986-87, only school record data were collected.

Chart A.1   Timeline for Beginning School Study Field Work and Coverage of Primary Data Sources (a Cohort of 790 Cases)*

Field Work & Data Sources	Yr.1 (82-83)		Yr.2 (83-84)		Yr.3 (84-85)		Yr.4 (85-86)		Yr.5 (86-87)		Yr.6 (87-88)		Yr.7[c] (88-89)		Yr.8 (89-90)		Yr.9 (90-91)		Yr.10 (91-92)		Yr.11 (92-93)		Yr.12 (93-94)		Yr.13 (94-95)		Yr.14 (95-96)	
	Fall	Sprg	Fall	Sprg	Fall	Sprg	Fall	Sprg	Fall	Sprg	Fall	Sprg	Fall	Sprg	Fall	Sprg	Fall	Sprg	Fall	Sprg	Fall	Sprg	Fall	Sprg	Fall	Sprg	Fall	Sprg
Student Interviews[a]	788	784	638	605		575		563		490		486	250	175	609	407	640	637		635		625		597		275[d]		pending[e]
Parent Questionnaires[a]	756		627	477		327	471				451		219		504		463		651		618							
Teacher Questionnaires	52	49	44	44			140				203		87		158		400											
# students covered		684		531			398				381		161		336		478											
BCPS Records[b]	705		596		617		557		510		538		479		462		442		362		≈401		≈277		pending[e]		pending[e]	
CAT Scores[b]	693	732	662	644	589	556	589	539	604	589	495	496		446		405			603[f]									
Life History Calendar																							552					
Tracking																										663		336*

[a] Through Year 7, only students (and their parents) in Baltimore City Public Schools were interviewed. Beginning in Year 8, coverage extends to all of the original cohort.

[b] Diminishing coverage over time reflects transfer out of the BCPS (and in the upper grades, dropout). School record information and testing data now are available for 153 members of the cohort who left the BCPS at some point. These data are now being processed and will be available for analysis when the proposed project commences.

[c] Figures in Year 7 are low because only youngsters who were making the transition to middle school that year were interviewed.

[d] In Year 13, just youngsters still in high school and dropouts were interviewed.

[e] These data are presently being processed.

[f] The CAT tests were not administered by BCPS from Year 9 forward. The BSS administered CAT tests during the Spring '91 through Fall '92 period.

* No BSS data collection for shaded periods.

Chart A.2   Major Categories of Information Available in the BSS Archive for Elementary Years

Category	Description
Cognitive Measures of Children	California Achievement Test, every grade, semi-annually (early fall and late spring) Teacher's marks, every grade, four quarters Retention/Promotion status, every grade Reading Levels, all years, four quarters Special Program Assignment (DEC, LLD, etc.), all years
Physical Development	Height, Weight, Handedness, measured fall and spring most years
Other School Record Data (collected in all years unless specified otherwise)	Student gender and ethnic identification Absence Lateness Student deportment, work habits, parent conference requests Special Problems (many areas, including speech, vision, social worker to home, attendance worker, special psychological testing, referrals to internal committees) Racial composition of schools and classrooms Classroom organization (reading groups - years 1 and 2); Curriculum tracking School moves and transfers
Non-Cognitive Measures of Children	Personal maturity/temperament ratings by teachers and parents (Zill Scale) Locus of Control scale, drawn from Stanford preschool measures for early grades; Rotter items later Self-esteem, Dickstein measure throughout; Rosenberg items later Various Harter Self-Esteem Scales, beginning yr 2 Achievement Responsibility Scales (Crandall), most years Depression (Kandel), beginning in year 6 Educational Expectations, all study years Body Image, all study years School Satisfaction (Epstein and McPartland), all study years

(continues)

Category	Description
(continued) **Family Background** (included in most or all parent interviews unless specified otherwise)	Mother's Education Father's Education Mother's Occupation Father's Occupation Poverty status of family (eligibility for free/reduced price meals) from BCPS Employment Status Household Moves, years 6 - 12 Household Possessions, years 8 - 10
Family Structure (included in most or all parent/student interviews)	Number of siblings Parent Configuration/Household Composition (Mother-Father, Mother-extended, Mother alone, others) Mother's age at child's birth Parent's marital status, separation, and divorce
Life History Calendar (Retrospective life histories by mothers, collected during years 11-12)	Mother's educational history Marital history: separation, divorce, live-in partners, contact with father Children: number, dates of birth, child care arrangements Household moves Mother's employment history Financial assistance: unemployment compensation, welfare/AFDC, child support/alimony, food stamps, public housing, etc. Retrospective estimate of total household income during year study child born, year began first grade, year finished elementary school, last year's income
Parents' Attitudes and Psychological Status (included in most or all parent interviews)	Expectations for their children (performance, educational level, occupations) Locus of Control (Rotter) Attribution of Responsibility Depression (Kandel) Life stress/personal problems of parents

(continues)

Category	Description
(continued) **Student's Home Environment** (collected in most or all parent/student interviews)	Chores Summer Activities Time on homework/where do homework, years 4 and beyond Stressful life events, parents, years 4 and beyond Retrospective history of child care arrangements, from birth, years 6 and 7 Parental supervision and monitoring of child Rating of student's peer popularity
Teacher Coverage (included in most or all teacher questionnaires)	Educational Background Work Experience Personal/biographical information (gender, marital status, family SES) Life Stress/personal problems Job Stress Classroom management practices and school climate Locus of Control (Rotter) Achievement Responsibility Scale (Crandall) Attitudes regarding study children

By the beginning of year 6 (fall 1987) 490 of the original 790 students (62%) remained in Baltimore City schools and were still enrolled in the Study. Those leaving the sample were disproportionately white and from higher educational and economic groups (See Table A.2). The original sample was 55% African American, had 67% on meal subsidy, and the mean parent education level was 11.9 years; the year 6 sample was 67% African American, had a meal subsidy level of 74%, and parents on average attended 11.6 years of school.

Beginning in the fall of 1988 (year 7) *all* Beginning School Study students were followed, including those who had left BCPS. A major effort was initiated at that time to trace and re-enroll students who had earlier dropped out of the study. By the end of year 13 (spring 1995), this continuing effort to re-enroll students had located 663 (84%) of the original 790 participants in the Beginning School Study . The follow-up rate of over 80% after thirteen years matches or exceeds other high-quality national surveys that cover much shorter intervals of time.

The original random sample compares well with the sample still active after 13 years. There are very few differences between these two groups on key variables measured in the fall of 1982 (see Table A.2), either in terms of means or standard deviations. For example, both groups have nearly identical scores (281 and 282) on the Reading Comprehension subtest of the California Achievement Test administered in the fall of 1982 when all students began first grade. Similarly, both the original

181

Table A.2 Attrition Analysis: Characteristics of Original Beginning School Study (BSS) Sample, Year 6 Sample, Year 13 Sample, and Students Who Left Beginning School Study by Year 13

	Original Sample			Yr 6 Sample			Yr 13 Sample			t-test	Not in Yr 13 Sample		
	Mean	S.D.	N	Mean	S.D.	N	Mean	S.D.	N		Mean	S.D.	N
California Achievement Test Scores													
Reading, Fall Yr 1	281	41.0	675	279	39.3	437	282	42.4	573		278	31.4	102
Reading, Fall Yr 3	386	55.7	589	381	54.6	448	388	55.8	519	*	372	53.2	70
Math, Fall Yr 1	293	32.0	693	290	30.8	447	294	32.5	586	*	284	26.9	107
Math, Fall Yr 3	380	41.7	590	376	39.7	449	382	42.1	519	*	362	34.1	71
Reading Mk, Yr 1 Q 1	1.88	.71	702	1.81	.71	452	1.91	.71	591	*	1.75	.67	111
Math Mk, Yr 1 Q 1	2.24	.84	702	2.17	.87	452	2.27	.84	591	+	2.11	.82	111
Proportion African-Am.	.55	.50	790	.67	.47	490	.55	.50	663		.51	.50	127
Proportion female	.51	.50	790	.52	.50	490	.53	.50	663		.37	.48	127
Proportion mother alone[a]	.20	.04	754	.22	.42	466	.19	.39	638	*	.25	.43	116
Proportion two parents[a]	.56	.50	754	.52	.50	466	.57	.50	638		.49	.50	116
Prop. mother/other adult[a]	.21	.41	754	.21	.41	466	.21	.40	638		.22	.41	116
Prop. meal subsidy, Yr 3	.67	.47	701	.74	.44	481	.65	.48	597	*	.76	.43	104
Occupational Prestige Scores (TSEI2)													
Mother's job	31.9	15.8	610	29.9	14.5	427	32.4	16.1	553	*	27.5	12.4	57
Father's job	33.3	18.1	518	29.8	15.2	343	33.6	18.2	475		30.0	16.6	43
Parent's education	11.9	2.59	753	11.6	2.44	464	12.0	2.62	636	*	11.4	2.40	117
Parent's abil est, Yr 1	3.65	.84	754	3.64	.85	467	3.67	.84	638		3.56	.87	116
Parent's expectations for student's marks													
Reading, Yr 1	2.67	.76	751	2.65	.74	465	2.71	.74	635	*	2.50	.84	116
Math, Yr 1	2.72	.72	749	2.65	.70	464	2.75	.70	632		2.56	.80	117

* p≤.05; + p≤.10
[a] In 4% of cases, mother was absent.
Note: Year 13 Sample contains 663, 84% of the Original Sample. T-tests compare year 13 Sample with those not in Year 13 Sample.

sample and the year 13 sample are 55% African-American. The proportion on meal subsidy differs by only two percentage points (67% and 65%). The number of years of parental education was also very close, 11.9 for the original sample versus 12.0 for the year 13 sample.

Although the year 13 sample closely matches the original sample, the 127 students who were lost from the sample do differ significantly from those remaining in the Beginning School Study. For example, they are disproportionately male (63% vs 47%), have parents with lower levels of education (11.4 years vs 12.00), are more often on meal subsidy (76% vs 65%), and have lower beginning Math scores (284 vs 294). (See Table A.2.)

Appendix B:
Indicators of Social Structure

Family Socioeconomic Status

Family Income: Meal Subsidy Status

Neither parents nor children were queried directly about family income until year 11 (1993) when retrospective data on family income were procured from the mothers of all students using a "Life History Calendar." (See section on Life History Calendar for further information on these questions.) Beginning in year 3 (1984-85), however, school records provided information regarding children's participation in the federal meal subsidy program. Children were eligible for free or reduced price meals based on family income and size. For example, in July 1, 1984, a family of four with a yearly income of $13,260 was eligible for full subsidy; one with an income of $18,870 was eligible for partial subsidy. The first figure is 1.30 times the federal poverty guideline and the second is 1.85 times this guideline. These income figures are revised annually by the federal government. School lunch information was available for at least one year for 716 (90.6%) of the full sample. The meal subsidy program participation rate of Beginning School Study students closely matches the overall meal subsidy rate for all Baltimore City children. For example, during year 5 (1986-87), 68.7% of Study students qualified for subsidized school lunches (see Table B.1), and the overall participation rate for Baltimore City elementary schools was 66.8% (Baltimore City Public Schools 1988).

Parent Education

During the first year of the study, parent education data were collected for one parent, usually (86%) the mother. Beginning in Spring 1984 the respondent parent was asked about the education level of both parents. Using pooled parent education data over the first eight years of the study, the mean years of education completed by mothers (95% of students) is 11.7 years; mean years of fathers' education (67% of students) is 12.2 years.

Parent Employment and Occupation

Beginning in year 1 parents were asked whether or not they worked, for how many hours, and whether or not there was another wage earner in the household. Specific information on parent occupation was gathered for both mother and father (if both lived with the student) beginning in year 2. Beginning in year 9 parental occupation was asked for parents who had any regular contact with the student. Parent responses were classified into 3-digit U.S. Bureau of the Census (1970) occupational codes, and these were transformed into Duncan SEI (Hauser and Featherman 1977) and updated Featherman-Stevens TSEI (Featherman and Stevens 1982) occupational status scores.

Table B.1   Income Eligibility[a] Guidelines for Free and Reduced Price Meals
               for a Family of Four and the Percent of Beginning School Study
               Sample Qualifying

Year	Free Meals	Reduced Price	Percent BSS Eligible for Meal Subsidy[b]
1984-85	$13,260	$18,870	67.0
1985-86	$13,845	$19,703	66.4
1986-87	$14,300	$20,350	68.7
1987-88	$14,560	$20,720	72.2
1988-89	$15,145	$21,553	62.8
1989-90	$15,730	$22,386	55.5

[a] The income eligibility guidelines for free and reduced price meals are developed by the U.S. Department of Agriculture and published in the Federal Register. The guidelines are obtained by multiplying the federal income poverty level by 1.85 for reduced price and 1.30 for free meals.
[b] Data come from information provided by Baltimore City Public Schools.

Pooling data over the first 9 years, information is available on mother's occupation for 610 students and for father's occupation for 518 students.

The parent occupation measures correlate well with the parent education measures. For mothers, the correlation between occupation and education ranges between .50 and .59. For fathers, these correlations are even higher--.59 to .71-- and compare quite favorably with those reported for fathers (.49 to .53) by Duncan, Featherman, and Duncan (1972).

Composite Socioeconomic Status Measure

A composite socioeconomic scale combines 5 variables: meal subsidy status and mother's and father's education and occupational status. Each variable is standardized and then the mean of the z-scores computed. If data were missing for any variable(s), the mean of the available variables was used. Nearly complete (99.5%) coverage is available for this composite socioeconomic measure, and its alpha reliability based on the full set of five items is .87 (N=386), and is from .74 to .84 even for 3 items. Two or more items were present for over 95% of the sample.

Home Possessions

Beginning in year 8, students were asked a series of 15 questions (adapted from National Opinion Research Center 1988) about possessions in the home, as follows: a place to study, newspaper, magazine subscription, encyclopedia/atlas, dictionary, typewriter, computer, dishwasher, clothes dryer, washing machine, microwave oven, over 50 books, VCR, pocket calculator, and room of own. In year 9, several new items were added: refrigerator, color TV, black and white TV, video camera, CD player, gun or rifle, telephone, file cabinet, and two or more bathrooms.

Beginning in year 9 parents were asked a similar series of questions about possessions in the home. This scale has not been directly used in estimating models cited in this book, but has been used as an indicator of specific conditions in homes of various socioeconomic levels.

Contextual Variables

Baltimore is unusual among American cities in the strength and viability of its neighborhoods. The city is a patchwork of clearly recognizable neighborhoods, most possessing a shared ethnic, cultural, and class identity as well as a colorful history. Cognizant of these community patterns, the City's official planning agencies have developed a network of health, recreational, and social services around the neighborhoods, and, most important for us, school catchment areas are generally drawn in terms of these same neighborhoods. For these reasons resources in schools and neighborhoods overlap. Among the 20 original schools in the Beginning School Study sample, in all cases except one, the students attending a given school resided in the neighborhood where the school was located.

To explore issues of school and neighborhood context, several variables were developed to proxy the socioeconomic level and racial mix of the original 20 schools and the neighborhoods in which they were located. (See Table B.2) All these variables were measured in 1982, and the school/neighborhood designations used for students in analyses for the first 5 years of the study were these same initial designations. Despite the considerable movement of students that occurred during the first 5 years (students had dispersed to 112 schools by the end of year 5), school context as measured by racial composition and economic level did not change much between years 1 and 5. For example, the correlation between the meal subsidy level of the schools the children attended in years 1 and 5 is .85, and the correlation between the percentage of African American students in the schools the children attended in years 1 and 5 is .92.

School Segregation Status

Baltimore has no large minority groups other than African-Americans. In 1980 African-Americans comprised 55% of the City population, whites 44%, and all other minority groups 1.3% (U.S. Bureau of the Census 1983). By 1990 the concentration of African-Americans had grown to 59%, of whites had fallen to 39%, and of other racial groups risen to 1.7% (U.S. Bureau of the Census 1991c). Two school-level dummy variables indicated whether the school was predominantly African American, predominantly white, or integrated (baseline category). The percentage of African American students averaged 99.5% in the 6 African American segregated schools, 6% in the 6 white segregated schools, and 48% in the 8 integrated schools (see Table B.1 for demographic characteristics of individual schools).

Table B.2   Characteristics of Original Schools in Beginning School Study
             Sample

School/ SES Category[a]	% Afr- Am	% Meal Subsidy	Yrs Parent Ed[b]	Neighbor- hood Househd Income[c] ($)	% Fam Below Poverty[d]	% Profess'l/ Manager[e]
Segregated African American Schools						
1 WC	100	83	11.87	11600	33.7	9.2
2 WC	99	76	11.63	11600	14.6	9.4
3 WC	100	88	11.73	10100	39.4	11.9
4 WC	99	68	11.51	11600	20.4	11.7
5 WC	100	79	11.07	7400	38.2	10.8
6 MC	99	52	12.70	15600	6.2	17.8
Average	99.5	74.3	11.75	11317	25.4	11.8
Segregated White Schools						
7 WC	1	30	10.91	14500	10.2	16.9
8 WC	4	39	10.72	12100	11.7	7.5
9 WC	5	50	10.61	12100	16.4	8.3
10 WC	6	33	10.55	16700	7.0	11.0
11 MC	10	14	12.55	17700	1.8	20.0
12 MC	10	53	10.20	14400	9.9	5.0
Average	6	36.5	10.92	14583	9.5	11.4
Integrated Schools						
13 WC	63	90	10.86	7400	39.0	9.9
14 WC	17	77	10.46	10500	22.5	6.4
15 WC	24	82	10.26	12100	11.7	7.5
16 MC	18	17	12.20	14400	11.1	15.9
17 WC	87	43	11.95	16500	3.7	28.6
18 MC	43	11	15.67	22700	2.0	63.5
19 MC	45	13	15.48	24200	2.9	57.2
20 MC	85	30	13.10	16300	8.6	31.0
Average	47.8	45.4	12.50	15512	12.7	27.5
20 School Ave.	50.8	51.4	11.80	13975	15.6	18.0

[a] SES designations for each school are either working class/inner city (WC) or middle class (MC).

[b] Average number of years of schooling for parents of study students in the school at the beginning of year 1.

[c] Median household income of neighborhood in which the school was located. Neighborhoods designations were the 26 Regional Planning Districts established for Baltimore by the Regional Planning Council and data came from the 1980 U.S. Census (Regional Planning Council 1983).

[d] Percent of families below the federal poverty level for the neighborhood in which each school is located. Neighborhood designations were developed by Baltimore City Planning Department and data came from the 1980 U.S. Census (Baltimore City Planning Department 1983).

[e] Percent of adults in professional or managerial occupations. Neighborhood designations were developed by Baltimore City Planning Department and data came from the 1980 U.S. Census (Baltimore City Department of Planning 1983).

School Level Parent Education

This school level measure is the average number of years of school completed by parents of study students measured at the beginning of year 1 in each of the 20 schools (range is from 10.2 years to 15.7 years).

School Level Meal Subsidy Rate

This is the percentage of children in each school who participated in the federal meal subsidy program in 1982-83 school year. Data come from the Baltimore City Public Schools (1988). Among the 20 Beginning School Study schools meal subsidy rates ranged from 11% to 90%. See above for a full description of meal subsidy eligibility guidelines.

Neighborhood Income

This is the median household income of the neighborhood in which the school was located (range from $7,400 to $24,200). Neighborhood designations were the 26 Regional Planning Districts established for Baltimore by the Regional Planning Council and data came from the 1980 U.S. Census (Regional Planning Council 1983). Each district included several census tracts and corresponded to commonly recognized neighborhood and community designations.

Neighborhood Family Poverty Rate

This family poverty measure is the percent of families below the federal poverty level in 1980 for the neighborhood in which each school is located. Neighborhoods are Baltimore City Department of Planning designations (266 neighborhoods) that relied on community association boundaries and generally recognized perceptions of neighborhood identity, and the data came from 1980 U.S. Census tabulations (Baltimore City Department of Planning 1983). Family poverty rates in the 20 Beginning School Study neighborhoods ranged from 1.8% to 39.4%.

Professional and Managerial Workers

This is the percentage of workers who held professional or managerial jobs for the neighborhood in which each school is located. Neighborhoods are Baltimore City Department of Planning designations that relied on community association boundaries and other generally recognized perceptions of neighborhood identity (Baltimore City Department of Planning 1983). Data comes from the 1980 U.S. Census. Percentage of professional and managerial workers varied from 5% to 63.5%.

Appendix C:
Measures of Student Performance and
Psychological Characteristics

Cognitive Growth and School Achievement

California Achievement Tests

Students' scores for the California Achievement Test (CAT) Form C (Grade 1 = *Level 11*, Grade 2 = *Level 12*, etc.) were collected from school records. To date, the Reading Comprehension and Mathematics Concepts and Applications subtests have been most often used in evaluations of Beginning School Study students' progress because (1) scale scores on these subtests are available continuously from grade one through grade 9, and (2) in first grade both of the subtests contain more items than other subtests, and were not subject to ceiling constraints.

During the first 6 years of the study, the Baltimore City Public Schools administered the California Achievement Test twice a year, fall and spring. During years 7 and 8, students took the test only in the spring. In year 9, Baltimore City Public Schools discontinued administration of the California Achievement Test system-wide, but by special arrangement school guidance counselors administered the Reading Comprehension and Math Concepts and Applications subtests to Beginning School Study students either singly or in small groups.

"Scale scores" are calibrated to measure growth over the student's 12-year school career (see California Achievement Test Technical Bulletin 1 1979, pp. 67-71). Correlations between fall and spring scores for the standardization sample in first grade are .45 and .69, respectively, for the Reading Comprehension and Math Concepts subtests. In subsequent years these correlations rise to over .80. Data for Beginning School Study students were similar--fall to spring correlations of .44 for the Reading Comprehension subtest and .63 for the Math Concepts subtest in year 1, and above .80 by year 4. The Kuder-Richardson 20 (homogeneity) reliabilities in the standardization sample are .68 and .83, respectively for Reading Comprehension and Math Concepts at the beginning of grade 1; by the end of grade 2 these reliabilities are consistently above .90 for both subtests (see Tables C.1a and C.1b for subtest reliability data on Beginning School Study sample and standardization sample).

Average scores of Beginning School Study children correspond well with those reported for the standardization sample (Tables C.1a (reading) and C.1b (math)). For Reading Comprehension at the beginning of grade 1, the Beginning School Study sample scored 3 points (1/15th of a s.d.) below the national sample; for Math Concepts and Applications, the Beginning School Study sample scored 6 points (1/6th of a s.d.) below the national sample.

Table C.1a   California Achievement Test, Form C, Reading Comprehension Subtest, Standardization Sample and BSS Sample: Means, Standard Deviations, and Reliability Data

| | Standardization Sample[a] | | | | BSS Sample | | | |
Year	Mean	S.D.	KR 20[b]	R[c]	Mean	S.D.	N	R[d]
Year 1: Fall	284	43.5	.68	0.45	281	41.0	675	0.44
Spring	336	47.2	.84		340	45.6	732	
Year 2: Fall	362	50.7	.89	0.71	345	51.5	656	0.66
Spring	388	52.7	.91		390	47.6	644	
Year 3: Fall	401	55.5	.91	0.79	386	55.7	589	0.78
Spring	424	57.2	.91		418	57.3	556	
Year 4: Fall	441	60.2	.91	0.82	421	66.3	555	0.85
Spring	460	67.5	.93		456	70.1	539	
Year 5: Fall	472	66.1	.92	0.83	455	68.6	578	0.86
Spring	488	68.4	.93		482	73.9	566	
Year 6: Fall	498	68.5	.91	0.84	481	66.6	492	0.83
Spring	514	73.1	.92		504	73.4	496	
Year 7: Fall	521	71.2	.91	0.83	--	--	--	--
Spring	534	76.8	.92		518	77.8	446	
Year 8: Fall	548	77.2	.88	0.81	--	--	--	--
Spring	563	82.6	.90		553	79.7	405	
Year 9: Fall	568	79.9	.89	0.81	--	--	--	--
Spring	577	84.5	.90		550	79.9	598[e]	

[a]From Tables 65-72, 82 and 103-111, *California Achievement Tests, Technical Bulletin 1*. Monterey, CA: CTB/McGraw-Hill, 1979. Pp. 74-81, 93-96, 120-134.

[b]Kuder-Richardson formula 20 (*KR 20*) is a measure of internal consistency. *KR 20* was used to estimate consistency of performance from item to item within each subtest.

[c]Test-retest reliability coefficient for the CAT Form C is the correlation between the fall and spring administrations of the test (6-month interval) for a national sample of students.

[d]Test-retest reliability coefficient for CAT Form C, BSS sample, is calculated each year from the fall and spring administrations of the test.

[e]The Year 9 testing of BSS students took place over a period of 18 months, from the spring of year 9 to the fall of year 11. When testing took place after the spring of year 9, scores were interpolated to correspond to what the student would have been expected to score if he had taken the test in the spring of year 9.

Table C.1b   California Achievement Test, Form C, Math Concepts and
Applications Subtest, Standardization Sample and BSS Sample:
Means, Standard Deviations, and Reliability Data

Year	Standardization Sample[a]				BSS Sample			
	Mean	S.D.	KR 20[b]	R[c]	Mean	S.D.	N	R[d]
Year 1: Fall	299	32.4	.83	0.69	293	32.0	693	0.63
Spring	334	36.4	.87		341	36.5	725	
Year 2: Fall	352	37.3	.87	0.81	341	37.2	662	0.78
Spring	376	41.6	.90		384	37.8	639	
Year 3: Fall	389	45.3	.92	0.83	380	41.7	590	0.85
Spring	413	46.6	.93		414	48.8	556	
Year 4: Fall	425	46.0	.91	0.83	413	50.9	555	0.88
Spring	444	50.7	.93		447	55.1	538	
Year 5: Fall	454	49.1	.92	0.83	448	54.8	575	0.86
Spring	473	56.8	.94		476	61.0	560	
Year 6: Fall	482	55.9	.89	0.84	476	60.0	495	0.88
Spring	499	63.1	.91		498	64.3	490	
Year 7: Fall	508	67.2	.91	0.84	--	--	--	--
Spring	522	72.5	.92		516	70.4	437	
Year 8: Fall	541	71.4	.91	0.85	--	--	--	--
Spring	556	78.4	.92		543	71.2	399	
Year 9: Fall	565	77.7	.92	0.85	--	--	--	--
Spring	577	83.6	.93		566	82.7	614[e]	

[a] From Tables 65-72, 82 and 103-111, *California Achievement Tests, Technical Bulletin 1.* 1979. Pp. 74-81, 93-96, 120-134.

[b] Kuder-Richardson formula 20 (*KR 20*) is a measure of internal consistency. *KR 20* was used to estimate consistency of performance from item to item within each subtest.

[c] Test-retest reliability coefficient for the CAT Form C is the correlation between the fall and spring administrations of the test (6-month interval) for a national sample of students.

[d] Test-retest reliability coefficient for CAT Form C, BSS sample, is calculated each year from the fall and spring administrations of the test.

[e] The year 9 testing of BSS students took place over a period of 18 months, from the spring of year 9 to the fall of year 11. When testing took place after the spring of year 9, scores were interpolated to correspond to what the student would have been expected to score if he had taken the test in the spring of year 9.

Academic Marks

Teachers gave marks in all four quarters each year, coded 4 for *excellent,* 3 for *good,* 2 for *satisfactory,* and 1 for *unsatisfactory.* During the elementary years, marks included reading, language, spelling, handwriting, mathematics, and science.

Non-Cognitive Measures

Student Academic and Occupational Expectations

Expectations for Marks. Every year students' expectations for their marks in reading, math, and conduct were obtained in interviews during the fall and spring before receipt of the first and fourth quarter report cards. Students were asked to "guess the marks you are going to get on your next report card" in reading (in later years English), math, and conduct. The expectations (mark estimates) given by students were coded in the same way as marks (see above).

Educational Aspirations. Beginning in year 4 students were asked to predict how far they thought they would go in school using a 4 point scale:

1 = finish 10th grade
2 = graduate from high school
3 = college
4 = more than college

Beginning in year 8, students were asked a series of questions about educational aspirations:

If nothing stood in your way, how far would you *like* to go in school?

Considering your situation, how far do you think you *actually will* go in school?

How far do your *parents* want you to go in school?

Students answered these questions on a 5-point scale:

1 = leave school as soon as possible
2 = finish high school
3 = get some vocational or college training after high school
4 = finish college
5 = more than college

The scale was later expanded to an 8-point scale to accommodate additional choices:

1 = leave school as soon as possible
2 = leave before high school graduation
3 = finish high school
4 = business or trade school after high school
5 = less than two years of college
6 = two or more years of college
7 = finish college (4 or 5 year degree)
8 = more than college (M.D., etc.)

School Satisfaction. A 4-item school satisfaction scale, developed from the Epstein and McPartland (1977) Quality of School Life Scale, was given beginning in year 1. Students were asked:

1. Would you say that school work is usually pretty dull or pretty interesting? If you could go to any school you wanted, would you go to this school, or some other school?
2. Do you like school a lot, think it's just OK, or not like it much at all?
3. Do you like your teacher a lot, think he/she is just OK, or not like him/her much at all?

Alpha reliabilities for this scale are in the .50 to .58 range.

Student's Occupational Aspirations. Beginning in year 2, an open-ended question was included: "If you could have any job when you grow up, what would you most like to be?" These job preferences were assigned Duncan SEI (Hauser and Featherman 1977) and updated Featherman-Stevens SEI (Featherman and Stevens 1982) occupational status scores.

Student Role Performance Measures

Absence and Lateness. The total number of *absences* and *latenesses* for each school year was taken from the end-of-year report cards. (See Table C.2.)

Conduct and Work Habits. Classroom conduct and study habits (effort, attention, class participation, "completes assignments", and "works independently") for the elementary grades were each coded 2 for *satisfactory* and 1 for *needs improvement.* A composite *Work Habits Scale* was created that summed these five study habit assessments. Internal reliability (Cronbach's alpha) for this scale is .85 or better. (See Table C.2.)

Parent-Teacher Conferences. The total number of parent conferences requested by the teacher was taken from report cards each year. (See Table C.2.)

Psychological Indicators

Chart A.2 lists psychological measures of students. Several measures relevant to this book are described below.

The Zill (1981) Scales. A 14-item scale developed by Zill and colleagues (National Survey of Children 1976) characterized the child's "behavioral and emotional adjustment to the learning and deportment demands of elementary school." Homeroom teachers and parents rated students on 14 items using a 6-interval grid format ranging from "exactly like" to "not at all like."

An initial factor analysis of *teachers'* ratings in grades one through four identified three sub-scales: *Cooperative-Compliance* (5 items), *Interest-Participation* (4 items), and *Attention Span-Restlessness* (4 items) (see Alexander, Entwisle, and Dauber 1993). Chart C.1 lists items on the 3 subscales. Alpha reliabilities are in the .74 to .85 range for years 1, 2, 4, and 6. Over the elementary years this factor structure does not differ by race, gender, or economic status (Alexander, Entwisle, and Dauber 1993).

Table C.2   Student Role Performance Measures, Years 1-5 by Gender

	Male			Female			Group Total		
	Mean	S.D.	N	Mean	S.D.	N	Mean	S.D.	N
Absence									
Year 1	12.55	11.51	346	13.98	11.73	356	13.28	11.64	702
Year 2	13.04	11.54	285	14.44	12.26	311	13.77	11.93	596
Year 3	11.32	9.66	291	13.59	11.46	308	12.49	10.68	599
Year 4	11.45	10.73	260	12.01	10.26	292	11.75	10.48	552
Year 5	11.76	11.05	240	10.29	9.49	272	10.98	10.27	512
Lateness									
Year 1	4.78	9.53	346	6.44	11.64	355	5.62	10.68	701
Year 2	4.23	8.20	287	4.98	8.28	314	4.62	8.24	601
Year 3	4.68	9.90	292	6.04	10.69	308	5.38	10.33	600
Year 4	5.11	9.50	259	5.26	10.45	292	5.19	10.00	551
Year 5	6.78	11.55	240	6.29	9.94	272	6.52	10.71	512
Conduct Mark, Quarter 4									
Year 1	1.71	.45	344	1.86	.34	355	1.79	.41	699
Year 2	1.65	.48	284	1.83	.37	309	1.74	.44	593
Year 3	1.54	.50	296	1.77	.42	318	1.66	.47	614
Year 4	1.53	.50	252	1.55	.50	284	1.54	.50	536
Year 5	1.52	.50	233	1.80	.40	267	1.67	.47	500
Work Habits, Quarter 4									
Year 1	8.56	1.79	342	9.04	1.51	354	8.81	1.67	696
Year 2	8.46	1.84	279	9.12	1.50	308	8.81	1.70	587
Year 3	7.88	2.00	288	8.91	1.65	315	8.42	1.90	603
Year 4	8.05	1.98	225	9.08	1.51	277	8.62	1.81	502
Year 5	8.04	1.86	232	8.98	1.59	265	8.55	1.78	497
Parent-Teacher Conference Requests (Proportion teacher requested conference)									
Year 1	.33	.47	344	.34	.47	357	.34	.47	701
Year 2	.30	.46	284	.23	.42	310	.26	.44	594
Year 3	.30	.46	296	.23	.42	315	.26	.44	611
Year 4	.35	.48	258	.25	.44	292	.30	.46	550
Year 5	.44	.50	228	.39	.49	258	.41	.49	486

Chart C.1   Zill Scale[a] Items, Three Dimensions Derived from Teacher
                 Responses [b]

Interest-Participation (I-P) 1. Very enthusiastic, interested in a lot of different things, likes to express his or her ideas 2. Usually in a happy mood; very cheerful 3. Is creative or imaginative 4. Keeps to himself or herself; spends a lot of time alone 5. Very timid, afraid of new things or new situations
Cooperation-Compliance (C-C) 1. Fights too much; teases, picks on or bullies other children 2. Tells lies or fibs 3. Has a very strong temper; loses it easily 4. Is polite, helpful, considerate of others
Attention Span-Restlessness (A-R) 1. Doesn't concentrate, doesn't pay attention for long 2. Rather high strung, tense, and nervous 3. Acts too young for his or her age, cries a lot or has tantrums 4. Is awfully restless, fidgets all the time, can't sit still

[a] *Source:* National Survey of Children 1976

[b] Teachers were asked to rate each study child on the qualities listed. Response options were: "exactly like," "very much like," "pretty much like," "somewhat like," "a little like," or "not at all like." Ratings were scored from 1 to 6, with high scores reflecting positive assessments.

Parents' ratings for the same 14-item Zill scale were available in years 2, 6, 8, and 9. Alpha reliabilities for the three subscales for the parent measure are in the .51 to .71 range. The higher reliabilities for the teacher data are consistent with the view that teachers hold more unitary views of children than parents do, perhaps because teachers see students mainly in a single setting (the classroom).

Peer Popularity. In the spring of each year, teachers were asked to give ratings of student popularity with peers. Teachers were asked, "On a scale from 5 (*most popular*) to 1 (*least popular*), guess the popularity of each child listed below." A list of Beginning School Study students in their classes was provided.

Dickstein Self-Esteem . The Dickstein self-esteem scale, initially developed with data from middle class elementary students in grades 1 through 6 (Dickstein 1972), was later used with a diverse sample of first, second, and third grade children from middle class and working class backgrounds between 1971 and 1976 (Entwisle and Hayduk 1978, 1982). It consists of 23 items related to skills and behaviors such as reading, running, learning new things, and so on. Scoring is from 1 ("I am very bad at ____ ") to 5 ("I am very good at ____ "). Twenty-one of these items comprise five subscales: *Character, Responsibility, Academic, Athletic,* and *Appearance* (see Chart C.2). Over the elementary years this structure appears to be invariant by race, gender, or economic status (see Pallas et al. 1990).

Chart C.2   Dickstein Self-Esteem Scale Items Included in Five Subscales

Character 1. Being polite 2. Obeying rules 3. Being kind 4. Being honest 5. Being cooperative
Responsibility 1. Being helpful 2. Being able to look after others 3. Being able to take care of yourself
Academic 1. Learning new things quickly 2. Being a good student (Yr 1) / Schoolwork 3. Doing arithmetic 4. Reading 5. Writing (Yr 1) / Handwriting
Athletic 1. Being good at sports 2. Playing ball 3. Running 4. Being strong 5. Gymnastics
Appearance 1. Being good looking 2. Being just the right weight 3. Being just the right height

Source: Dickstein 1972.

Depression Scale. Beginning in year 6 students completed a 6-item scale developed by Kandel and Davies (1982) to measure depressive mood. Students were asked how often they experienced various feelings:

Feeling too tired

Having trouble going to sleep or staying asleep

Feeling unhappy, sad or depressed

Feeling hopeless about the future

Feeling nervous or tense

Worrying too much about things

Item coding was from 1 ("a lot") to 3 ("not at all"). Kandel and Davies (1982) report Cronbach alpha reliability as .79. For the Beginning School Study student sample in year 6 the reliability is .55.

Harter Scales. Beginning in year 2 students completed the *Scholastic Competence* and the *Global Self-Worth* subscales from the *Harter Self-Perception Profile for*

Children (Harter 1985a). The Scholastic Competence subscale measures the child's perception of his/her competence or ability within the realm of scholastic performance. The Global Self-Worth scale assesses the child's global perception of self-worth or esteem as a person--the extent to which the child likes the self as a person, is happy about the way he/she is leading his/her life, and is generally happy with the way he/she is. Each subscale contains 6 items. For each item, a child states whether he or she is more like the kids described in one of two statements. For example, students are asked to choose between:

Some kids feel that they are very good at their schoolwork
BUT
Other kids worry about whether they can do the schoolwork assigned to them.

After making a first choice, the child is then asked whether the statement selected is "sort of true for me" or "really true for me." Thus four possible responses are available for each item with scoring from 1 (least adequate self-judgement) to 4 (most adequate self-judgement). See Chart C.3 for an abbreviated summary of individual scale items.

The internal consistency reliability for the Scholastic Competence scale is .80, and for the Global Self-Worth scale is .84 (Harter 1985a). Cronbach alphas for the Beginning School Study sample are in the .51 to .59 range for the Scholastic Competence scale and .55 to .70 for the Global Self-Worth scale.

In year 6, items from *Harter's Social Support Scale for Children* (Harter 1985b) were administered. The 6-item parent scale assesses the extent to which children feel their parents understand them, want to hear about their problems, care about their feelings, treat them like a person who really matters, like them the way they are, and act as though what their children do is important. Similarly, the 6-item classmate support scale taps the extent to which children's classmates like them the way they are, are friendly, don't make fun of them, listen to what they say, and ask them to join in play or games. The format for these scales was the same as that described above for the Self-Perception Profile scales. See Chart C.3 for summary of individual scale items.

Published reliabilities for the social support scales are .82 for the parent scale and .79 for the classmate scale (Harter 1985b). For the Beginning School Study sample, these reliabilities are .62 and .69, respectively.

Height, Weight, and Satisfaction with Height/Weight

Twice yearly children's height (beginning in grade 1) and weight (beginning in year 4) were measured. Beginning in year 1 students were also asked about their satisfaction with their height and their weight. These were 2 of the 23 items on the Dickstein (1972) self-esteem instrument (see above for discussion of Dickstein self-esteem scale).

Chart C.3   Scale Items from the Harter Scales [a]

| **Scholastic Competence** |
| 1. Good at schoolwork |
| 2. Just as smart as others |
| 3. Can figure out answers |
| 4. Do schoolwork quickly |
| 5. Remember things easily |
| 6. Do well at classwork |
| **Global Self-Worth** |
| 1. Happy the way I am |
| 2. Feel good the way I act |
| 3. Happy with self as a person |
| 4. Want to stay the same |
| 5. Do things fine |
| 6. Am a good person |
| **Parental Support** |
| 1. Do understand them |
| 2. Listen to problems |
| 3. Care about their feelings |
| 4. Treat them like a person |
| 5. Like the way they are |
| 6. What children do important |
| **Classmate Support** |
| 1. Like them the way they are |
| 2. Can become friends with |
| 3. Don't make fun of them |
| 4. Pay attention to what they say |
| 5. Get asked to play |
| 6. Play with at recess |

[a] *Source*: Harter 1985a, 1985b.

Appendix D:
School Record Information

Grade retention status and Special Education assignment are available every year (see Table D.1). Retention rates are highest in grades 1 and 2--nearly 17% in first grade and 10% in second grade. Special Education placements were most often made after grades 1 or 2, and usually occurred after at least one retention.

By the beginning of year 8, 49% of the 486 students still remaining in BCPS were in eighth grade, i.e., "on time." The remaining 51% were either one grade level behind (29.2%) or further behind (10.5%), or were in Special Education placements (10.9%).

By year 13 of the Beginning School Study , of the 655 students still being followed, 47% had graduated from high school, 26% were still in high school, and 27% had dropped out of school.

Grade Retention

Grade retention status is available every year from school records, and is coded 1 for *retained* and 0 for *promoted*. A cumulative measure of grade retention in grades 1 through 5 was also created which indicated whether student was ever retained through the first 5 grades. Coding was 1 for *retained at least once* and 0 for *never retained*. The cumulative retention rate through grade 5 was 44%.

Special Education Placement

Receipt of Special Education services was determined from school records. Coding is 1=*receipt of any Special Education* or 0 = *no Special Education services*.

Reading Groups

Reading group placements are based on teachers' reports from the fall and spring of grades 1 and 2. Each responding teacher was asked how many reading groups were in each class. Then, for each child participating in the study, each teacher was asked to note the number of the child's reading group: 1 was the highest group, 2 the next highest, and so on. In order to make comparisons across classrooms with different numbers of reading groups, the groups were ranked on the basis of their position relative to the other groups in the same class. Students were classified according to a 3-category ranking: 1 *lowest group in their classroom*, 2 *intermediate level group*, or 3 *highest level group*. Reading group level for grade 2 is available only for students who did not repeat grade 1.

Table D.1   BSS Grade Retention and Special Education Placements, Years 1-8[a]

Year of School	On-Time Students[b]		Off-Time Students		First Retention[c]		Second Retention		Retained Twice		Spec. Ed. Students[d]		N Left System	N Still in System
	N	%	N	%	N	%	N	%	N	%	N	%		
2	626	83.0	126	16.7	127	16.8	–	–	–	–	2	0.3	21	754
3	520	72.7	165	23	68	9.5	1	0.1	1	0.1	30	4.2	39	715
4	417	64.2	192	29.6	47	7.2	3	0.5	3	0.5	40	6.2	66	649
5	369	60.1	193	31.4	21	3.4	19	3.1	22	3.6	52	8.5	35	614
6	309	56.2	177	32.2	10	1.8	11	2.0	25	4.5	64	11.6	64	550
7	265	52.1	173	34.0	22	4.3	4	0.8	22	4.3	71	13.9	41	509
8	240	49.4	193	39.7	22	4.5	25	5.1	51	11.0	53	10.9	23	486

[a] The year 1 sample (N = 775) omitted 15 of the 790 students because of gaps in their grade assignment records or because of other inconsistencies that could not be reconciled.

[b] "On-Time" category includes a few students (never more than 4) who skipped a grade and are a grade ahead.

[c] "Retained for First Time" category includes a small number of students who are also counted in the "Special Education" category (1 in year 2, 7 in year 3, 2 in year 4, 1 in year 5, 1 in year 6, and 4 in year 7). These students were assigned to Special Education and then also retained in grade.

[d] Students in Special Education category include only those whose problems were severe enough to warrant placement in separate Special Education classes. In this table they do not have a regular grade level assignment and thus do not appear in either the "on-time" or "off-time" category. In addition, a larger number of Special Education students whose problems were less severe, received special education pull-out instruction in reading and/or math. They are included in the grade level tallies for "on-time" and "off-time" students. During the 8-year period, 144 students received pull-out instruction at some point, 60 in year 1 and 59 in year 2.

Reading Instructional Level

This was taken from report cards and indicates the instructional level of the reader the student was using in a given quarter. Coding was as follows: 1 = *Pre-Readiness, Readiness*; 2 = *PrePrimer*, 3 = *Primer*, 4 = *Grade 1 Level*; 5 = *Grade 2 Level*; etc.

Total Number of Low Placements in First Grade

Low placements in first grade are considered to be retention in grade 1, assignment to Special Education, and low reading group placement. Sixty-nine percent of Beginning School Study students were spared any low placement, 17% had one low placement, 9% had two, and 5% had all three.

Middle School Course Placement

Course Placement in English, Reading, and Math in Middle School

In middle school, curriculum tracking begins in reading, English, and math. In math, advanced students took pre-algebra or algebra. In language, advanced students could take a foreign language or move on to literary criticism and creative or expository writing. Children in lower-level reading/English classes were limited to remedial reading, rules of grammar, vocabulary building, and the like, while those in lower-level math classes worked on number skills.

Different criteria were used to classify courses in the various subject areas. All reading courses were considered *remedial*. English and math courses were classified as 1, *remedial*; 2, *regular*, or 3 *advanced*. In English, students were assigned to *remedial* courses when they failed to pass the Baltimore City Reading and Writing Proficiency tests. Students who satisfied various screening criteria (e.g., scoring above grade level on standardized tests or receiving grades of 80 or above in all subjects) could be tracked into *advanced* level courses (either "enriched" or the higher level "advanced academic"). In math, *remedial* meant assignment to Special Education classes in math, and *advanced* meant participation in "advanced academic" (but not "enriched") pre-algebra or algebra courses. Thus the classification *advanced* in a math course was more exclusive than *advanced* in an English course, and those classified as *remedial* in math were only those receiving Special Education services in math.

Foreign Language in Grade 6

Foreign language tracking simply distinguished "any" foreign language from "none."

Total Number of High Placements in Grade 6

High placements in grade 6 are considered to be placement in *advanced* level courses in English and math, taking a foreign language, and *not* taking a reading course. Only 9% of students in grade 6 had high placements in all four curricular areas and 54% had no high level course placements.

Total Number of Low Placements in Grade 6

Low placements in grade 6 are considered to be placement in *remedial* English and math, *not* taking a foreign language, and taking a reading course. Thirteen percent of sixth graders were classified as low in all four areas and only 12% escaped any low placements.

Special Problem Referrals

Every year beginning in year 1, information was procured from each student's school on the student's referrals to various screening committees or resources--for example, promotional, attendance, or screening committees or referrals to a reading resource specialist or to speech therapy. A dichotomous indicator was created that indicates whether or not the student had received any referrals to screening committees or extra resources for that year.

Kindergarten Attendance

At the beginning of first grade, parents were asked, "Did your child attend kindergarten?" Responses were coded 1 = *not at all,* 2 =*one half year or less with half-day sessions,* 3 = *one full year with half-day sessions,* or 4 = *full year with full-day sessions.*

School Moves

Each student's history of school transfers was reconstructed using school system data from the beginning of first grade. School records allowed for a maximum of three *within-year* moves annually. Summer moves (*between-year transfers*) were identified by comparing spring school enrollments against those for the following fall. Transfer out of the system was inferred when the record of school identifications terminated. Children's mobility history after leaving the City system is unknown. By the end of the fifth year of the Beginning School Study , children enrolled in the original 20 schools had dispersed to 112 schools within the system as well as to an unknown number of schools outside the system (28% were enrolled in schools outside Baltimore city).

Appendix E:
Parent Characteristics, Family Structure, and Home Environment

Parental Measures

Interviews with parents provided data on parental expectations for children's performance in school and psychological data on parents themselves (see Chart A.2). Parents completed items taken from several psychological scales: Locus of Control (Rotter 1966 and Mischel, Zeiss, and Zeiss 1974), Depression (Kandel and Davies 1982), life stress/personal problems (Holmes and Rahe 1967), sex role attitudes, parental attitudes toward their own school experience, and parental opinions on factors important for student achievement (ability, effort, or personality).

Two measures adapted from an earlier study (Entwisle and Hayduk 1982) assessed the psychological resources provided by parents: (1) parents' estimate of the child's ability to do schoolwork and (2) parents' expectations for children's marks in reading, math, and conduct.

Parents' Ability Estimate

Every year parents were asked, "How do you think your child compares with other children in his/her school in terms of ability to do school work?" This item was coded from 1 (*among the poorest*) to 5 (*among the best*).

Parents' Mark Expectations

To assess parents' expectations about how well their children would perform on their first report card each year, parents were asked their "best guesses" for their child's first mark in reading, math and conduct. For math and reading, these responses were coded 4 for *excellent*, 3 for *good*, 2 for *satisfactory* and 1 for *unsatisfactory*. For conduct, the coding was 2 for *"satisfactory"* or 1 for *"needs improvement."*

Parents' Educational Aspirations for Student

Beginning in year 1 parents were queried about their educational aspirations for their children. Parents were asked "How far do you expect your child will go in school?" and they responded on a 5-point scale:

    1 = Not finish high school
    2 = Finish high school
    3 = Finish 1 or 2 years college
    4 = Finish 4 years college
    5 = More than college (M.D., etc.)

Beginning in year 3 the choices were expanded to an 8-point scale:

1 = Grade nine or less
2 = Some high school
3 = Finish high school (or G.E.D.)
4 = Business or trade school after high school
5 = Less than two years of college
6 = Two or more years of college
7 = Finish college (four- or five-year degree)
8 = More than college (M.D., etc.)

Parent Interviewed in Year 4

Coded 1 for parents who completed the parent interview in year 4; 0 for no interview. (Used in regression models, Chapter 5.)

Rotter Locus of Control Scale

Beginning in year 6, a 6-item scale adapted from the Rotter (1966) Internal-External Control Scale was used to assess parent's locus of control. Parents were asked which of two alternative statements "is closer to your thinking." For example:

Bad luck has a lot to do with unhappy things in people's lives.
OR
The mistakes people make cause their bad luck.

The internal reliability (Cronbach's alpha) for parents in the Beginning School Study sample in year 6 was .47.

Depression Scale

Beginning in year 6, parents were administered the 6-item scale developed by Kandel and Davies (1982) to measure depressive mood (same scale as that administered to students). See Appendix C for detailed description of this depression scale. The reliability (Cronbach alpha) for the Beginning School Study sample parents in year 6 was .81.

Family Structure and Home Environment

Data on students' families include: whether the father lived in the household, presence of other adults besides parents or siblings, number of siblings, mother's age at child's birth, and a calendar of parental marriage, separation and divorce.

Household Composition

At the beginning of year 1, 56% of children lived with both mother and father (including stepfathers), 20% lived with only the mother, 21% lived with the mother and other adults (most often (40%) the grandmother), and 3.7% lived in a household where the mother was absent. (See Table E.1.) Fifty-seven percent of children classified as mother-absent were living with fathers (either alone or with another adult). Stepfathers are combined with biological fathers in defining mother-father homes because the number of stepfather families is too small to sustain separate analysis (only 8% of fathers are stepfathers). However, analyses involving children who live in mother-father families were repeated omitting those with stepfathers and this omission did not change either the findings or their level of significance.

Mother's Age at Student's Birth

The mother's birth date, used with the child's birth date, determined the mother's age at the student's birth.

Number of Siblings

Parents were asked in the fall of 1982 how many older brothers, older sisters, younger brothers, and younger sisters the study child had.

Parental Involvement, Monitoring, and Supervision

During the early years, information was collected about parental story-reading, student TV watching, home chores, allowances, summer activities and trips, child care arrangements, homework habits and supervision, parents' involvement with the school, parents' monitoring activities, and parental knowledge of the child's problems and strengths. (See Table E.2 for measures relating to parental involvement and supervision.)

Parent Story Reading. In years 1 and 2, parents were asked: "Yesterday, did you read stories with your child? How long?" Responses were coded 0 *less than 10 minutes* or 1 *10 minutes or more.*

Hours Child Watched TV. At the beginning of year 3 parents were asked: "On a typical weekday, how many hours did your child watch TV?"

Did Parents See School Records. In years 1 and 2, parents were asked if they had "ever seen any of your child's school records or test scores?" Parents' responses were coded either 0 *no* or 1 *yes.*

Summer Activities. At the beginning of year 3 parents were asked about the organized activities their child had participated in during the previous summer. See Table E.2 for listing of possible choices. A composite measure of number of summer activities was created by summing the total number of activities for each child.

Summer Trips. At the beginning of year 3 parents were asked about the day trips and overnight trips their child had been on during the previous summer. See Table E.2 for full listing of possible summer trips. A composite measure of number of summer trips was created by summing the total number of summer trips for each child.

Table E.1   BSS Family Characteristics

Family Characteristic	Mean Value/Percent
Family Composition (1982)	
Mother-Father	56%
Mother & Other Adult	21%
Mother Alone	20%
Mother Absent	4%
Mother's Marital Status (1982)	
Never-Married	25%
Separated or Divorced	17%
Widowed	1%
Married	57%
Number of Siblings (1982)	1.46
Age of Mother at Student's Birth	23.9
Mother's Years of Schooling[a]	11.7
Father's Years of Schooling[a]	12.2
Mother's Occupational Status[b]	31.9
Father's Occupational Status[b]	33.3

[a]Mean mother's and father's years of schooling derived from data pooled over the first eight years of the study.
[b]Updated Featherman-Stevens occupational status scores (Featherman and Stevens 1982).

Parent's Personal Problems and Life Stress

Beginning in year 3, parents reported on their own personal problems and stressful life events such as trouble with the boss, job loss, financial difficulties, divorce, separation, remarriage, death of spouse or other family member or close friend, illness or injury, and problems with teenage children. Parents responded with "yes" or "no" as to whether or not they had experienced each event during the past year *and* over the past 5 years. This scale was adapted from Holmes and Rahe (1967). (See Table E.2 for specific items in scale.)

Life History Calendar

During year 11 (1993) a retrospective Life History Calendar asked students' mothers about key events in their lives such as marriages, divorce, live-in partners, children's births, living arrangements, household moves, study child's contact with father, education, work, financial assistance, and family income (see Chart A.2). The Life History Calendar provided data on whether single parents were divorced, separated,

Table E.2   Home Environment: Parental Involvement, Monitoring, and
             Supervision, Parent's Personal Problems/Life Stress

VARIABLE	YEARS
Have you ever seen any of your child's school records or test scores?	1, 2
How often in past year have you been in the building where your child went to school?	6, 7, 8
Who helps the child with reading/English homework? Math? Other?	6, 7, 8
Who usually checks to see if homework is completed?	8
Yesterday, did you read stories with your child? How long?	1, 2
During the summer, who looked after your child most often during the day?	3, 6, 7, 8
During the summer when did your child watch TV?	6, 7, 8
Yesterday (or most recent school day) how long did your child watch TV?	1, 2
On a typical weekday how many hours did your child watch TV?	3
Who usually watches TV with your child?	3
At what age do you think children are pretty much responsible for how they spend their free time?	6, 7, 8
How far do you expect your child will go in school?	1, 2, 3, 4, 6, 7, 8

Composite Measure of Number of Summer Trips:
 This past summer did your child go on any day trips? Kinds of trips and who accompanied child:
     State or city park
     Washington, D.C. (or other large city)
     Amusement park
     Zoo, Aquarium, Science Center
     Fairs or carnivals
     Ocean City or other beach
     Swimming at pool or elsewhere
     Sports (baseball, etc.)
     Fishing, crabbing, or boating
     Other
	3

This past summer did your child go on any overnight trips? Where? Who accompanied?	3

VARIABLE	YEARS
Composite Measure of Number of Summer Activities: Which of following did your child do this past summer during school vacation? Music or dance lessons Swimming or gymnastics lessons City Recreation Center Daycare center Summer school or tutoring in math or reading Bible school Little League or other organized sport with coach Went to library Took books home from the library	3
Home Chores: Chores your child was supposed to do this past summer: Make own bed Clean up after meals Run errands at the store Babysit or watch younger children Mow your grass Help clean your car Other housecleaning (vacuuming, sweeping, etc.)	3, 6, 7, 8
Did your child get paid or receive an allowance for doing chores at home?	3, 6, 7, 8
Did your child get paid for doing chores for other people?	6, 7, 8
Parents' Personal Problems and Life Stress: (Holmes and Rahe 1967) Please indicate which of the following events happened to you during this past year: Trouble with your boss Trouble with the law Serious financial problems (such as lien foreclosure, loss of welfare payments) Lost your job Divorced or separated Married or remarried Birth or adoption of a child Death of close family member or friend Death of spouse Serious illness or injury of family member Serious personal illness or injury Serious problem with your teenaged children Took a second job Moved from one house to another (Beginning Year 6)	3, 4, 6, 7, 8

or never-married. Calendars were received from 566 mothers and from 41 non-mother caretakers.

Mother's Marital Status. Information obtained from the Life History Calendar was used to create an indicator of mother's marital status at the time the student entered first grade. Mothers were categorized as *never married* (25%), *divorced or separated* (17%), *married* (57%), and *widowed* (1%). The number of widowed mothers was too small to sustain analysis so they were excluded from consideration.

Appendix F:
Teacher Measures

Starting in first grade, Beginning School Study teachers were queried about their expectations and evaluations of study students, as well as about their own background, attitudes toward teaching, and their current school environment. Teachers also completed several psychological assessment instruments.

Personal teacher data include gender, ethnic background, age, marital status, socioeconomic status of family of origin, educational background, and years of teaching experience. Teachers also completed schedules similar to those administered to parents on personal problems/life stress (Holmes and Rahe 1967) and locus of control (Rotter 1966). Teachers were asked about their job conditions, marking criteria, classroom organization practices, perceptions of school climate, and job satisfaction/stress (Pettegrew and Wolf 1982).

Teacher Mark Expectations

During the late spring of each year (years 1 through 9) teachers were asked to guess the mark that students would receive on the first report card in the following school year in reading/English and math. These responses are coded from 1 to 4 in the same way as student marks and parent's mark expectations (see Appendix E).

Classroom Chores

In year 4 teachers were asked to name three students in their class "on whom you could or would rely to help" with each of 5 classroom chores:

Take notes to the office
Pass out or collect papers
Clean blackboards, help with a TV or other equipment
Escort visitors around school
Put up posters, fix bulletin boards

The names were categorized as to gender of student, and a tally was made of the total number of girls chosen as helpers.

School Climate

Beginning in year 1, teachers were asked to assess the general atmosphere of their school by completing a School Climate scale composed of 4 items adapted from Pettegrew and Wolf (1982):

For most faculty, teaching here is: *very unpleasant* or *very pleasant*
The climate in this school is: *very tense* or *very warm*
Student-faculty relations here are: *very poor* or *very good*
Trying to do your job right here is: *very frustrating* or *very rewarding*

The alpha reliability of this scale was .92 for the data collected in year 1.

References

Aiken, Lewis. 1971. Verbal Factors and Mathematics Learning: A Review of Research. *Journal for Research in Mathematics Education* 2:304-13.

Alexander, Karl L., Martha A. Cook, and Edward L. McDill. 1978. Curriculum Tracking and Educational Stratification. *American Sociological Review* 43:47-66.

------, and Bruce K. Eckland. 1975a. Basic Attainment Processes. *Sociology of Education* 48:457-95.

------, and Bruce K. Eckland. 1975b. School Experiences and Status Attainment. In *Adolescence in the Life Cycle*, ed. S. E. Dragastin and Glen H. Elder, 171-210. New York: Wiley.

------, and Bruce K. Eckland. 1980. The "Exploration in Equality of Opportunity" Sample of 1955 High School Sophomores. In *Research in Sociology of Education and Socialization Vol 1*, ed. Alan C. Kerckhoff, 31-58. Greenwich CT: JAI Press.

------, and Doris R. Entwisle. 1988. Achievement in the First Two Years of School: Patterns and Processes. Serial No. 218. *Monographs of the Society for Research in Child Development* 53 (2).

------, and Doris R. Entwisle. 1996a. Schools and Children at Risk. In *Family-School Links: How Do They Affect Educational Outcomes?* eds. Alan Booth and Judith F. Dunn, 67-88. Mahway, N.J.: Erlbaum.

------, and Doris R. Entwisle. 1996b. Educational Tracking in the Early Years: First Grade Placements and Middle School Constraints. In *Generating Social Stratification: Toward a New Research Agenda*, ed. Alan C. Kerckhoff, 83-113. New York: Westview Press.

------, and Doris R. Entwisle. In Preparation. Development in Tandem: Self-Image from First Grade into High School.

------, Doris R. Entwisle, and Susan L. Dauber. 1993. First Grade Classroom Behavior: Its Short- and Long-Term Consequences for School Performance. *Child Development* 64:801-14.

------, Doris R. Entwisle, and Susan L. Dauber. 1994. *On the Success of Failure: A Reassessment of the Effects of Retention in the Primary Grades*. Cambridge, MA: Cambridge University Press.

------, Doris R. Entwisle, and Susan L. Dauber. 1996. Children in Motion: School Transfers and Elementary School Performance. *Journal of Educational Research* 90 (1):3-12.

------, Doris R. Entwisle, and Carrie S. Horsey. 1997. From First Grade Forward: Early Foundations of High School Dropout. *Sociology of Education*, in press.

------, Doris R. Entwisle, and Nettie Legters. 1995. On the Multiple Faces of First Grade Tracking. Presented at Annual Meeting of the Southern Sociological Society. Atlanta, Ga.

------, Doris R. Entwisle, and Maxine S. Thompson. 1987. School Performance, Status Relations and the Structure of Sentiment: Bringing the Teacher Back In. *American Sociological Review* 52:665-82.

Alpert, Judith L. 1975. Do Teachers Adapt Methods and Materials to Ability Groups in Reading? *California Journal of Educational Research* 26:120-23.

Alwin, Duane F., and Arland Thornton. 1984. Family Origins and the Schooling Process: Early Versus Late Influence of Parental Characteristics. *American Sociological Review* 49:784-802.

Astone, Nan M., and Sara S. McLanahan. 1989. Family Structure and Success in High School: The Role of Parental Socialization. Presented at Meeting of Population Association of America. Baltimore, MD.

------, and Sara S. McLanahan. 1991. Family Structure, Parental Practices and High School Completion. *American Sociological Review* 56:309-20.

Averch, Harvey A., S. J. Carroll, T. S. Donaldson, H. J. Kiesling, and J. Pincus. 1972. *How Effective Is Schooling?* Santa Monica, CA: Rand Corporation.

Bachman, Jerald G., S. Green, and I. D. Wirtanen. 1971. *Youth in Transition Series.* Vol. 3, *Dropping Out — Problem or Symptom?* Ann Arbor, MI: Institute for Social Research.

------, P. M. O'Malley, and J. Johnston. 1978. *Adolescence to Adulthood: Change and Stability in the Lives of Young Men.* Ann Arbor, MI: Institute for Social Research.

Baltimore City Department of Planning. 1983. *Neighborhood Statistics Program.* Baltimore: Baltimore City Department of Planning.

Baltimore City Public Schools. 1988. School Profiles: School Year 1987-88. Office of the Superintendent of Public Instruction. Baltimore, MD, February.

------. 1991. *Maryland School Performance Program Report, 1991, School System and Schools-Baltimore City.* Baltimore, MD: Baltimore City Public Schools.

------. 1992. *End-of-the-Year Race/Sex Demographics by School Frequencies for 1990-91.* Unpublished Data. Baltimore, MD: Baltimore City Public Schools Department of Research and Evaluation.

Barnett, W. Steven. 1996. Long-Term Effects of Early Childhood Care and Education on Disadvantaged Children's Cognitive Development and School Success. *The Future of Children* 5 (3):25-50.

Barr, Rebecca, and Robert Dreeben. 1983. *How Schools Work.* Chicago: University of Chicago Press.

Barrington, Byron L., and Bryan Hendricks. 1989. Differentiating Characteristics of High School Graduates, Dropouts, and Nongraduates. *Journal of Educational Research* 82 (6):309-19.

Beller, E. Kuno. 1983. The Philadelphia Study: The Impact of Preschool on Intellectual and Socioemotional Development. In *As the Twig Is Bent: Lasting Effects of Preschool Programs*, ed. The Consortium for Longitudinal Studies, 333-76. Hillsdale, NJ: Erlbaum.

Bellisimo, Y., C. H, Sacks. 1995. Changes over Time in Kindergarten Holding Out: Parents and School Contexts. *Early Childhood Research Quarterly* 10:105-222.

Benbow, Camilla P., and Julian C. Stanley. 1980. Sex Differences in Mathematical Ability: Fact or Artifact? *Science* 210:1262-64.

Berrueta-Clement, John R., Lawrence J. Schweinhart, W. Steven Barnett, Ann S.

Epstein, and David P. Weikart. 1984. *Changed Lives: The Effect of the Perry Preschool Program on Youths Through Age 19.* Monograph of the High/Scope Educational Research Foundation. Ypsilanti, MI: High Scope Press.

Bianchi, Susan M. 1984. Children's Progress Through School: A Research Note. *Sociology of Education* 57:184-92.

------, and Edith McArthur. 1991. *Family Disruption and Economic Hardship: The Short-Run Picture for Children.* U. S. Bureau of the Census, Current Population Reports. Series P-70, Vol. No. 23. Washington, D.C.:U. S. Government Printing Office.

Bing, Elizabeth. 1963. Effects of Childrearing Practices on Development of Differential Cognitive Abilities. *Child Development* 34:631-48.

Bisanz, Jeffrey, Maria Dunn, and Frederick J. Morrison. 1995. Effects of Age and Schooling on the Acquisition of Elementary Quantitative Skills. *Developmental Psychology* 31:221-36.

Blake, Judith. 1981. Family Size and the Quality of Children. *Demography* 18:421-42.

------. 1989. *Family Size and Achievement.* Berkeley, CA: University of California Press.

Blau, Peter M., and Otis D. Duncan. 1967. *The American Occupational Structure.* New York: Wiley.

Bloom, Benjamin. 1964. *Stability and Change in Human Characteristics.* New York: John Wiley and Sons.

Blumenfeld, Phyllis C., Paul R. Pintrich, and V. L. Hamilton. 1986. Children's Concepts of Ability, Effort and Conduct. *American Educational Research Journal* 23:95-104.

------, Paul R. Pintrich, Judith Meece, and Kathleen Wessels. 1982. The Formation and Role of Self Perceptions of Ability in Elementary Classrooms. *The Elementary School Journal* 82:401-20.

Bond, Guy L., and Robert Dykstra. 1967. The Cooperative Research Program in First Grade Reading Instruction. *Reading Research Quarterly* 2 (4):1-42.

Booth, Alan, and Judith F. Dunn. 1996. *Family-School Links: How Do They Affect Educational Outcomes?* Mahwah, NJ: Erlbaum.

Bossert, Steven T. 1981. Understanding Sex Differences in Children's Classroom Experiences. *Elementary School Journal* 81:255-66.

Brandon, Peter. 1993-1994. The Connection Between Family Structure and Entitlements Affecting Poor Young Children. *Focus, 15*(3):27-34.

Brauth, Steven E., William S. Hall, and Robert J. eds. Dooling. 1991. *Plasticity of Development.* Cambridge, MA: MIT Press.

Broman, Sarah H., P. L. Nichols, and W.A. Kennedy. 1975. *Preschool IQ: Prenatal and Early Developmental Correlates.* Hillsdale, NJ: Erlbaum.

Bronfenbrenner, Urie. 1974. Is Early Intervention Effective? *Teachers College* 76:279-303.

------. 1991. What Do Families Do? *Family Affairs* 4:1-6.

------, and Ann C. Crouter. 1983. The Evolution of Environmental Models in Development Research. In *Handbook of Child Psychology Volume 1*, ed. Paul Mussen. New York: Wiley.

Brooks-Gunn, Jeanne, Greg J. Duncan, and Pamela K. Klebanov. 1993. Do Neighborhoods Influence Child and Adolescent Development? *American Journal of Sociology* 99:353-95.

------, Guang Guo and Frank F. Furstenberg. 1993. Who Drops out and Who Continues Beyond High School? A 20-Year Follow-Up of Black Urban Youth. *Journal of Research on Adolescence* 3:271-94.

Brophy, Jere E. 1985. Interactions of Male and Female Students with Male and Female Teachers. In *Gender Influences in Classroom Interaction*, eds. Louis Cherry Wilkinson and Cora Bagley Marrett, 115-42. New York: Academic.

Brophy, Jere E., and Thomas Good. 1970. Teachers' Communication of Differential Expectations for Children's Classroom Performance. *Journal of Educational Psychology* 61:367-74.

Brumberg, Joan J. 1988. *Fasting Girls*. Cambridge, MA: Harvard.

Bruno, Rosalind R., and Andrea Adams. 1994. *School Enrollment: Social and Economic Characteristics of Students: October 1993*. U.S. Bureau of the Census, Current Population Reports. P20-479. Washington D.C.: U.S. Government Printing Office.

Bryant, W. Keith, and Cathleen D. Zick. 1996. An Examination of Parent-Child Shared Time. *Journal of Marriage and the Family* 58:227-37.

Butler, Susan R., Herbert W. Marsh, Marlene J. Sheppard, and John L. Sheppard. 1985. Seven Year Longitudinal Study of the Early Prediction of Reading Achievement. *Journal of Educational Psychology* 77:349-61.

Cahan, Sorel, and Nora Cohen. 1989. Age Versus Schooling Effects on Intelligence Development. *Child Development* 60:1237-49.

Cairns, Robert B., Beverley D. Cairns, and Holly J. Neckerman. 1989. Early School Dropout: Configurations and Determinants. *Child Development* 60:1437-52.

California Achievement Test. 1979. *Technical Bulletin 1, Forms C and D, Levels 10-19*. Monterey, CA: McGraw-Hill.

Cameron, Mary Bridget, and Barry J. Wilson. 1990. The Effects of Chronological Age, Gender and Delay of Entry on Academic Achievements and Retention: Implications for Academic Redshirting. *Psychology in the Schools* 27:260-63.

Carter, Launor F. 1983. *A Study of Compensatory and Elementary Education: The Sustaining Effects Study*. Prepared for System Development Corporation. Santa Monica: CA, U.S. Department of Education.

------. 1984. The Sustaining Effects Study of Compensatory and Elementary Education. *Educational Researcher* 13:4-13.

Cassidy, Jude. 1988. Child-Mother Attachment and the Self in Six-Year-Olds. *Child Development* 59 (1):121-34.

Ceci, Stephen J. 1991. How Much Does Schooling Influence General Intelligence and Its Cognitive Components? A Reassessment of the Evidence. *Developmental Psychology* 5:703-22.

Central Advisory Council for Education. 1967. *Children and Their Primary Schools.* London: Her Majesty's Stationery Office.

Chase-Lansdale, P. Lindsay, Jeanne Brooks-Gunn, and Elise S. Zamsky. 1994. Young African American Multigenerational Families in Poverty: Quality of Mothering and Grandmothering. *Child Development* 65:373-93.

Cicarelli, Victor, et al. 1969. *The Impact of Head Start: An Evaluation of Head Start on Children's Cognitive and Affective Development.* Report presented to the Office of Economic Opportunity, Pursuant to Contract B89-4536. Report No. PB 184 328. U.S. Institute for Applied Technology: Westinghouse Learning Corporation for Federal Scientific and Technical Information.

Coleman, James S. 1988. Social Capital in the Creation of Human Capital. *American Journal of Sociology* 94 (Supplement):S95-S120.

------. 1992. Some Points in Educational Choice. *Sociology of Education* 65:260-62.

------, Ernest Q. Campbell, Charles J. Hobson, James McPartland, Alexander Mood, F. D. Weinfeld, and R. L. York. 1966. *Equality of Educational Opportunity.* Washington, D.C.: U.S. Government Printing Office.

Colletta, Nancy Donohue. 1983. Stressful Lives: The Situation of Divorced Mothers and Their Children. *Journal of Divorce* 6:19-31.

Collins, J. 1986. Differential Instruction in Reading Groups. In *The Social Construction of Literacy*, ed. J. Cook-Gumperz, 117-36. Cambridge, England: Cambridge University Press.

Connell, James P., Elizabeth Clifford, and Warren Crichlow. 1992. Gender and Ethnic Variation in Contextual Influences on Adolescent School Performance. Paper Presented at Society for Research in Adolescence. Washington, D.C., March.

Consortium of Longitudinal Studies. 1983. *As the Twig Is Bent: Lasting Effect of Preschool Programs.* Hillsdale, NJ: Erlbaum.

Cooper, Harris, Barbara Nye, Kelly Charlton, James Lindsay, and Scott Greathouse. 1996. The Effects of Summer Vacation on Achievement Test Scores: A Narrative and Meta-Analytic Review. *Review of Educational Research* 66:227-68.

Corbett, Thomas. 1993. Child Poverty and Welfare Reform: Progress or Paralysis. *Focus* 15 (1):1-17.

Crandall, Virginia, W. Katkovsky, and V. Crandall. 1965. Children's Beliefs of Their Control of Reinforcements in Intellectual Academic Achievement Behaviors. *Child Development* 36:91-109.

Crouter, Ann C., Shelley M. MacDermid, Susan M. McHale, and Maureen Perry-Jenkins. 1990. Parental Monitoring and Perceptions of Children's School Performance and Conduct in Dual- and Single-Earner Families. *Developmental Psychology* 26 (4):649-57.

Dauber, Susan L. 1993. Educational Expectations Versus Educational Trajectory: Social Psychological and School Organizational Perspectives on Adolescent Educational Attainment. Unpublished Doctoral Dissertation. Baltimore, MD: The Johns Hopkins University.

------, Karl L. Alexander, and Doris R. Entwisle. 1993. Characteristics of Retainees and Early Precursors of Retention in Grade: Who Is Held Back? *Merrill-Palmer*

Quarterly 39:326-43.

------, Karl L. Alexander, and Doris R. Entwisle. 1996. Tracking and Transitions Through the Middle Grades: Channeling Educational Trajectories. *Sociology of Education* 69:290-307.

David, Jane. 1974. Follow Through Summer Study: A Two-Part Investigation of the Impact of Exposure to Schooling on Achievement Growth. Doctoral Dissertation. Cambridge, MA: Harvard Graduate School of Education.

------, and S. H. Pelavin. 1978. Secondary Analysis: In Compensatory Education Programs. *New Directions for Program Evaluation* 4:31-44.

Dawson, Deborah A. 1991. Family Structure and Children's Health and Well-Being: Data from the 1988 National Health Interview Survey on Child Health. *Journal of Marriage and the Family* 53:573-84.

deGroot, A. D. 1951. Short Articles and Notes: War and the Intelligence of Youth. *Journal of Abnormal and Social Psychology* 46:596-97.

Dickstein, Ellen B. 1972. The Development of Self-Esteem: Theory and Measurement. Unpublished Doctoral Dissertation. Baltimore, MD: Johns Hopkins University Press.

Doma, V. 1969. The Intellectual Development and the Achievement at School of Different-Sexed Fraternal Twins. *Educational Testing Service International Newsletter* 7:7-8.

Dornbusch, Sanford M., J. Merrill Carlsmith, S. J. Bushwall, Philip L. Ritter, H. Leiderman, A. H. Hastorf, and Ruth T. Gross. 1985. Single Parents, Extended Households, and the Control of Adolescents. *Child Development* 56:326-41.

------, and W. R. Scott. 1975. *Evaluation and the Exercise of Authority*. San Francisco: Jossey-Bass.

Douglas, J. W. B., and J. M. Ross. 1965. The Effects of Absence on Primary School Performance. *British Journal of Educational Psychology* 35:28-40.

Dreeben, Robert, and Rebecca Barr. 1988. The Formation and Instruction of Ability Groups. *American Journal of Education* 97:34-64.

DuBois, David L., Robert D. Felner, Stephen Brand, Angela M. Adan, and Elizabeth G. Evans. 1992. A Prospective Study of Life Stress, Social Support, and Adaptation in Early Adolescence. *Child Development* 63:542-57.

------, Robert D. Felner, Henry Meares, and Marion Krier. 1994. Prospective Investigation of the Effects of Socioeconomic Disadvantage, Life Stress, and Social Support on Early Adolescent Adjustment. *Journal of Abnormal Psychology* 103:511-22.

Duncan, Greg J., and D. Laren. 1990. *Neighborhood Correlates of Teen Births and Dropping Out: Preliminary Results from the PSID-Geocode File*. Ann Arbor, MI: Survey Research Center, University of Michigan.

------, and Willard L. Rodgers. 1991. Has Children's Poverty Become More Persistent? *American Sociological Review* 56:538-50.

Duncan, Otis D., David L. Featherman, and Beverly Duncan. 1972. *Socioeconomic Background and Achievement*. New York: Seminar Press.

Durkheim, Emile. 1973. *On Morality and Society; Selected Writings*. Chicago:

University of Chicago Press.

Dwyer, Carol A. 1973. Sex Differences in Reading. *Review of Educational Research* 43:455-60.

Eccles, Jacquelynne S., and Phyllis Blumenfeld. 1985. Classroom Experience and Student Gender: Are There Differences and Do They Matter? In *Gender Influences in Classroom Interaction*, eds. Louise Cherry Wilkinson and Cora Bagley Marrett, 79-114. New York: Academic Press.

------, Carol Midgley, and T. Adler. 1984. Grade-Related Changes in the School Environment: Effects on Achievement Motivation. In *The Development of Achievement Motivation*, ed. John G. Nicholls, 283-331. Greenwich, CT: JAI Press.

Eder, Donna. 1981. Ability Grouping as a Self-Fulfilling Prophecy: A Micro-Analysis of Teacher-Student Interaction. *Sociology of Education* 54:151-62.

Edgar, Eugene, Mervette Heggelund, and Mary Fisher. 1988. A Longitudinal Study of Graduates of Special Education Preschools: Educational Placement after Preschool. *Topics In Early Childhood Special Education* 8:61-74.

Eggebean, David, J., and D. T. Lichter. 1991. Race, Family Structure, and Changing Poverty among American Children. *American Sociological Review* 56:801-17.

Elder, Glen H. Jr. 1974. *Children of the Great Depression: Social Change in Life Experience*. Chicago: University of Chicago Press.

------, Jeffrey K. Liker, and C. E. Cross. 1984. Parent Child Behavior in the Great Depression: Life Course and Intergenerational Influences. In *Lifespan Development and Behavior Volume 6*, eds. Paul E. Baltes and Orville G. Brim, 109-58. New York: Academic Press.

Elster, Arthur B., Robert Ketterlinus, and Michael E. Lamb. 1990. Association Between Parenthood and Problem Behavior in a National Sample of Adolescents. *Pediatrics* 85:1044-50.

Ensminger, Margaret E., and Anita L. Slusarcick. 1992. Paths to High School Graduation or Dropout: A Longitudinal Study of a First-Grade Cohort. *Sociology of Education* 65:95-113.

Entwisle, Doris R. 1990. Schools and the Adolescent. In *At the Threshold: The Developing Adolescent*, eds. Shirley S. Feldman and Glen R Elliott, 197-224. Cambridge, MA: Harvard University Press.

------. 1995. The Role of Schools in Sustaining Benefits of Early Childhood Programs. *The Future of Children* 5:133-44.

------, and Karl L. Alexander. 1988. Factors Affecting Achievement Test Scores and Marks Received by Black and White First Graders. *The Elementary School Journal* 88:449-71.

------, and Karl L. Alexander. 1989. Early Schooling as a 'Critical Period' Phenomenon. In *Sociology of Education and Socialization*, eds. K. Namboodiri and R.G. Corwin, 27-55. Greenwich, CT: JAI Press.

------, and Karl L. Alexander. 1990. Beginning School Math Competence. *Child Development* 61:454-71.

------, and Karl L. Alexander. 1992. Summer Setback: Race, Poverty, School

Composition, and Mathematics Achievement in the First Two Years of School. *American Sociological Review* 57:72-84.

------, and Karl L. Alexander. 1993. Entry into Schools: The Beginning School Transition and Educational Stratification in the United States. In *Annual Review of Sociology*, 19, 401-23. Palo Alto, CA: Annual Reviews, Inc.

------, and Karl L. Alexander. 1994. Winter Setback: School Racial Composition and Learning to Read. *American Sociological Review* 59:446-60.

------, and Karl L. Alexander. 1995. A Parent's Economic Shadow: Family Structure Versus Family Resources as Influences on Early School Achievement. *Journal of Marriage and the Family* 57:399-409.

------, and Karl L. Alexander. 1996a. Further Comments on Seasonal Learning. In *Family-School Links: How Do They Affect Educational Outcomes?* eds. Alan Booth and Judith F. Dunn, 125-36. Mahwah, NJ: Erlbaum.

------, and Karl L. Alexander. 1996b. Family Type and Children's Growth in Reading and Math over the Primary Grades. *Journal of Marriage and the Family* 58: 341-45.

------, and Karl L. Alexander. 1997. The Handicap of Being Male: Early School Decisions. Unpublished Manuscript.

------, and Karl L. Alexander, Doris Cadigan, and Aaron M. Pallas. Kindergarten Experience: Cognitive Effects or Socialization. *American Educational Research Journal* 24:337-64.

------, Karl L. Alexander, and Linda S. Olson. 1994. The Gender Gap in Math: Its Possible Origins in Neighborhood Effects. *American Sociological Review* 59:822-38.

------, and David B. Baker. 1983. Gender and Young Children's Expectations for Performance in Arithmetic. *Developmental Psychology* 19:200-09.

------, and Leslie A. Hayduk. 1981. Academic Expectations and the School Attainment of Young Children. *Sociology of Education* 54:34-50.

------, and Leslie A. Hayduk. 1978. *Too Great Expectations: The Academic Outlook of Young Children*. Baltimore: Johns Hopkins University Press.

------, and Leslie A. Hayduk. 1982. *Early Schooling: Cognitive and Affective Outcomes*. Baltimore: Johns Hopkins University Press.

------, and Leslie A. Hayduk. 1988. Lasting Effects of Elementary School. *Sociology of Education* 61:147-59.

------, and Murray Webster, Jr. 1976. Raising Children's Performance Expectations. *Social Science Research* 1:147-58.

Epstein, Joyce. 1988. *Single Parents and the Schools: The Effect of Marital Status on Parent and Teacher Evaluations*. Report No. 353. Johns Hopkins University. Baltimore, MD: Center for Social Organization of Schools.

------, and James M. McPartland. 1977. *The Quality of School Life Scale*. New York: Houghton Mifflin.

Epstein, Seymour. 1973. The Self-Concept Revisited. *American Psychologist* 28:404-16.

Estes, William Kaye. 1970. *Learning Theory and Mental Development.* New York: Academic Press.

Estrada, Peggy, William F. Arsenio, Robert D. Hess, and Susan D. Holloway. 1987. Affective Quality of the Mother-Child Relationship: Longitudinal Consequences for Children's School Relevant Cognitive Functioning. *Developmental Psychology* 23:210-15.

Falbo, Toni. 1982. Only Children in America. In *Sibling Relationships: Their Nature and Significance Across the Life Span,* eds. Michael E. Lamb and Brian Sutton-Smith. Hillsdale, NJ: Erlbaum.

Farkas, George, Robert Grobe, David Sheehan, and Yuan Shuan. 1990. Cultural Resources and School Success: Gender, Ethnicity and Poverty Groups Within an Urban School District. *American Sociological Review* 55:127-42.

Farley, Reynolds, and Walter Ernest Allen. 1987. *The Color Line and Quality of Life in America.* New York: Russell Sage.

Featherman, David L., and G. Stevens. 1982. A Revised Socioeconomic Index of Occupational Status: Application in Analysis of Sex Differences in Attainment. In *Social Structure and Behavior: Essays in Honor of William Hamilton Sewell,* eds. Robert M. Hauser, David Mechanic, Archibald O. Haller and T. S. Hauser, 141-82. New York: Academic Press.

Feingold, Alan. 1988. Cognitive Gender Differences Are Disappearing. *American Psychologist* 43:95-103.

Felmlee, Diane, and Donna Eder. 1983. Contextual Effects in the Classroom: The Impact of Ability Groups on Student Attention. *Sociology of Education* 56:77-87.

Fennema, Elizabeth, and Julia Sherman. 1977. Sex-Related Differences in Mathematics Achievement, Spatial Visualization, and Affective Factors. *American Educational Research Journal* 14:51-71.

Ferri, Elsa. 1976. *Growing up in a One-Parent Family: A Long Term Study of Child Development.* London: National Foundation for Educational Research.

Fine, Michelle. 1991. *Framing Dropouts: Notes on the Politics of an Urban Public High School.* Albany, NY: State University of New York Press.

Finlayson, H. J. 1977. Non-Promotion and Self-Concept Development. *Phi Delta Kappan* 59:205-06.

Finn, Jeremy D. 1972. Expectations and the Educational Environment. *Review of Educational Research* 42:387-409.

Fitzsimmons, Stephen J., Julia Cheever, Emily Macunovich, and Diane Leonard. 1969. School Failures: Now and Tomorrow. *Developmental Psychology* 1:134-46.

Flanagan, John C., Frederick B. Davis, John T. Dailey, Marion F. Shaycoft, David B. Orr, Isadore Goldberg, and Clinton A. Neyman. 1964. *Project Talent.* Pittsburgh, PA: University of Pittsburgh School of Education.

Fox, Lynn H., Linda Brody, and Dianne Tobin. 1980. *Women and the Mathematical Mystique.* Baltimore, MD: Johns Hopkins University Press.

------, Dianne Tobin, and Linda Brody. 1979. Sex Role Socialization and Achievement in Mathematics. In *Sex-Related Differences in Cognitive Functioning:*

Developmental Issues, eds. Michele A. Wittig and Anne C. Peterson, 303-34. New York: Academic Press.

Furstenberg, Frank F., Jr. 1976. *Unplanned Parenthood: The Social Consequences of Teenage Childbearing*. New York: Free Press.

------. 1987. The New Extended Family: The Experience of Parents and Children after Marriage. In *Remarriage and Stepparenting: Current Research and Theory*, eds. K. Pasley and M. Ininger-Tallman, 42-61. New York: Guilford.

------, Jeanne Brooks-Gunn, and S. P. Morgan. 1987. *Adolescent Mothers in Later Life*. Cambridge: Cambridge University Press.

------, and Mary Elizabeth Hughes. 1995. *The Influence of Neighborhoods on Children's Development: A Theoretical Perspective and a Research Agenda*. Institute for Research on Poverty Special Report 60c. *Indicators of Children's Well-Being: Conference Papers*, Vol. III May 1995. Madison, WI: Institute for Research on Poverty. 81-102.

Garfinkel, Irwin, and Sara S. McLanahan. 1986. *Single Mothers and Their Children: A New American Dilemma*. Washington, D.C.: Urban Institute Press.

Gottfredson, Denise C. 1982. Personality and Persistence in Education: A Longitudinal Study. *Journal of Personality and Social Psychology* 43:532-45.

Gray, Susan W., Barbara K. Ramsey, and Rupert A. Klaus. 1983. The Early Training Project 1962-1980. In *As the Twig Is Bent: Lasting Effects of Preschool Programs*, ed. The Consortium for Longitudinal Studies, 37-70. Hillsdale, NJ: Erlbaum.

Green, Robert Lee, Louis J. Hofman, Richard J. Morse, Marilyn E. Hayes, and Robert F. Morgan. 1964. *The Educational Status of Children in a District Without Public Schools*. Cooperative Research Project. Michigan State University: Bureau of Educational Research.

Grissmer, David W., Shelia Nataraj Kirby, Mark Berends, and Stephanie Williamson. 1994. *Student Achievement and the Changing American Family*. Santa Monica, CA: Rand Corporation.

Guttmann, Joseph, Nehemia Geva, and Shelly Gefen. 1988. Teachers' and School Children's Stereotypic Perceptions of the Child of Divorce. *American Educational Research Journal* 25:555-71.

Haller, Emil J. 1985. Pupil Race and Elementary School Ability Grouping: Are Teachers Biased Against Black Children? *American Educational Research Journal* 22:456-83.

------, and Sharon A. Davis. 1980. Does Socioeconomic Status Bias the Assignment of Elementary School Students to Reading Groups? *American Educational Research Journal* 17:409-18.

Hallinan, Maureen T., and Aage B. Sørensen. 1983. The Formation and Stability of Instructional Groups. *American Sociological Review* 48:838-51.

------, and Aage B. Sørenson. 1987. Ability Grouping and Sex Differences in Mathematics Achievement. *Sociology of Education* 60:63-72.

Hammond, Pierce A., and Joy A. Frechtling. 1979. Twelve, Nine and Three Month Achievement Gains of Low and Average Achieving Elementary School Students. Paper presented at American Educational Research Association Annual Meeting.

San Francisco.

Harnqvist, K. 1977. Enduring Effects of Schooling: A Neglected Area in Educational Research. *Educational Researcher* 6:5-11.

Harter, Susan. 1985a. *Manual for the Self-Perception Profile for Children*. Denver, CO: University of Denver.

------. 1985b. *Manual for the Social Support Scale for Children*. Denver, CO: University of Denver.

Hartup, Willard. 1989. Social Relationships and Their Developmental Significance. *American Psychologist* 44:120-26.

Harvard Education Letter. 1991. Retention: Can We Stop Failing Kids? *Harvard Education Letter* 7:1-3.

Hauser, Robert L., and David L. Featherman. 1977. *The Process of Stratification: Trends and Analysis*. New York: Academic Press.

Hauser, Robert M. 1971. *Socioeconomic Background and Educational Performance*. American Sociological Association. Washington, D.C.: Rose Monograph Series.

Haveman, Robert, and Barbara Wolfe. 1994. *Succeeding Generations*. New York: Russell Sage.

Hayes, Donald P., and Judith Grether. 1969. The School Year and Vacations: When Do Students Learn? Paper presented at the Eastern Sociological Association meeting. New York, April. Subsequently Published in *Cornell Journal of Social Relations* 17 (1983): 56-71.

------, and J. P. King. 1974. *The Development of Reading Achievement Differentials During the School Year and Vacations*. Ithaca, NY: Cornell University.

Heller, Kirby A. 1982. Effects of Special Education Placement on Educable Mentally Retarded Children. In *Children in Special Education: A Strategy for Equity*, eds. Kirby A. Heller, Wayne H. Holtzman, and Samuel Messick, 262-99. Washington, D.C.: National Academy Press.

Hess, Robert D., and Teresa M. McDevitt. 1984. Some Cognitive Consequences of Maternal Intervention Techniques: A Longitudinal Study. *Child Development* 55:2017-30.

------, Susan D. Holloway, W. Patrick Dickson, and Gary G. Price. 1984. Maternal Variables as Predictors of Children's School Readiness and Later Achievement in Vocabulary and Mathematics in Sixth Grade. *Child Development* 55:1902-12.

------, and V. C. Shipman. 1965. Early Experience and the Socialization of Cognitive Modes in Children. *Child Development* 36:869-88.

Hetherington, E. Mavis, Kathleen A. Camara, and David L. Featherman. 1983. Achievement and Intellectual Functioning in One-Parent Families. In *Achievement and Achievement Motives*, ed. Janet Spence, 205-84. San Francisco: W. H. Freeman.

Heyneman, Stephen P., and William A. Loxley. 1983. The Effect of Primary-School Quality on Academic Achievement Across Twenty-Nine High- and Low-Income Countries. *American Journal of Sociology* 88:1162-94.

Heyns, Barbara. 1978. *Summer Learning and the Effects of Schooling*. New York: Academic Press.

------. 1986. Summer Programs and Compensatory Education: The Future of an Idea. Working paper, National Institute of Education, Chapter One Study Team, Conference on the Effects of Alternative Designs in Compensatory Education. Washington, D.C.

------. 1987. Schooling and Cognitive Development: Is There a Season for Learning? *Child Development* 58:1151-60.

Hilton, Thomas L., and Gosta W. Berglund. 1974. Sex Differences in Mathematics Achievement: A Longitudinal Study. *Journal of Educational Research* 67:231-37.

Hinshaw, Stephen P. 1992. Externalizing Behavior Problems and Academic Underachievement in Childhood and Adolescence: Causal Relationships and Underlying Mechanisms. *Psychological Bulletin* 111:127-55.

Ho, Esther Sui-Chu, and J. Douglas Willms. 1996. Effects of Parent Involvement on Eighth-Grade Achievement. *Sociology of Education* 69:126-41.

Hofferth, Sandra L. 1987. The Children of Teen Childbearers. In *Risking the Future*, eds. Sandra L. Hofferth and Cheryl D. Hayes, 174-206. Washington, D.C.: National Academy Press.

Holmes, C. Thomas. 1989. Grade Level Retention Effects: A Meta-Analysis of Research Studies. In *Flunking Grades: Research and Policies on Retention*, eds. Lorrie A. Shepard and Mary Lee Smith. London: Falmer Press.

Holmes, Thomas H., and Richard H. Rahe. 1967. The Social Readjustment Rating Scale. *Journal of Psychometric Research* 11:213-18.

Husén, Torsten. 1969. *Talent, Opportunity and Career*. Stockholm: Almqvist and Wiksell.

------, and Albert Tuijnman. 1991. The Contribution of Formal Schooling to the Increase in Intellectual Capital. *Educational Researcher* 20:17-25.

Huston, Aletha C. 1983. Sex-Typing. In *Handbook of Child Psychology Vol 4*, ed. Paul H. Mussen. New York: Wiley.

------. 1994. Children in Poverty: Designing Research to Affect Policy. *Social Policy Report*. Society for Research in Child Development, 8(2):1-15, Ann Arbor, MI: University of Michigan.

Huttenlocher, Janellen, Susan Levine, and Jack Vevea. 1997. Environmental Effects on Cognitive Growth: Evidence from Time Period Comparisons. Unpublished paper.

Hyde, Janet S. 1990. Meta-Analysis and the Psychology of Gender Differences. *Signs: Journal of Women in Culture and Society* 16:55-73.

------, Elizabeth Fennema, and Susan J. Lamon. 1990. Gender Differences in Mathematics Performance: A Meta-Analysis. *Psychological Bulletin* 107:139-55.

Jackson, Gregg B. 1975. The Research Evidence on the Effects of Grade Retention. *Review of Educational Research* 45:613-35.

Jargowsky, Paul A., and Mary Jo Bane. 1990. Ghetto Poverty: Basic Questions. In *Inner-City Poverty in the United States.*, eds. Laurence E. Lynn and Michael G. H. McGeary. Washington D.C.: National Academy Press.

Jarrett, Robin L. 1995. Growing up Poor: The Family Experiences of Socially Mobile Youth in Low-Income African American Neighborhoods. *Journal of Adolescent*

Research 10:111-35.

Jencks, Christopher, Marshall Smith, Henry Acland, Mary Jo Bane, David Cohen, Herbert Gintis, Barbara Heyns, and Stephan Michelson. 1972. *Inequality: A Reassessment of the Effects of Family and Schooling in America.* New York: Basic.

------. 1985. How Much Do High School Students Learn? *Sociology of Education* 58:128-53.

------, and Susan Mayer. 1988. *The Social Consequences of Growing up in a Poor Neighborhood: A Review.* Evanston, IL: Center for Urban Affairs and Policy Research, Northwestern University.

------, and Susan Mayer. 1990. The Social Consequences of Growing up in a Poor Neighborhood. In *Inner-City Poverty in the United States.*, eds. Laurence E. Lynn and McGeary Michael G. H., 111-86. Washington D.C.: National Academy Press.

Jensen, Arthur R. 1969. How Much Can We Boost I. Q. and Scholastic Achievement? *Harvard Educational Review* 39:1-123.

Johnson, Jennifer. 1995. Limited Choices. Unpublished Doctoral Dissertation. Baltimore, MD: Johns Hopkins University.

Jones, Molly M., and Garrett K. Mandeville. 1990. The Effect of Age at School Entry on Reading Achievement Scores among South Carolina Students. *Remedial and Special Education* 11:56-62.

Kandel, Denise B., and Mark Davies. 1982. Epidemiology of Depressive Mood in Adolescents. *Archives of General Psychiatry* 39:1205-12.

Karweit, Nancy. 1973. *Rainy Days and Mondays: An Analysis of Factors Related to Absence from School.* Report No. 162. Baltimore, MD: Center for the Social Organization of Schools.

------. 1976. A Reanalysis of the Effect of Quantity of Schooling on Achievement. *Sociology of Education* 49:236-46.

------. 1992. Retention Policy. In *Encyclopedia of Educational Research*, ed. Marvin Alkin, 1114-18. New York: MacMillan.

Kellam, Sheppard G. 1990. Developmental Epidemiologic Framework for Family Research on Depression and Aggression. In *Depression and Aggression in Family Interaction*, eds. G. R. Patterson, 11-48. Hillsdale, NJ: Erlbaum.

------. 1994. The Social Adaptation of Children in Classrooms: A Measure of Family Childrearing Effectiveness. In *Exploring Family Relationships with Other Social Contexts*, ed. Ross D. Parke and Sheppard G. Kellam, 147-68. Hillsdale, N.J.: Erlbaum..

------, J. D. Branch, K. C. Agrawal, and Margaret E. Ensminger. 1975. *Mental Health and Going to School: The Woodlawn Program of Assessment, Early Intervention, and Evaluation.* Chicago: University of Chicago Press.

------, Margaret E. Ensminger, and R. Jay Turner. 1977. Family Structure and the Mental Health of Children: Concurrent and Longitudinal Community- Wide Studies. *Archives of General Psychiatry* 34:1012-22.

------, Lisa Werthamer-Larsson, Lawrence J. Dolan, C. H. Brown, J. Laudolff, G. Edelsohn, and Leonard Wheeler. 1991. Developmental Epidemiologically-based

Preventive Trials: Baseline Modeling of Early Target Behaviors and Depressive Symptoms. *American Journal of Community Psychology* 19:563-84.

Kerckhoff, Alan C. 1993. *Diverging Pathways: Social Structure and Career Deflections.* New York: Cambridge University Press.

Kilgore, Sally B. 1991. The Organizational Context of Tracking in Schools. *American Sociological Review* 56:189-203.

Klibanoff, Leonard S., and Sue A. Haggart. 1981. *Report # 8: Summer Growth and the Effectiveness of Summer School.* Technical Report to the Office of Program Evaluation. U.S. Department of Education, Mountain View, CA: RMC Research Corporation.

Kohn, Melvin. 1977. *Class and Conformity: A Study in Values.* Chicago: University of Chicago Press.

Kraus, Philip E. 1973. *Yesterday's Children.* New York: Wiley.

Kurdek, Lawrence A., and Ronald J. Sinclair. 1988. Relation of Eighth Graders' Family Structure, Gender, and Family Environment with Academic Performance and School Behavior. *Journal of Educational Psychology* 80:90-94.

Lareau, Annette. 1987. Social Class Differences in Family-School Relationships: The Importance of Cultural Capital. *Sociology of Education* 60:73-85.

------. 1992. Gender Differences in Parent Involvement in Schooling. In *Education and Gender Equality,* ed. J. Wrigley, 207-24. London, England: Falmer Press.

Lash, Andrea A., and Sandra L. Kirkpatrick. 1990. A Classroom Perspective on Student Mobility. *Elementary School Journal* 91:171-91.

LaVeist, Thomas A. 1992. The Political Empowerment and Health Status of African Americans: Mapping a New Territory. *American Journal of Sociology* 97:1080-95.

Lazar, Irving, and Richard Darlington. 1982. Lasting Effects of Early Education: A Report from the Consortium for Longitudinal Studies. *Monographs of the Society for Research in Child Development* 47 (2-3).

Lee, Valerie, Anthony, S. Bryk, and Julia B. Smith. 1993. The Organization of Effective Secondary Schools. In *Review of Research in Education,* ed. Linda Darling-Hammond, 171-267. Washington D.C.: American Educational Research Association.

Leinhardt, Gaea, and Allan Pallay. 1982. Restrictive Educational Settings: Exile or Haven? *Review of Educational Research* 54:557-78.

Lever, Janet. 1976. Sex Differences in the Games Children Play. *Social Problems* 23:478-87.

Lloyd, Kim M., and Sonia Miner. 1993. Sibsize and Educational Achievement among Individuals from Non-Intact Families: The Case of Whites, Blacks and Hispanics. Paper presented at American Sociological Association meeting. Miami, FL, August.

Luster, Tom, and Harriette McAdoo. 1996. Family and Child Influences on Educational Attainment: A Secondary Analysis of the High/Scope Perry Preschool Data. *Developmental Psychology* 32:26-39.

Madden, Nancy A., and Robert E. Slavin. 1983. Mainstreaming Students with Mild Handicaps: Academic and Social Outcomes. *Review of Educational Research* 53:519-69.

Marjoribanks, Kevin. 1979. *Families and Their Learning Environments*. London: Routledge.

Maryland State Department of Education. 1976. *Maryland Accountability Program Report, Year II, School Year 1974-75*. Maryland State Department of Education, Division of Research, Evaluation and Information Systems.

------. 1990. *The Fact Book 1989-90: A Statistical Handbook*. Baltimore, MD: Maryland State Department of Education.

------. 1992. *Maryland School Performance Report, 1992 State and School Systems*. Baltimore, MD: Maryland State Department of Education.

------. 1994. *Maryland School Performance Report, 1994 State and School Systems*. Baltimore, MD: Maryland State Department of Education.

Mayer, Susan E. 1991. How Much Does a High School's Racial and Socioeconomic Mix Affect Graduation and Teenage Fertility Rates? In *The Urban Underclass*, eds. Christopher Jencks and Penelope E. Peterson, 321-41. Washington, D.C.: Brookings.

McCandless, Boyd, A. Roberts, and T. Stannes. 1972. Teachers' Marks, Achievement Test Scores, and Aptitude Relations with Respect to Social Class, Race, and Sex. *Journal of Educational Psychology* 63:153-59.

McDill, Edward L., Mary S. McDill, and J. Timothy Sprehe. 1969. *Strategies for Success in Compensatory Education: An Appraisal of Evaluation Research*. Baltimore: John Hopkins University Press.

------, Gary Natriello, and Aaron M. Pallas. 1985. Raising Standards and Retaining Students: The Impact of the Reform Recommendations on Potential Dropouts. *Review of Educational Research* 55:415-33.

------, Gary Natriello, and Aaron M. Pallas. 1986. A Population at Risk: Potential Consequences of Tougher School Standards for Student Dropouts. *American Journal of Education* 94:135-81.

McLanahan, Sara S. 1983. Family Structure and Stress: A Longitudinal Comparison of Two-Parent and Female-Headed Families. *Journal of Marriage and the Family* 45:347-53.

------, and Larry Bumpass. 1988a. Intergenerational Consequences of Family Disruption. *American Journal of Sociology* 94:130-52.

------, and Larry Bumpass. 1988b. A Note on the Effect of Family Structure on School Enrollment. In *Divided Opportunities*, eds. Gary Sandefur and Marta Tienda, 195-201. New York: Plenum.

------, and Gary Sandefur. 1994. *Growing up with a Single Parent: What Hurts, What Helps*. Cambridge, MA: Harvard.

McLoyd, Vonnie. 1989. Socialization and Development in a Changing Economy: The Effects of Paternal Income and Job Loss on Children. *American Psychologist* 44:293-302.

------. 1990. The Impact of Economic Hardship on Black Families and Children: Psychological Distress, Parenting, and Socioemotional Development. *Child Development* 62:311-46.

McPartland, James M., J. R. Coldiron, and Jomills H. Braddock. 1987. *School*

226 References

Structures and Classroom Practices in Elementary, Middle and Secondary Schools. Report No. 14. Baltimore: Johns Hopkins University, Center for Research on Elementary and Middle Schools.

Medrich, Elliott A., Judith Roizen, Victor Rubin, and Stuart Buckley. 1982. *The Serious Business of Growing Up*. Berkeley, CA: University of California Press.

Menaghan, Elizabeth G., and Toby L. Parcel. 1991. Stability and Change in Children's Home Environments: The Effects of Parental Occupational Experiences and Family Conditions. Presented at the Society for Research in Child Development meeting, Seattle, Washington, April.

Mercy, James A., and Lala C. Steelman. 1982. Familial Influences on the Intellectual Attainment of Children. *American Sociological Review* 47:532-42.

Meyer, Linda A. 1984. Long-Term Academic Effects of Direct Instruction: Project Follow Through. *The Elementary School Journal* 84:380-94.

Miller, Louise B., and Rondeall P. Bizzell. 1983. The Louisville Experiment: A Comparison of Four Programs. In *As the Twig Is Bent: Lasting Effects of Preschool Programs*, ed. The Consortium for Longitudinal Studies, 171-200. Hillsdale, NJ: Erlbaum.

Moore, Kristin A. 1995. *Nonmarital Childbearing in the United States*. Report to Congress on Out-of-Wedlock Childbearing. National Center for Health Statistics, Department of Health and Human Services. Public Health Service 95-1257-1. Hyattsville, MD: US Department of Health and Human Services.

------, and N. O. Snyder. 1991. Cognitive Attainment Among First-Born Children of Adolescent-Mothers. *American Sociological Review* 56:612-24.

Mischel, W., R. Zeiss, and A. Zeiss. 1974. Locus of Control: Current Trends in Theory and Research. *Journal of Personality and Social Psychology* 29:265-78.

Morris, John, John Ehren, Barbara Lenz, and B. Keith. 1991. Building a Model to Predict Which Fourth Through Eighth Graders Will Drop out in High School. *Journal of Experimental Education* 59:286-93.

------. 1976. A Seven Year Check on the Possible Effects of Attitudes, Motives, and Behavior Patterns on Change in Economic Status. In *Five Thousand American Families- Patterns of Economic Progress Vol 4*, eds. Greg J. Duncan and James N. Morgan, 421-28. Ann Arbor, MI: Institute for Social Research, University of Michigan.

Morrison, Donna Ruane. The Divorce Process and Children's Well-Being: A Longitudinal Analysis. 1992. Unpublished Doctoral Dissertation. Baltimore, MD: The Johns Hopkins University.

Morrison, Fredrick J., Elizabeth M Griffith, and Gary L. Williamson. 1993. Two Strikes from the Start: Individual Differences in Early Literacy. Presented at Society for Research in Child Development meetings. New Orleans, LA., March.

------, Lisa Smith, and Maurcen Dow-Ehrensberger. 1995. Education and Cognitive Development: A Natural Experiment. *Developmental Psychology* 31:789-99.

Mosteller, Frederick, and Daniel P. Moynihan. 1972. *On Equality of Educational Opportunity*. New York: Vintage.

Mueser, Peter. 1979. The Effects of Non-Cognitive Traits. In *Who Gets Ahead? The*

Determinants of Economic Success in America, ed. Christopher Jencks, 122-58. New York: Basic.

Murnane, Richard J. 1975. *The Impact of School Resources on the Learning of Inner City Children*. Cambridge, MA: Ballinger.

National Center for Education Statistics. 1990. *A Profile of the American Eighth Grader: NELS 88 Student Descriptive Summary*. U.S. Department of Education, Office of Educational Research and Improvement. Washington, D.C.: U. S. Government Printing Office.

National Opinion Research Center. 1988. *Eighth grade questionnaire NELS:88*. Prepared for U.S. Department of Education, Center for Education Statistics. Chicago, IL: University of Chicago.

National Survey of Children. 1976. New York: Foundation for Child Development.

Neckerman, Kathryn M., and William J. Wilson. 1988. Schools and Poor Communities. In *School Success for Students at Risk*, ed. Council of Chief State School Officers, 25-44. San Diego, CA: Harcourt-Brace-Jovanovich.

Newport, Elissa L. 1991. Contrasting Conceptions of the Critical Period for Language. In *The Epigenesis of the Mind: Essays on Biology and Cognition*, eds. S. Carey and R. Gelman, 111-30. Hillsdale, NJ: Erlbaum.

O'Connell, Martin, and Carolyn C. Rogers. 1980. The Legitimacy Status of First Births to U.S. Women Aged 15-24, 1939-1978. *Family Planning Perspectives* 12:16-25.

Olneck, Michael R., and David B. Bills. 1980. What Makes Sammy Run? An Empirical Assessment of the Bowles-Gintis Correspondence Theory. *American Journal of Education* 89 (1):27-61.

Page, Ellis B. 1958. Teacher's Comments and Student Performance: A Seventy Four Classroom Experiment in School Motivation. *Journal of Educational Psychology* 49:173-81.

Pallas, Aaron M. 1984. The Determinants of High School Dropouts. Unpublished Doctoral Dissertation. Baltimore: Johns Hopkins University.

------, Doris R. Entwisle, Karl L. Alexander, and Doris Cadigan. 1987. Children Who Do Exceptionally Well in First Grade. *Sociology of Education* 60:257-71.

------, Doris R. Entwisle, Karl L. Alexander, and M. Frank Stluka. 1994. Ability-Group Effects: Instructional, Social or Institutional? *Sociology of Education* 67:27-46.

------, Doris R. Entwisle, Karl L. Alexander, and Peter Weinstein. 1990. Social Structure and the Development of Self-Esteem in Young Children. *Social Psychology Quarterly* 53 (4):302-15.

------, Gary Natriello, and Edward L. McDill. 1989. The Changing Nature of the Disadvantaged Population: Current Dimensions and Future Trends. *Educational Researcher* 18:16-22.

Palmer, Francis H. 1983. The Harlem Study: Effects by Type of Training, Age of Training, and Social Class. In *As the Twig Is Bent. Lasting Effects of Preschool Programs*, ed. The Consortium for Longitudinal Studies, 201-36. Hillsdale, N. J.: Erlbaum.

Parke, Ross D., and Sheppard G. Kellam. 1994. *Exploring Family Relationships with Other Social Contexts*. Hillsdale, N.J.: Erlbaum.

------, Thomas G. Power, Barbara R. Tinsley, and Shelley Hymel. 1980. The Father's Role in the Family System. In *Parent-Infant Relationships*, ed. P. M. Taylor, 117-36. New York: Grune and Stratton.

Parker, Steven, Steven Greer, and Barry Zuckerman. 1988. Double Jeopardy: The Impact of Poverty on Early Child Development. *Pediatric Clinics of North America* 35:1227-40.

Parsons, Jacquelynne E., Terry F. Adler, and Caroline M. Kaczala. 1982. Socialization of Achievement Attitudes and Beliefs: Parental Influences. *Child Development* 53:322-39.

------, and Diane N. Ruble. 1977. The Development of Achievement-Related Expectancies. *Child Development* 48:1075-79.

Pedersen, Eigil, Therese A. Faucher, and William W. Eaton. 1978. A New Perspective on the Effects of First-Grade Teachers on Children's Subsequent Adult Status. *Harvard Educational Review* 48:1-31.

Pelavin, S. H., and J. L. David. 1977. *Evaluating Long-Term Achievement: An Analysis of Longitudinal Data from Compensatory Educational Programs*. EPRC 4537-15. Prepared for Office of the Assistant Secretary for Education, Department of Health, Education and Welfare. Washington, D.C.: SRI International Educational Policy Research Center.

Pettegrew, Loyd S., and Glenda E. Wolf. 1982. Validating Measures of Teacher Stress. *American Educational Research Journal* 19:373-96.

Pianta, Robert C., L. Alan Sroufe, and Byron Egeland. 1989. Continuity and Discontinuity in Maternal Sensitivity at 6, 24 and 42 Months of Age in a High-Risk Sample. *Child Development* 60:481-87.

Pope, Jean, B. Lehrer, and J. Stevens. 1980. A Multiphasic Reading Screening Procedure. *Journal of Learning Disabilities* 13:98-102.

Prawat, Richard, and Robert Jarvis. 1980. Gender Differences as a Factor in Teachers' Perceptions of Students. *Journal of Educational Psychology* 72:743-49.

Purkey, William Watson. 1970. *Self Concept and School Achievement*. Englewood Cliffs, N.J.: Prentice-Hall.

Rainwater, Lee, and Timothy M. Smeeding. 1995. U.S. Doing Poorly Compared to Others. *News and Issues* 5(3):4-5. National Center for Children in Poverty, New York.

Regional Planning Council. 1983. *Census '80: Income and Poverty Status Report for Regional Planning Districts*. Baltimore, MD: Regional Planning Council, January.

Rehberg, Richard A, and Evelyn R. Rosenthal. 1978. *Class and Merit in the American High School*. White Plains, NY: Longman.

Reuman, David A. 1989. How Social Comparison Mediates the Relation Between Ability-Grouping Practices and Students' Achievement Expectancies in Mathematics. *Journal of Educational Psychology* 81:178-89.

Reynolds, Arthur J. 1989. A Structural Model of First-Grade Outcomes for an Urban, Low Socioeconomic Status, Minority Population. *Journal of Educational*

Psychology 81:594-603.

------. 1991. Early Schooling of Children at Risk. *American Educational Research Journal* 28:393-422.

------. 1992. Grade Retention and School Adjustment: An Explanatory Analysis. *Educational Evaluation and Policy Analysis* 14:101-21.

------. 1994. Effects of a Preschool plus Follow-On Intervention for Children at Risk. *Developmental Psychology* 30:787-804.

Richman, N., J. Stevenson, and P. J. Graham. 1982. *Pre-School to School: A Behavioral Study*. London: Academic Press.

Rist, Ray. 1970. Social Class and Teacher Expectations: The Self-Fulfilling Prophecy in Ghetto Education. *Harvard Educational Review* 40:411-51.

Roderick, Melissa. 1993. The Path to Dropping Out: Evidence for Intervention. *American Sociological Review* 15:351-57.

Rosenbaum, James E. 1976. *Making Inequality*. New York: Wiley.

------. 1980. Some Implications of Educational Grouping. *Review of Research in Education* 8:361-401.

------. 1984. The Social Organization of Instructional Grouping. In *The Social Context of Instruction: Group Organization and Group Process*, eds. Penelope L. Peterson, Louise Cherry Wilkinson and Maureen Hallinan, 53-68. San Diego, CA: Academic.

Rosenberg, Morris and Roberta G. Simmons. 1971. *Black and White Self-Esteem: The Urban School Child*. Arnold M. and Caroline Rose Monograph Series. Washington, D.C.: American Sociological Association.

------. 1979. *Conceiving the Self*. New York: Basic.

Rosenthal, Robert. 1968. *Pygmalion in the Classroom: Teacher Expectation and Pupils' Intellectual Development*. New York: Holt, Rinehart, and Winston.

Rotter, Julian B. 1966. Generalized Expectancies for Internal Versus External Control of Reinforcement. *Psychology Monographs: General and Applied* 80:1-28.

Rowan, Brian, and Andrew W. Miracle. 1983. Systems of Ability Grouping and the Stratification of Achievement in Elementary Schools. *Sociology of Education* 56:133-44.

Royce, Jacqueline M., Richard B. Darlington, and Harry W. Murray. 1983. Pooled Analyses: Findings Across Studies. In *As the Twig Is Bent: Lasting Effects of Preschool Programs*, ed. The Consortium for Longitudinal Studies. Hillsdale, NJ: Erlbaum.

Ruggles, Patricia. 1992. Measuring Poverty. University of Wisconsin, Institute for Research on Poverty, Madison. *Focus* 14 (1):1-9.

Salzman, Stephanie A. 1987. Meta-Analysis of Studies Investigating the Effects of Father Absence on Children's Cognitive Performance. Paper presented at American Educational Research Association meeting. Washington, D.C., April.

Sameroff, Arnold. 1985. Foreword. In *Low Achieving Children*, eds. Sarah Broman, Ellen Bien, and Peter Shaughnessy, vii-xi. Hillsdale, NJ: Erlbaum.

Sampson, Robert J. 1992. Family Management and Child Development: Insights from

Social Disorganization Theory. In *Advances in Criminology Theory, Vol 3: Fact, Frameworks, and Forecasts*, ed. J. McCord, 63-93. New Brunswick, NJ: Transaction.

Santrock, John W., and R. L. Tracy. 1978. The Effects of Children's Family Structure Status on the Development of Stereotypes by Teachers. *Journal of Educational Psychology* 70:754-57.

Saxe, Geoffrey B, Steven R. Guberman, and Maryl Gearheart. 1987. Social Processes in Early Number Development. *Monographs of Society for Research in Child Development* 52 (Serial No. 216).

Schneider, Barbara L. 1980. Production Analysis of Gains in Achievement. Paper Presented at American Educational Research Association Meeting. Boston.

------, and James S. Coleman. 1993. *Parents, Their Children, and Schools*. Boulder, CO: Westview.

Schweinhart, Lawrence J., and David Weikart. 1983. The Effects of the Perry Preschool Program on Youths Through Age 15--A Summary. In *As the Twig Is Bent: Lasting Effects of Preschool Programs*, ed. The Consortium for Longitudinal Studies, 71-102. Hillsdale, NJ: Erlbaum.

Seaver, W. Burleigh. 1973. Effects of Naturally-Induced Teacher Expectancies. *Journal of Personality and Social Psychology* 28:333-42.

Seginer, Rachel. 1983. Parents' Expectations and Children's Academic Achievements: A Literature Review. *Merrill-Palmer Quarterly* 29:1-23.

Sewell, William H, and Robert M. Hauser. 1976. Causes and Consequences of Higher Education: Models of the Status Attainment Process. In *Schooling and Achievement in American Society*, eds. William H. Sewell, Robert M Hauser, and David L. Featherman, 9-28. New York: Academic Press.

Shepard, Lorrie A, and Mary Lee Smith. 1989. *Flunking Grades: Research and Policies on Retention*. London: Falmer.

Simmons, Roberta G., and Dale A. Blyth. 1987. *Moving into Adolescence: The Impact of Pubertal Change and School Context*. Hawthorn, NY: Aldine De Gruyter.

Simner, Marvin L., and Michael J. Barnes. 1991. Relationship between First-Grade Marks and the High School Dropout Problem. *Journal of School Psychology* 29:331-35.

Sleet, David A. 1985. Differences in the Social Complexity of Children's Play Choices. *Perceptual and Motor Skills* 60:283-87.

Smith, M. S. 1972. Equality of Educational Opportunity: The Basic Findings Reconsidered. In *Equality of Educational Opportunity*, eds. Frederick Mosteller and Daniel P. Moynihan, 230-342. New York: Vintage.

Smith, Thomas M., Gayle T. Rogers, Nabeel Alsalam, Marianne Perie, Rebecca P. Mahoney, and Valerie Martin. 1994. *The Condition of Education*. NCES 94-194. Washington, D.C.: U.S. Department of Education.

Sørensen, Aage B., and Maureen Hallinan. 1984. Effects of Race on Assignment to Ability Groups. In *The Social Context of Instruction: Group Organization and Group Processes*, eds. Penelope L. Peterson, Louise Cherry Wilkinson, and

Maureen T. Hallinan, 85-103. New York: Academic.

Sorenson, Elaine. 1991. *Exploring the Reasons Behind the Narrowing Gender Gap in Earnings*. Washington, D.C.: Urban Institute.

Spencer, Margaret B. 1992. Neighborhood Features, Self-Esteem, and Achievement Orientation. Paper presented at Society for Research in Adolescence meeting. Washington, D.C., March.

St. John, Nancy. 1975. *School Desegregation: Outcomes for Children*. New York: Wiley.

Stack, Carol B. 1974. *All Our Kin*. New York: Harper & Row.

Stallings, John A. 1975. Relationships Between Classroom Instructional Practices and Child Development. Presented at American Educational Research Association. Washington, D.C..

Staples, Robert R., and Alfredo Mirande. 1980. Racial and Cultural Variations among American Families: A Decennial Review of the Literature on Minority Families. *Journal of Marriage and the Family* 42:157-73.

Stephens, John M. 1956. *Educational Psychology*. New York: Holt, Rinehart and Winston.

Stevenson, David L., and David P. Baker. 1987. The Family-School Relation and the Child's School Performance. *Child Development* 58:1348-57.

Stevenson, Harold W., and Richard S. Newman. 1986. Long-Term Prediction of Achievement and Attitudes in Mathematics and Reading. *Child Development* 57:646-59.

------, and James Stigler. 1992. *The Learning Gap: Why Our Schools Are Failing and What We Can Learn from Japanese and Chinese Education*. New York: Summit.

Stewart, A. 1993. *Head Start: A Fact Sheet*. Washington, D.C.: Congressional Research Service.

Strodtbeck, Fred. 1958. Family Interaction, Values and Achievement. In *Talent and Society*, ed. David C. McClelland, 135-94. Princeton, NJ: Van Nostrand.

Stroup, Atlee L., and Lee N. Robins. 1972. Elementary School Predictors of High School Dropout among Black Males. *Sociology of Education* 45:212-22.

Sullivan, Harry S. 1953. *Conceptions of Modern Psychiatry, 2nd Edition*. New York: Norton.

Sundius, M. Jane. 1996. Making the Mark: Family Resources and Their Effect on Children's First Grade Report Cards. Unpublished Doctoral Dissertation. Baltimore, MD: Johns Hopkins University.

Sutton-Smith, Brian, and Benjamin G. Rosenberg. 1970. *The Sibling*. New York: Holt, Rinehart & Winston.

Tanner, James M. 1973. Growing Up. *Scientific American* 229 (3): 35-43.

Teachman, Jay D., Kathleen Paasch, and Karen Carver. 1996. Social Capital and Dropping out of School Early. *Journal of Marriage and the Family* 58:773-83.

Thompson, Maxine S., Karl L. Alexander, Doris R. Entwisle, and M. Jane Sundius. 1992. The Influence of Family Composition on Children's Conformity to the Student Role. *American Educational Research Journal* 29:405-24.

Tienda, Marta. 1991. Poor People and Poor Places: Deciphering Neighborhood Effects on Poverty Outcomes. In *Macro-Micro Linkages in Sociology*, ed. Joan Huber, 244-62. Maberry, CA: Sage.

Tuck, Kathy D. 1989. A Study of Students Who Left: D.C. Public School Dropouts. Presented at American Educational Research Association meetings. San Francisco, CA, March.

U.S. Bureau of the Census. 1973. Characteristics of the Population. Part 22, Maryland. In *Census of the Population: 1970, Vol. 1*. Washington, D.C.: U.S. Government Printing Office.

------. 1983. *Census of Population: 1980 Vol 1. Characteristics of the Population*. Washington, D.C.: U.S. Government Printing Office.

------. 1987. *Geographic Mobility: 1985* Current Population Reports, Series P-20, *No. 420*. Washington, D.C.: U.S. Government Printing Office.

------. 1990a. *Household and Family Characteristics: March 1990 and 1989*. Current Population Report P-20, No. 447. Washington, D.C.: U.S. Government Printing Office.

------. 1990b. *Statistical Abstract of the U.S.* Washington, D.C.: Bureau of the Census.

------. 1991a. *Statistical Abstract of the U.S.* Washington, D.C.: Bureau of the Census.

------. 1991b. *Marital Status and Living Arrangements. March 1990*. Current Population Reports, Series P-20, No. 450. Washington, D.C.: U.S. Government Printing Office.

------. 1992a. *Marital Status and Living Arrangements: March 1992*. Current Population Reports. Series P-20, No. 468. Washington, D.C.: U.S. Government Printing Office.

------. 1992b. *School Enrollment -Social and Economic Characteristics of Students: October 1990*. Current Population Reports. P-20, No. 460. Washington, D.C.: U.S. Government Printing Office.

------. 1992c. *Statistical Abstract of the U.S.* Washington, D.C.: Bureau of the Census.

------. 1993. *Money Income of Households, Families, and Persons in the United States: 1992*. Current Population Reports. P-60, No. 184. Washington, D.C.: U.S. Government Printing Office.

------. 1994. *Statistical Abstract of the U.S.* Washington, D.C.: Bureau of the Census.

------. 1995a. *Child Support for Custodial Mothers and Fathers: 1991*. August, 1995. Current Population Reports, Series P-20, No. 187. Washington, D.C.: U.S. Government Printing Office.

------. 1995b. *Statistical Abstract of the U.S.* Washington, D.C.: Bureau of the Census.

U.S. Department of Education. 1991. *Trends in Academic Progress*. National Center for Education Statistics. Washington, D.C.: U.S. Department of Education.

------. 1994a. *The Condition of Education*. National Center for Education Statistics 94-104. Washington, D.C.: U.S. Department of Education.

------. 1994b. *Access to Early Childhood Programs for Children at Risk*. National Center for Education Statistics 93 (372).

------. 1995. *The Condition of Education.* National Center for Education Statistics 95-273. Washington, D.C.: U.S. Department of Education.

------. 1994a. *The Condition of Education.* National Center for Education Statistics 94-104. Washington, D.C.: U.S. Department of Education.

Varnhagen, Connie K., Frederick J. Morrison, and Robin Everall. 1994. Age and Schooling Effects in Story Recall and Story Production. *Developmental Psychology* 30:969-79.

Veenman, Simon. 1995. Cognitive and Noncognitive Effects of Multigrade and Multi-Age Classes: A Best-Evidence Synthesis. *Review of Educational Research* 65:319-81.

W. T. Grant Foundation. 1988. *The Forgotten Half: Pathways to Success for America's Youth and Young Families.* Washington, D.C.: Youth and America's Future: William T. Grant Commission on Work, Family and Citizenship.

Wadsworth, M. E. 1986. Effects of Parenting Style and Preschool Experience on Children's Verbal Attainment: Results of a British Longitudinal Study. *Early Childhood Research Quarterly* 1:237-38.

Walberg, Herbert J. 1984. Improving the Productivity of America's Schools. *Educational Leadership*, May, 19-27.

Walker, Deborah K, Judith D. Singer, Judith S. Palfrey, Michele Orza, and Marta Wenger. 1988. Who Leaves and Who Stays in Special Education: A 2-Year Follow-Up Study. *Exceptional Children* 54:393-402.

Weiss, Robert S. 1979. *Going It Alone: The Family Life and Social Situation of the Single Parent.* New York: Basic.

------. 1984. The Impact of Marital Dissolution on Income and Consumption in Single-Parent Households. *Journal of Marriage and the Family* 46:115-28.

Weller, L. David, Carl J. Schnittjer, and Bertha A. Tuten. 1992. Predicting Achievement in Grades Three Through Ten Using the Metropolitan Readiness Test. *Journal of Research in Childhood Education* 6:121-29.

Werner, Earl E. 1980. Environmental Interaction in Minimal Brain Dysfunctions. In *Handbook of Minimal Brain Dysfunctions: A Critical View*, eds. Herbert E. Rie and Ellen D. Rie. New York: Wiley.

Werthamer-Larsson, Lisa, Sheppard G. Kellam, and Leonard Wheeler. 1991. Effect of First Grade Classroom Environment on Shy Behavior, Aggressive Behavior, and Concentration Problems. *American Journal of Community Psychology* 19:585-602.

Whalen, Thomas E., and Mary Ann Fried. 1973. Geographic Mobility and Its Effects on Student Achievement. *Journal of Educational Research* 67:163-65.

White, Karl L. 1982. The Relation between Socioeconomic Status and Academic Achievement. *Psychological Bulletin* 91:461-81.

Wiley, David, E., and Annegret Harnischfeger. 1974. *Explosion of a Myth: Quantity of Schooling and Exposure to Instruction, Major Educational Vehicles.* Report No. 8, Department of Education. Studies of Educative Process. Chicago: University of Chicago.

Wilson, William J. 1987. *The Truly Disadvantaged.* Chicago: The University of

Chicago Press.

Woodhead, Martin. 1988. When Psychology Informs Public Policy: The Case of Early Childhood Intervention. *American Psychologist* 43:443-54.

Zill, Nicholas. 1981. American Children: Happy, Healthy, and Insecure. Report on Foundation for Child Development's National Survey of Children. New York: The Foundation for Child Development.

------. 1994. Understanding Why Children in Step-Families Have More Learning and Behavior Problems than Children in Nuclear Families. In *Stepfamilies: Who Benefits? Who Does Not?* eds. Alan Booth and Judith F. Dunn, 97-108. Hillsdale, NJ: Erlbaum.

------. 1996. Family Change and Student Achievement: What We Have Learned, What It Means for Schools. In *Family-School Links: How Do They Affect Educational Outcomes?* eds. Alan Booth and Judy Dunn, 139-74. Mahwah, NJ: Erlbaum.

------, and Carolyn C. Rogers. 1988. Recent Trends in the Well-Being of Children in the United States and Their Implications for Public Policy. In *The Changing American Family and Public Policy*, ed. Andrew H. Cherlin, 26-116. Washington, D.C.: Urban Institute.

Index

About the Book and Authors

Educational sociologists have paid relatively littlle attention to children in middle childhood (ages 6 to 12, whereas developmental psychologists have emphasized factors internal to the child much more than the social contexts in explaining children's development. *Children, Schools, and Inequality* redresses that imbalance. It examines elementary school outcomes (e.g., test scores, grades, retention rates) in light of the socioeconomic variation in schools and neighborhoods, the organizational patterns across elementary schools, and the ways in which family structure intersects with children's school performance. Adding data from the Baltimore Beginning School Study to information culled from the fields of sociology, child development, and education, this book suggests why the gap between the school achievement of poor children and those who are better off has been so difficult to close. Doris Entwisle, Karl Alexander, and Linda Steffel Olson show why the first-grade transition—how children negotiate entry into full-time schooling—is a crucial period. They also show that events over that time have repercussions that echo throughout children's entire school careers. Currently the only study of this life transition to cover a comprehensive sample and to suggest straightforward remedies for urban schools, *Children, Schools, and Inequality* can inform educators, practicioners, and policymakers as well as researchers in the sociology of education and child development.

Doris R. Entwisle and Karl L. Alexander are professors of sociology, both at Johns Hopkins University. **Linda Steffel Olson** is senior research assistant in the Department of Sociology at Johns Hopkins University.